NATALIE TRICE is a PR Director  international TV channels and Financ entrepreneurs at the forefront of their i Natalie has worked with them all.

Today, as well as retained clients, N world the fundamentals of PR and gives them the skills and confidence to go out and talk to the media. With her ideas, contacts and cheerleading approach, her clients secure the column inches and airwaves that help them to stand out from the crowd, and shine.

Cast Life – A Parent's Guide to DDH was Natalie's first book and sits alongside her charity, DDH UK, which supports thousands of people around the world dealing with hip dysplasia, a condition one of her sons has been treated for over the past decade.

PR SCHOOL
YOUR TIME TO

shine

SilverWood

Published in 2019 by SilverWood Books

SilverWood Books Ltd
14 Small Street, Bristol, BS1 1DE, United Kingdom
www.silverwoodbooks.co.uk

Copyright © Natalie Trice 2019

The right of Natalie Trice to be identified as the author of this work
has been asserted in accordance with the Copyright, Designs
and Patents Act 1988 Sections 77 and 78.

All rights reserved. No part of this publication may be reproduced,
stored in a retrieval system, or transmitted in any form or by any means,
electronic, mechanical, photocopying, recording or otherwise,
without prior permission of the copyright holder.

ISBN 978-1-78132-922-1 (paperback)
ISBN 978-1-78132-923-8 (ebook)

British Library Cataloguing in Publication Data
A CIP catalogue record for this book is available from
the British Library

Page design and typesetting by SilverWood Books
Printed on responsibly sourced paper

"*This book is a must-have for any small business owner wanting to get their head around PR. Natalie shares all of her wealth of experience and knowledge in an easy to follow book. Highly recommended.*"

Ruth Kudzi, author and business coach

"*This book takes the drama out of publicity. Natalie has a calm way of slowly convincing you that PR might be easier than you think. Brilliant advice and tips you can easily try. And the best thing is the link to Natalie's online support, so, you don't feel alone. Read the book, join the FB group and ask for help as you progress. Thank you, Natalie, for sharing your wisdom.*"

Eleanor Tweddell, business mentor

"*I cannot recommend this book more to my small-business friends! For most of us at the beginning, PR is like some mythical creature that you've heard legends about but haven't experienced yourself. This book gives valuable insights in an understandable way for anyone looking to get their foot in the door of this exclusive world.*"

Dawn Beth Baxter, social media coach

"*As a newcomer to the world of PR, I found Natalie's book absolutely invaluable. Accessible, written in terms the layperson will understand, and utterly inspiring. I found her DIY guide to creating a press pack incredibly useful, and the version for my business is now ready to go for my press work. Go, Natalie!*"

Denise Spragg, owner of The Sangha House

Dedicated to Roxy, the brightest star that ever did shine x

Contents

Acknowledgements

PR School has been a labour of love, and one I wouldn't have been able to write without the support of my husband, Oliver, and my two gorgeous sons, Eddie and Lucas.

If my first PR boss, Althea Taylor-Salmon, hadn't had faith in me and recognised the raw potential that walked into her London office in 1998, there'd be no PR School today, so thank you. That goes for every business and client who put their faith in me over the past 23 years.

Thank you to Greta Solomon for answering my Facebook post when I was wondering if this book was ever going to come together. It did, and you played a starring role.

Jo Henderson – I owe you, and you too, Octavia Holmes, as well as my family.

The comments from business owners, bloggers and journalists, helped bring my teaching to life in this book, so thank you for your time and feedback. Heidi, Emma-Jane, Hazel, Kelly and Gail – cheers to you all.

Jessica Killingley – you're a rock-star legend. Thank you today, tomorrow and forever. Ruth Kudzi – those ten friends we talked about – you are right there, thank you.

Thank you to the members of the PR School Facebook community who have been the givers of comments, quotes, virtual coffee and hugs.

Photos can make or break a story, so thank you to Antonina Mamzenko who provided some excellent photography hints and tips. If you ever need yours taken by a pro, she's the one.

Hannah Martin thank you for writing the foreword for this book and I am delighted that you are now a client.

Kate Gannon and Kelly Kemp, you are my dream team.

And, of course, thank you for buying this book. I hope my words will give you the courage to get out there and tell your story so you shine the way I know you are meant to.

Natalie x

Foreword

PR has the power to make your small business successful. The right exposure in the right publication or website can get your name and offering in front of thousands of potential customers – and lead to coveted brand awareness and sales.

And the best thing about PR? If you know how to do it, you can do it yourself.

You don't need a big-name PR firm to represent you to get media coverage today. All *you* need is a little know-how, and plenty of willingness to do the work.

When we launched Talented Ladies Club six years ago, I didn't have a clue about PR. Since then I've learned and applied PR techniques and strategies, and landed coverage in, among others, *The Sunday Times*, *Daily Mail*, *The Guardian*, *The Telegraph*, *Psychologies*, *Stylist* and *Woman & Home*, and I've appeared on Radio 4's *Woman's Hour*, the *Victoria Derbyshire* show on BBC Two, Channel 4, and Sky News.

I've achieved all this coverage myself, without hiring an agency, and using techniques you can apply yourself today.

So, if I did all that, you can too. And this book will teach you how.

The value of all that coverage has been priceless to us. It's put our brand on the map, and introduced us to some of the 82,000 people who now read our website every month. Just imagine what a little know-how will do for your business, too.

Hannah Martin
Talented Ladies Club
talentedladiesclub.com

Introduction

My name is Natalie Trice and whether you're an artist or an author, an activist or an aromatherapist, a Pilates teacher or a personal trainer, a nutritionist or a stylist, I want to help you get to grips with PR so that you can confidently tell your story and shine.

You probably don't have a publicist working on your behalf, but that doesn't matter because this book will give you the tools, and confidence, to run your PR like a pro, and put your business in the media spotlight.

I want to inspire you to think bigger than ever, and empower you so that you can go on an exciting new adventure with your business.

A Bit About Me

In 2011 I reached a turning point in my life and closed the PR agency I had built up and loved.

After spending years working for major companies like Epson, CNN and the Discovery Channel, I set up Tally PR so I could be a working mum on my terms. The business was growing, I was working with bigger brands and considering taking on a junior team member, but I also had two little boys, Eddie and Lucas.

Lucas was diagnosed with developmental dysplasia of the hip (DDH) when he was three months old, and while this isn't a life-threatening condition, it has certainly been life-changing for us. Overnight we went from soft play and baby massage, to hospital appointments, X-rays and operations.

My business needed me to be in London several times a week, but my son needed me to be at home with him while he was recovering from surgery. He was stuck in casts and pretty immobile, when he should have been running around with his older brother.

I thought I was superhuman and that I could do it all, but during a rare weekend away with my husband, I finally admitted that I was just one woman with too many plates to spin and something needed to give. I made the heartbreakingly difficult choice to stop working for a while, close the business I had worked so hard to build, and give my family the time and support they needed.

I went back to the office the following Monday and spoke to my clients, who were amazingly supportive. Final reports were written, journalists and contacts were emailed, files were packed up, and while my out of office was switched on, my passion for PR didn't ever turn off.

Without my business I felt as if my identity was slipping away from me. It soon became clear that while being a stay-at-home mum meant I could navigate the murky waters of DDH for Lucas, I missed my work and I simply wasn't fulfilled by going to soft play sessions and hanging out in coffee shops. I needed something more, so I started a blog and that's when I thought about writing a book. I did my research, took a course, sent out emails to publishers and secured a deal that led to me writing *Cast Life*.

Two days before Lucas had a major operation to break and realign his pelvis, I launched *Cast Life* and over 70 people came to the party. They did buy the book, we raised nearly £1,000 and I knew from the tears in their eyes that they felt my emotions as I told my brave son's story.

I am now part of the Advisory Board of the International Hip Dysplasia Institute in the United States, which is an honour and one that has helped position me as an expert in the field. I never thought I would attend steering groups at Great Ormond Street Hospital in London, be part of research-funding applications or take part in hip clinics at University Hospital Southampton, but I do.

So, What Does This Have To Do With PR And You?

Well, the money raised at the launch event, the interviews and media coverage to raise awareness of DDH around the world, the seat on boards and the ability to support people around the world has all come from the PR work I have done.

I admit that I have my career experiences, but I wanted you to know that I understand what it is like to go out there and do it for yourself, by yourself.

Our story is proof of what happens when you take that brave step and embrace your vulnerability and do the self-promotion that helps you move forwards.

I wanted other parents to know that they weren't alone, that someone else 'got it'. To do that, I had to let them know we were there to help them, and now, they do:

"Reading Cast Life *really helped me when we started on this long hip journey. It gave me lots of information and practical ideas through the eyes of an experienced parent."*

Rachael

"The DDH UK page helped me keep sane! It was so welcoming, I got my answers, my fears lessened, and I realised I wasn't in this alone. It is such an amazing support and without this group I don't know how I'd have made it through."

Tammy

"Cast Life and DDH UK made me realise that although I'm in Australia, I'm never alone in my daughter's hip journey! The information was so useful, easy to read, and I read it in one sitting and use it to help other mums here in Australia. My copy is well loved."

Michelle

These comments illustrate the power of telling your story, of opening up to the world and reaching out to others, and if you are nodding in agreement, then you have picked up the right book for you.

Your PR journey might be a steep learning curve, and there might be times when you think you can't do it, but stick with it because this could be the missing piece in your puzzle.

'Look at me' isn't something many of us are comfortable with, but if you don't shout about who you are and what you do, someone else will, which means they'll own the pages on magazines that could be yours.

Alison Simpson, Digital Content Editor of WeAreTheCity, perfectly sums things up when she says, *"Don't be afraid to blow your own horn! I think sometimes we have a tendency to hide our achievements, or to play*

them down, when really we should be shouting them from the rooftops –
especially when it comes to promoting your own brand."

It's time to stop those voices that shout you aren't good enough, aren't famous enough and aren't talented enough to talk about yourself; instead we are going to focus on your talents, your successes and let the press know all about them.

Being seen in the media on a consistent basis can help to raise the profile of your business, increase traffic to your website, boost your sales and client list, and could position you as an expert in your field.

The combination of all of these factors will not only create a thriving business, but it can also boost your confidence so that you shine brighter than ever.

Interviews in *Red* magazine, product round-ups on HuffPost and taking part in TED Talks won't happen overnight, but if you don't make a start, they will never happen at all.

There are always going to be reasons not to turn on your PR machine:

> You don't have the time.
> You don't have the money.
> You don't have your own office.
> You don't have the contacts.
> You aren't good enough.
> STOP!
> You can do this.

I believe that if you are good enough to have happy (delighted, even) paying clients then you are good enough to talk to the press about who you are and what you do.

The sooner you take that leap of faith, the more opportunities you are going to find and the sooner you will see your name in the spotlight.

Don't worry about what anyone else thinks, or what they are doing; this is your time to shine and I am here to make sure that is exactly what you do.

Don't think of this as a text book, but rather a journal for your PR adventure and the start of something new and exciting.

Scribble in the margins.

Use the text boxes to make notes.

Do the homework exercises, do them twice, do them until you feel confident enough to shine.

Highlight the bits that really resonate with you.

Underline relevant points.

Make a mess.

Stick things in and add Post-it Notes.

Make this *your* copy of *PR School* and I have a feeling it will take you somewhere amazing.

If you're looking for dry, academic guidelines, *PR School* isn't for you, but if you are ready to feel empowered and inspired and want to learn the skills to get you noticed using a confident voice, you are in the right place.

If you like what you're reading as you work through this book, come and get involved with the PR School community online. We will welcome you with open arms and you'll get even more expert advice, support and ideas to help you and your business to shine, as well as the chance to find new contacts and media opportunities.

So, let's get to work. We have a lot to do.

Natalie x

P.S. Remember that what happens in PR School, stays in PR School!

Lesson One

Getting to Grips with PR

Do you feel like PR is a VIP club reserved for celebrities and major players?

Have you got a story to tell, but hold back from talking about yourself because you don't want people to think you are bragging?

Are you dying to get in touch with influencers about your clothing brand, but not sure where to start?

Want to drive sales and raise your profile but fed up with spending money on ads and getting no return?

If you have said yes to one, some or all of these, then PR School is the perfect place for you.

I am not saying that this book will teach you everything it has taken me, and my colleagues, years to fine-tune, but it will put you on the right path.

What PR Is Not – The Myths Dispelled

There are many misconceptions about PR, and I feel that it's worth me clearing up some of this confusion before we move on.

PR is most definitely NOT free; it is an investment of time, resources, energy, products and creativity, all of which are precious and need to be used wisely.

PR isn't just about the column inches and air time – exposure needs to tie into your 'why' if it is going to help you grow your business and allow you to shine.

Giving stuff away for the sake of it isn't PR, but working with an engaged influencer on Instagram could help you build your brand, which means it could be worth sending them products and investing in that relationship.

PR isn't just about parties and having fun, and while it isn't ER, there is a serious side to this communication activity.

Stalking journalists on Twitter and spamming bloggers isn't PR, but it is kind of creepy and could get you into trouble.

Showing off isn't PR, it is boring and won't help you get ahead.

PR isn't about using lies to cover up your mistakes, it's about being honest and transparent so that you earn trust and respect.

PR isn't just about scheduling social media content and letting it lie dormant, it's about using that information to educate, inspire and engage with the people who matter to you.

PR isn't just for big businesses, it is also for hard-working, inspirational people just like you.

Talking off the record isn't PR, it's a mistake, so please never do it.

PR isn't a one-off press release, it's a long-term vision and strategy that can have a big impact on your business.

Automated pitches, endless follow-ups and ignoring deadlines and image requests aren't PR, they are poor practice and won't help you build the credibility you are looking for.

Copying a press release to every journalist in the country isn't PR, it is foolish and I've seen this lazy mistake go viral, on more than one occasion.

You see, PR isn't always easy to get right, but if you are willing to learn and put in the time and energy, it can be very worthwhile.

PR takes courage, determination and hard work, so it isn't for the faint-hearted.

PR isn't something that you will learn overnight, but it is something you can master over time.

I hope this has made things a little clearer and that you are now ready to start your PR adventure.

What PR Really Is About

The Chartered Institute of Public Relations[1] says, *"Public Relations is about reputation – the result of what you do, what you say and what others say about you."*

They continue, *"Public Relations is the discipline which looks after reputation, with the aim of earning understanding and support and influencing opinion and behaviour. It is the planned and sustained effort to establish and maintain goodwill and mutual understanding between an organisation and its publics."*

What this essentially means is that PR is what other people say about you, not what you say about yourself.

Favourable mentions of your business in the media, in my opinion, hold more value than a paid advert because you aren't dictating the message, someone else is.

To make life easier, why not think about it as a **P**ersonal **R**ecommendation by a third party?

If *Grazia*, *Stella* and *Style* all love your T-shirts because of the organic cotton fabric and on-trend leopard print design, people will flock to your website and you may sell out of stock, fast. Put a small ad in each of those publications, and not only will your budget be gone in seconds, but I doubt that you will get the same return.

While PR includes a broad range of areas, including corporate, investor, internal and crisis communications, social media management and community relations, at the heart of this book, we are looking at media relations and how you can use it in your business.

Media relations is about building relationships with the press, so that they answer your emails, take your calls, come to your events, review your products and then tell your story to their readers.

When I talk about the media in this book, I am not just referring to newspapers, magazines and TV channels. Websites, online magazines, blogs, vlogs, podcasts and social media feeds are all on the rise and as a small business owner this means there are more opportunities than ever for you to elevate your brand and get people talking about you.

From *Forbes* and *Women's Health*, to *Stylist* and mindbodygreen, PR opportunities are out there for the taking every hour, day, week and month of the year.

Think about the women who are interviewed by Oprah who started their now successful businesses at their kitchen tables.

Look at the tales of triumph and tragedy that are told on the pages of newspapers all of the time.

Reviews of books, restaurants and the latest cars are featured on blogs day in, day out. Every year gorgeous products appear in the Christmas shopping guides of *Country Living*, *Fabulous* and *Stella*.

All of this is the work of PR and something that is within your reach.

It is important to remember that PR is part of the overall communications mix and should be integrated into your brand image, website, social media feeds and marketing campaigns. However, it is important to keep those **P**ersonal **R**ecommendations front of mind at all times, as this what we are aiming for with your PR efforts.

How PR Can Work for You

If you are serious about investing your time, energy and resources in PR and working with the media to promote your business, then you need to be clear about why you are doing it and what you want to achieve.

At this point, I recommend you watch Simon Sinek's first TED Talk[2], so you can consider your 'why', and I think his powerful words will get you thinking about your business in a new and exciting way.

My 'why' for writing this book wasn't to sell thousands of copies (but that would be nice), it was about becoming the 'go to' PR consultant for people who want to learn to shine. This might not happen today, tomorrow or even this year, but as I write more books, more blog posts and communicate on social media, I get closer to that goal.

If you know what your 'why' is, then it is easier to get out of bed in the morning, decision-making becomes clearer, connecting with people happens more naturally and your PR activities will flow because you know what you are aiming for and why you are doing things.

No one does PR for nothing and if they do, it's a waste of time, effort and money. Yes, it's a pretty good feeling when you see yourself in print, but PR is more than an ego boost or a vanity project; if it is done well it can be a game changer.

Being in *Harper's Bazaar* is fantastic and you might be the most talked-about person on social media for a week or two, but if the feature doesn't include the name of your business and your website, it's a wasted opportunity when it comes to sales and traffic.

It doesn't matter what your 'why' is, but you need to have one as this will direct your energy, keep you going when you want to give up, and help measure your success.

There are many different reasons why people and organisations do PR, so let's have a look at them.

To Raise Awareness of Products and Services

Let's say you're a nutritionist, you are known in your local area and your social media feeds are doing OK, but you want more people to join your group coaching sessions online as this is where the real money is to be made. Your story is that you overcame bulimia in your 20s and are now healthy, eat well and work with women aged 30 to 45 who want to deal with food issues and move forwards. You email the Features Editor at *Top Santé*, they love your story and interview you as part of a three-person case study and your business and website are included both in print and online. The magazine reaches thousands of women and when the story goes live you start to get more enquiries from potential clients as well as more media opportunities, and so it goes on. This is PR working well, and it is what I want for you.

To Change Perceptions

While not easy to do, it is possible to change perceptions and consumer behaviour, and PR can certainly play a role in this. Skoda, Greggs and many other businesses have all used PR as part of their communication efforts and have changed the way the public have viewed them and their products.

To Find New Opportunities

Improved recruitment, sponsorships, award nominations and new business wins can all be the product of successful PR activities and sustained media exposure. If people keep seeing your name pop up in the press, then in time they will start to sit up, take notice and want to be a part of what you are doing.

To Drive Website Traffic

If you want people to go to your website, to sign up for your newsletter, to download your e-book or buy your products, PR is great as it can help with Search Engine Optimisation (SEO).

SEO is not a one-off marketing activity. It touches and interacts with every other aspect of marketing and communications, including PR. Therefore, it should be a strong consideration when devising a PR strategy, and Natalie Weaving, Director at The Typeface Group Ltd, has some good reasons why:

Backlinks and Domain Authority
When it comes to SEO, PR can be a useful way to build or increase the number of authoritative backlinks to your website. However, for this to work properly, your website needs to be performing well. For example, it needs to load quickly, be mobile responsive and have content that your audience expects to find from your business. You can check how your website is performing with the free Moz toolbar which displays your Domain Authority. Domain Authority is one of the main measures an online media outlet looks at when deciding whether to link back to you or not. It should also be a consideration when you are looking to grow your online presence. This is because if a website's Domain Authority is poor, it will negatively impact the rankings of the site that is linking to it.

What is Domain Authority?
A Domain Authority (DA) is a trust score given to a website based on whether a site is well maintained, secure and following SEO best practice. The score was developed by Moz (a software company) and it is based on the algorithms which search engines use when crawling and ranking your website. To put it simply, if your website SEO is poor – or even non-existent – and you do not have many backlinks to your site from authoritative sources, then you will be stuck with a low score.

Having said that, you will also have a low score if your website is relatively new or if you are blogging regularly. This is because DA is an average of Page Authority, which starts at zero whenever a new page – such as a blog post – is added. However, the benefits of having a blog still outweigh this small negative. You can overcome this by ensuring that everything you do add to your website is optimised and considered. This will help you to achieve those high-quality links from top media outlets.

Relevant and well written content
Another fundamental SEO consideration is providing content that

your audience would potentially want to read when they land on your site. This content should not only be useful to the audience, but it should also show you as a thought leader in your chosen field. Your website and the content you put on it could easily make the difference between you or your competitor getting the opportunity to comment in the national press or be interviewed on TV.

If your content is well written, relevant and full of expert opinion, you have a much better chance of being picked up by the media than one that is static, out-of-date and full of sickly buzzwords or clichés. The reason for this is simple – a media outlet will trust you if they can see that you can write well and know your subject inside and out. This just makes the job of a time-poor journalist so much easier.

Intent of the user

A huge change has happened that has meant keywords for blog content is not as important as it once was. It is now about the readability of the content and relevance to what you actually do and offer. With search engines using AI to decide what the person searching is actually looking for, keyword stuffing is no longer a practice that will ensure the discoverability.

This does not mean keywords are dead. It means that you don't have to force keywords into a beautifully written piece of content if there isn't one that fits. Simply ensuring that your website is keyword rich across the board will support your rankings as it will mean it is full of the words or phrases people are searching for in the first place.

Adding high-quality content to your site consistently will not only help grow your business as customers can find you easily, but it will also send trust signals to Google if people are then engaging with your site. This, in turn, will help your DA and ranking. That means that it will help journalists to find you in search results, too. So, make sure whenever anyone lands on your website that your contact details are easy to get hold of too.

To sum it up, SEO and PR support each other. Good SEO practices can increase your PR opportunities and PR opportunities from authoritative sources can support your SEO activity.

To Boost Sales

Having your wedding flowers showcased in a bridal magazine, your chocolates being included in a Father's Day round-up in *The Mail on Sunday*, or taking part in an interview in *Devon Life* about how you produce local organic gin, can see sales shooting through the roof and take you to great places.

To Put a Charity on the Map

If you are reading this book and work with a charity, then be assured that PR can be an amazing way to put that cause on the map. People facing challenging situations need support, and if you do your PR right, they will find you, and believe me, you will shine. You may also find that PR will help you to find volunteers to help your cause and increase donations.

To Gain Credibility

Maybe you work with mothers looking for a career change and after establishing a relationship with the features assistant at *Balance* magazine, she emails you for a comment about regaining your confidence after maternity leave. Your expert advice appears in the magazine and instantly gives your credibility a boost because the publication trusts you and thinks you can help their audience. People will read your words, check your website and hopefully come to you for help. The more often your name is seen, the more your target audience will trust you and that builds a credibility that no advert can match.

To Recruit Staff

As your exposure increases and people keep seeing you in the press, you will be regarded as a market leader by customers and competitors as well as potential talent. When I was working in the TV world, Cartoon Network had a great reputation for training staff and the opportunity to travel, and when I started working there, I knew it wasn't just hype.

To Influence Government Policy

It might sound like a tall order, but policy can be changed as a result of PR efforts. Knife crime, gangs, youth culture – are all current issues we are worried about but if PR is part of the communications mix, things can hopefully change.

To Attract Investors

While you are busy thinking about where you want to be seen, you never know who might see you when you do shine. Being in the media on an ongoing basis can really help to put you on the radar of investors and potentially open the doors to new opportunities.

To Build Goodwill

Maybe you're a property developer and have bought a piece of land in a run-down part of town and have planning permission to redevelop the site. PR can help you show the local community what is in it for them. Maybe a new school and leisure centre will be built and better health-care facilities provided, together with new jobs, and if this is communicated in the right way, you could be facing a very different audience.

To Manage a Crisis

PR isn't just about generating positive news, it can also help to handle bad publicity. Whether it's customer information being hacked, an environmental scandal or an outbreak of food poisoning, crisis management can help deal with a bad situation. It is always a good idea to have a plan in place to deal with a crisis, and I would never suggest ignoring a problem, as it won't go away and could make you look worse, which isn't what you want. When a problem comes along, don't panic and don't make knee-jerk decisions as this can add flames to the fire. Take a deep breath, look at the situation, speak to other parties involved, respond to the event with an honest, calm statement on your blog, answer comments on social media and learn. If things get really out of hand, you might need to ask for the help of a professional, and if that's what it takes to get back on track, do it.

To Become an Expert in Your Field

This doesn't happen overnight but if you focus, and put in the hard work, the rewards are worth it. You can't wait around for the people at TED to call you to do a talk or for a Dragon to just hand over the investment you need. Be brave and pitch yourself as a speaker, panellist, or workshop leader at a local level. Start small and once you have a few events under your belt, pitch for bigger conferences and industry events and not only will you polish your pitch, but you'll gain more and more exposure and gradually you will be seen as an expert, and then the sky is the limit.

To Get People to Attend an Event

Whether it's the opening of a new shop, a charity auction, or Santa fun run, PR can help get people to attend an event and get involved. One example is if a local celebrity is turning on the Christmas lights and there's a chance to win £1,000 on the night – this could be what it takes to get the evening paper interested in what's going on and write about it so that a record number of people come out on the night and get involved.

For Validation

Not many people think about this, but being seen in the press can give you validation amongst family, friends and peers. Very often when you are running a business for yourself, especially in the early days, people don't always get it and, even worse, they don't always take it seriously as they think a nine-to-five job is more sensible. A feature in *Elle* or an interview in *Forbes* can change that view and you will shine in a whole new light.

There are no two ways about it: to do your own PR you need to be brave.

You need to believe in who you are and what you do.

PR is about shutting down the voices that are telling you not to shout about your successes, and going out there and sharing your story anyway.

It's about making your visions and dreams come to life by taking up the offers that start to come your way because of the work you have put in.

Chloe Leibowitz, an award-winning life coach, comments on this: *"Take every opportunity that comes your way – even when it terrifies you!! We often talk ourselves out of things due to fear, and that voice that talks to us and tells us that perhaps we can't do it, we're not good enough, we're a fraud!! It's all nonsense, but it can hold us back so much, and can be followed by the kick in the stomach when someone else gets the coverage you know would be so good for you and your business. If you speak up about what you do, and have confidence in your brand, you will be much more likely to get that press attention."*

I am not saying it will be easy.

You may feel scared at times, but doing it even if it terrifies you could be the best thing you have ever done for you, your confidence and your business.

PR School Homework: My 'Why'

What would I like to achieve from doing PR?

....

....

....

....

....

....

In PR and Business – Be You

When you are thinking about doing PR for your business, it is vital to remain true to yourself and your brand at all times.

Getting media attention and shining might not be an innate trait for you, but it's something you can build up slowly over time.

Doing the exercises in this book will help you to do that and give you the confidence to push through your fears when it comes to PR and putting yourself out there and into the spotlight.

The media, influencers and your target audience are looking for not only great products and services, but authenticity too. It is pretty much impossible to pretend you are something you are not, and being real and authentic is the way forward when it comes to PR.

If you aren't authentic then your story won't quite ring true, your messages will be mixed, your tone of voice will seem out of place and your social media feeds will be mismatched.

Rebecca Ffrancon, personal stylist and colour consultant agrees: *"It definitely takes courage to be authentic and to really put yourself out there. I was so worried about being trolled and rejected and disliked, but actually none of that has happened, yet! I've turned my mindset around to think of it as a filter – the last thing you want is people following you who aren't interested in you, don't like you (and will ultimately never become a client). For me, the idea of NOT being authentic and creating a different persona to my own never really crossed my mind – you'd have to remember what you've said to who and how you've said it. I much prefer the simplicity of being me."*

Look at the businesses you buy from, who are true to themselves and offer great products and services that people invest in, and they are the ones that are successful.

Think about the people who inspire you, and I am pretty sure that they will be the ones who have a story that feels real when you read about them in the paper or listen to them talking about their journey on podcasts.

Be real, be honest, show yourself as someone who values progress over perfection.

Show up with an inspiring story or share how you overcame a challenge that took you off course and on to new horizons, and people are far more likely to buy into that than an easy ride to the top that is probably too good to be true.

What's Stopping You?

There is no question about it, putting yourself out there can be hard, terrifying even. While some of us want to be known, and even well known, at the same time we don't want to look like we are showing off. But plenty of other people are doing it and doing it well and no one thinks they are smug, they think they are smart.

Let's face it, there is always going to be a reason NOT to step outside your comfort zone when it comes to doing your own PR:

The children are too young.
You have just gone through a messy divorce and aren't in the right space.
You need to lose that extra half a stone so your photos look better.
You'd like to be in your new offices so you feel ready to go for it.
It's important for your blog to look perfect before you can post anything on it.
You just aren't quite ready to say, "Here I am, and this is what I do."

I meet so many people who say all these things, and more, and when we talk about it and get to the heart of the matter, what is really causing their hesitation and procrastination is confidence, or a lack of it.

Award-nominated author, business coach and mentor, Ruth Kudzi knows only too well that this can happen, and says, *"I have spoken to hundreds of clients and they often talk about lacking the confidence to be visible and put themselves out there with their business ideas. Regularly, in the same breath they comment about other people who have been successful in terms of business and are featured in the press who they feel don't have as many qualifications or skills. Much of what they say may well be true – they could be more experienced than X, maybe they are even better at their job, but the key difference is X has been busy self-promoting."*

She adds, *"Confidence in terms of taking action and visibility are two of the biggest predictors of success. In terms of clients, the ones who have the most profitable businesses are those who believe they can and do."*

There we have it, taking action and being visible are needed if you want to move forward and elevate your business, and that is what we are going to do, together.

This might sound a bit left field, but what holds some people back is the fear of success, rather than failure. Think about it for a moment: you're a fantastic coach and secure a series of mentions in newspaper features and blog posts, and eventually you are interviewed in *Psychologies* magazine. All of a sudden everyone wants to talk to you and you freak out and don't know what to do next, or where to turn.

The truth of the matter is, if you get those media wins, then you deserve to shout about it and the more you do it, the easier it will become. When you have *The Times* calling you for a comment about healthy eating because a freelance journalist went to one of your talks at their kid's school, or there's a request to review your pop-up restaurant from *Time Out* because their intern follows you on Twitter, it will have been so worth it and you can then shout even louder.

Taking the first step by writing a blog post, doing a Facebook Live, or writing an email to your local paper, might feel like a massive step, but I guarantee you will feel great once it's done.

Doing that one thing today could be the beginning of something so much bigger. Something you've never even dreamt of.

Don't worry about what anyone else thinks, or what they're doing, because this is your time to own your space and shine, so let's step up to the mark and make it happen.

PR School Homework: PR and Me

What does PR mean to me?

....

....

What is stopping me from promoting myself and shining?

....

....

Who is stopping me from taking part in PR?

....

....

What one thing could I do TODAY to start my PR journey?

....

....

How would I feel if I took that first PR step?

....

....

How would doing that benefit my business?

....

....

Lesson Two

Be Your Own Media Maker

The digital age means can we decide on the content and messages we send out to the world and therefore have a say in the image we create for ourselves and our businesses.

While there is still huge scope to work with and appear in the mass media, if you can move beyond the idea that only being in magazines and newspapers equals successful PR, then you are a click away from opportunities that will help you grow and shine.

As a small business owner with access to Twitter, Facebook, Instagram and LinkedIn as well as websites, blogs and vlogs, you can spread your news faster and cast your net wider than ever before.

Whether you're a virtual assistant, maths tutor or web designer, you can do this for yourself from your smartphone or laptop. At the click of a button and the swipe of a screen, you can instantly connect with the media, manage your reputation and give potential clients a taste of who you are and what you can do for them.

Encouraging people to watch your Facebook Lives or download a free e-book is a fantastic way to get them interested in what you have to say and leave them wanting to know more.

If you create interesting, engaging stories about your brand and react to breaking news and current affairs, you are starting to position yourself as an expert who is part of the conversation.

The world has changed beyond recognition and if you want people to talk about you and you want to get ahead and shine, you need to get involved and take advantage of what's on offer to you right here, right now.

Content Is Key to Success

To be your own media maker, you need to create content that people not only want to read, but also want to share with others, because this can help you to potentially reach more people than ever.

No one wants to read your content. This is a harsh statement but one that served Jackie Scully, Deputy Managing Director of a leading London content marketing agency, well as an editor and writer in the first decade of her career. If she wanted people to read and share her work, she needed to give them a reason to do so. Content is everywhere (just visit internetlivestats.com to see the dizzying amount being published online right now), but great content isn't, so here are her 11 tips to help you cut through the noise and get people talking:

Just start

This is the hardest part. If you hold out for that great first line, you may never publish a post. The more you write, the easier writing will become. Words are ideas are for publishing and sharing – not lurking in your drafts folder. Don't let the perfect be the enemy of the good.

Find your angle

Given the number of communications channels now available, it can often feel like everyone's a writer. So how do you create content people want to read and share? You choose an angle. My first ever running blog was published in *The Guardian*. Why? Because I ran my first 10k with a hip full of metal and no hair the week before my last chemotherapy treatment for cancer. My first HuffPost column about running a marathon wasn't just about running. It was about the confessions of a first-time marathon runner recovering from cancer treatment. And, my second (which led to multiple media interviews and saw my now-husband and I being profiled as one of the main human-interest marathon stories in April 2017) was about trying to train for a marathon while planning a wedding for the same day and trying to raise thousands for charity. I found my angle – and you can too.

Use your best idea first

I speak to lots of bloggers who tell me that they are saving their best ideas while they build their blog. Saving for what, I ask? Great ideas are only great when people can hear about them. With great ideas come a following and the flow of many other great ideas (there is no limited supply of great ideas). Only by starting big can you see just how much bigger you can go.

Make it personal

People buy people, so if part of your plan is to build your personal brand, let people get to know you through your words and actions. Don't be afraid to share your experiences, vulnerabilities and fears and bare a bit of that soul.

Keep it short

Short sentences, short paragraphs, short posts. Attention spans favour list-based articles online (otherwise known as listicles) so think about whether what you have to say can be easily broken into bite-sized pieces. If in doubt, cut it out. Oh, and if you are writing a list, choose an odd number of points (e.g. seven ways to…). Choose even numbers and people will think you've rounded up and your points are less powerful as a result.

Raise a smile

Humour is your friend. And humour based on shared experiences, your very best friend. One of my most-shared posts isn't an emotional cancer-related piece, but a listicle about spotting the signs you might love running too much. If you can find your equivalent of a sweaty pile of Lycra and a drawer dedicated to running medals for your subject, people will laugh along with you.

Make it visual

It is a truth universally acknowledged that if you include more images in posts, those posts are more likely to be shared and remembered. And don't worry if you're not a great photographer. If the picture helps with the storytelling and is high enough resolution (around 1MB is usually a good rule of thumb for most purposes online), it will do the job.

Consider your audience

One of my favourite books about content is Jonah Berger's 'Contagious'. In it, he talks about how to be interesting and create content worth sharing. His thoughts on social currency are really clever and so simple when you think about it. If you write something that will make people look good if they share it (surprising, delighting, informing etc.), they are more likely to share it. If readers can answer the question: 'What's in it for me?' you're on the right track.

Find your cheerleaders

The biggest mistake people make when trying to create shareable content is thinking everyone in the same space is a competitor. Find people writing about similar things and they are more likely to be interested in what you have to say and want to share it with their like-minded networks. With content sharing comes community. And, like all good networkers, if you celebrate other people, provide helpful comments and also share their content and ideas, you will draw people to you. It takes confidence, but kindness is the best currency there is.

Think practical, not promotional

Whether you are promoting a product, a service or a cause, start from the point of view of the problem you are trying to solve rather than simply promoting the solution. Tips and helpful guidance provide real practical value for readers and will encourage that all-important content sharing. By contrast, promotional pieces won't get you promoted. Be helpful and people will thank you for it.

And one for luck – see what I did there to avoid it being an even list!

Don't forget to link

You've written your helpful, personal, funny and surprising content that will make anyone sharing it look good. So now what? Remember to include appropriate links to other content or your services/products/fundraising page/social media at the end so that people know what you want them to do next. Without the right calls to action (basically links to take the reader forward in some way) people are likely to move on to something else and leave you behind.

Now you know what you have to do, and have your content ready and waiting to be used, you need to start using it.

Let's go.

Get Involved in Social Media

If you aren't active on social media, you need to be because it can be an amazing business, PR and growth tool and is another way to be your own media maker and show the world who you are and what you do.

Social media isn't something to be scared of, and it won't take over your life, but it could take you places you thought were only for the major players.

People who follow you and interact with you are more likely to come to you for expert comment, to use your services or buy your products because they will have seen your posts and have a good feeling for what you stand for.

You can spend lots of time worrying about which platform to work on, how big it is and how many users it has, but what you actually need to do is work out what your target audience use, and hang out in the same places.

While Instagram can be brilliant for a photographer who wants to reach couples getting married, an HR consultant might find LinkedIn the place to find potential clients looking for work as well as sharing their opinions on the current employment situation with their peers and the media. Again, it's a platform where you can stand out as an expert, so use it.

If you are targeting mums, it might be that they are mainly using Facebook, but if you want to get the attention of the media, Twitter could be the place for you as there are continuous requests for stories on there via the #journorequest hashtag.

The temptation might be to get out there and run accounts on all platforms, but I am not sure that is the best way forward, unless you have loads of time or an assistant who can do it all and respond to people in a timely, appropriate manner.

Claire Sparksman, social media marketing consultant and founder of Be Social London, thinks social media is brilliant for PR: *"You can share your story, build brand awareness, create and develop relationships and have conversations with people. You can raise awareness of events, launches, a new product or book, fundraising, collaborations, new work or initiatives – or just sing about your brand!*

"The strategy behind using social for PR is the same across all your social platforms but you should always tailor your messages so they work for each platform and each audience on that platform (your audience may not be the same on different platforms).

"Always tailor your message to your audience. Think about how you can combine your message with what will resonate with them."

Social Media – What Is What?

You don't want to have too many plates spinning, so let's have a look at the options so you can decide what the most appropriate channels for you are. This way, you'll be able to create great content and engage with people and make meaningful connections.

Twitter

Twitter can be a fantastic PR tool and with a 2018 survey by Muck Rack[3] showing that 27% of journalists cite Twitter as their primary news source, this is a good place to be seen.

It's super easy to find, follow and communicate with the media and influencers, as well as customers, and thanks to hashtags like #journorequest there are excellent media opportunities up for grabs on the platform that you may otherwise never discover. Journalists use this to share details about the features they are working on and need an expert comment or interview for. As they are actively looking for help, this is a great time to contact them via a reply tweet, direct message (DM) or email them and make inroads with your PR.

If you can't help directly each time, retweeting their request so they can reach the right people, or asking them to share the final piece so you can share with your followers, can be helpful and show willing. This might not get you in the press, but helps to be part of the conversation and by being in touch with them, and on their radar, you never know where it could lead in the future.

As I said, it is all about conversations, so the more you participate and engage with people, the more you will get out of it and the more opportunities will come along. Remember, this works both ways, so if you see something that you know would be of interest to someone you know, tell them about it. They will thank you, I am sure.

Facebook

With over two billion monthly active users (when I wrote this book in 2019), Facebook is a pretty good place to be if you want to connect with customers, influencers and the media. It is easy to navigate and post information, you can run competitions, share your wins so your network can celebrate with you and it is great if you want to create a page, group or community.

While making your voice heard and your brand seen can take time, it is really worth doing. The DDH UK closed group has nearly 3,000 members from around the world who come to us for support. Over in the PR School Facebook group, journalists and influencers are constantly looking for stories from businesses, so it is worth joining and seeing if there is a fit for you. With both, I post at least three times a day, but in the early days and as you're finding your way, I'd suggest adding new posts three to five times a week, and as your following grows and people find out about you, you'll want to do it more, believe me, because it will really help you to shine and attract the right attention.

I spend way too much time on Facebook, but it has led to a huge number of opportunities for me and my clients, and I would encourage you to set up an account and start playing around with it to build your knowledge and confidence. Find groups that work for you and your business, as well your PR.

Instagram

Instagram is growing fast and it is all about great photos and telling stories, which is what we are all about at PR School. Not only is it a place to find media contacts but, maybe more importantly, it's where food, lifestyle, luxury and fashion brands hang out together with influencers.

If you have strong visual content, photos and videos, Instagram is a great place for you to be seen. For example, if you sell cool personalised T-shirts and want to ramp up your sales, Instagram could be the place for you as you can add images of customers wearing their shirts around the world, as well as influencers sporting them by the pool or in a club, and before you know it, new customers will come looking for you to get a piece of the action.

Tamara Stringer, social media consultant and owner of Incredibly Social, has some great tips on getting started with Instagram:

It's all about the images
Use good quality images and think about what you are writing in the caption – people love a story, so make it interesting and engaging. Ask questions because people love to feel part of your story.

Be consistent
Don't just post for the sake of it – be realistic with your time and the number of posts you can create and stick to it!

Use Instagram stories
Stories are the best way of getting your account seen and ideally you should post 3–10 stories a day to ensure you are remaining in people's minds. If you can, talk to the camera and use subtitles or summarise what you have said with text as most people watch stories with the volume off. Stories are great for behind the scenes and do not need to be too polished, they are a relaxed way to get your story across.

Think of Instagram as a virtual shop window
If you view Instagram as your shop window you will see how important it is to make it interesting to look at, so people will come in and find out more.

People love to see people
What I mean by this is to post pictures of yourself in action, doing what you love, with people who work with you. Doing this makes your brand feel more authentic to the people you want to talk to.

Test things out
If you try something and it doesn't work – change things up, see which posts get the most engagement and try and recreate similar ones. Do your research – look at what is working for similar businesses and think about how you can rework it for your brand.

Be creative, think big and you will shine on this welcoming platform that is inspiring and so easy to use.

LinkedIn

LinkedIn is good if you have a service-based business, such as coaching, HR, marketing or sales. You can connect with journalists as well as posting about your areas of expertise so that people know you are there for comment. This is a more formal platform, so your content needs to be more professional in manner, as does the way you communicate your messages and share your news stories and events that you want other people to attend.

There are many groups you can join and this can be a brilliant way to find those all-important awards to enter and conferences to speak at.

Emma Wyatt, social media consultant at Social Conversations by Emma, understands about getting to grips with LinkedIn: *"LinkedIn is an amazing platform to grow your personal brand and visibility and while it takes time to do this, it can be done without any advertising budget.*

"It is important to have a complete profile with stunning profile and cover images. Write a to the point headline and create a clear summary to intrigue the reader to connect with you and ask for a conversation to find out more.

"Plan to be on the platform daily, post about your expertise and join conversations that other people are having around your subject/industry. Connect with the key people you want to work with; build and nurture your relationship with them. Help them to find out more about you, why you do what you do and why your story is of interest to them and their readers."

I do use LinkedIn for business, but I know it's a case of the more effort you put in, the better the engagement and the bigger the results. So, I'd better get on with it and take Emma's advice.

Helen Campbell, Business Coach at Jazz Cat, is no stranger to the power of LinkedIn and doesn't believe it is just an online CV service or a way of showing recruiters you're 'open'. She sees it as an incredibly useful platform to publicise and market your business in an authentic way.

Helen says, *"Spend a little time on LinkedIn and you'll notice quality content which you can learn from and share, and use as inspiration for creating your own. You may also start to notice media requests on LinkedIn – if you connect with editors and journalists – as well as seeing speaking opportunities at conferences and events. My recent LinkedIn goal was to secure a book deal. I focused for a whole year on creating and posting longer articles, which were relatable and shareable, on the topic of my book. I also connected with people who worked in publishing, which helped me to appear in the feeds of relevant decision-makers. In less than a year of doing this I was approached with a book deal. I'd suggest spending at least six months giving it a really good go before deciding whether it's a platform you enjoy and can learn from. If you love a long read and enjoy writing, you may find it becomes your favourite platform fairly quickly."*

Pinterest

I will be honest here, I don't use Pinterest, but with over 250 million active monthly users (again, in 2019 when I wrote this) I think it is somewhere I need to start hanging out[4].

Jocasta Tribe, founder of Marketing for Mums, agrees and says, *"Pinterest is great for an e-commerce brand to drive traffic to a particular product page of a website as 93% people use Pinterest to help them plan for a purchase[5] and a staggering 86% of millennials say they use Pinterest to 'plan life moments, big and small'. If you want to reach women then Pinterest is the place to be as it has the biggest female to male ratio of all the other platforms."*

She added, *"Rather than selling a product, Pinterest is a great place for building a brand identity with the different boards enabling you to tell different brand stories. This is especially great if you have a visual business – maybe you are a photographer or interior designer – because the content is based upon impactful, beautiful images and that is what people are looking for on this platform."*

Getting the Best from Social Media

Simply having a social media account isn't enough to cut through the increasing noise and the desire to be heard. It's a bit like having a pair of wellies, but leaving them in the cupboard when it rains!

Nicola Scoon, online marketing specialist, has some great tips when it comes to social media:

Have a plan

One of the pieces of advice you'll always hear about social media is to stay consistent. But how do you stay consistent and post something new every single day? By planning!

If you can, set aside time at the start of each month to plan your social media content for the month ahead. Get ahead and batch tasks by writing out social media posts, creating graphics or finding photos, and scheduling everything using a tool like Hootsuite or SmarterQueue.

Planning and scheduling a month's worth of content gives you a base to start from, reducing the pressure on you to come up with a masterpiece on the fly.

Focus your efforts where your audience is

With so many social media platforms around, how do you know which one to spend your time on? We all have our own personal preferences, but to start with it's best to spend time building up a presence on the channels that your ideal audience uses.

Focusing on one or two social media platforms means that you're giving yourself enough space to create and share really great content, and to build up a community around what you do. When you've established a community or following you're happy with, you can then branch out and experiment with other social media platforms and encourage your followers to find you there too.

Not sure where to find your audience? Set aside some time to work on your client persona and pinpoint what your customer likes and where they look for ideas, inspiration or news. You can also look at similar businesses to see where they have the most engaged following.

Have fun with it!

Social media platforms like Facebook and Instagram offer you the perfect place to share more about who you are, what inspires you and the people behind your business. The little touches like sharing the inspiration behind the name of your product or a funny moment from the office can make people feel closer to you.

It's also a great opportunity to have some fun and experiment. Find some qualities that are common amongst your audience and create content around them – this might be sharing a meme, asking a question about a trending topic or a caption competition. The fast-moving nature of social media means that you have more freedom to try something new. If it doesn't work you can try something different next time, but if it does it could quickly go viral!

Engagement is everything

Once you've created your content and scheduled it, there is still a lot to consider so that your social media presence really stands out. Plan out time in your day to check in regularly and reply to comments, share content from others and take part in conversations with your community. Not only does this mean building deeper connections with your audience and potential customers, but it does wonders for your PR and brand awareness too.

Do what you love and outsource the rest

We all get to a point in our businesses where we run out of time to do everything. If social media doesn't excite you, or there are aspects of it you don't enjoy (like scheduling), consider outsourcing those parts or hiring an assistant. Look for someone who can translate your brand voice into engaging content and use it as an opportunity to grow your following and community even further.

From this, I hope it is clear that social media is a great place to find PR opportunities as well as making connections and building valuable relationships with the media, peers and customers. While it takes time, stick with it and as you start to shine and become more recognised and trusted, you will be glad you did because you never know who might be watching and what that could lead to.

PR School Homework: Social Media Platforms

Take an hour out, with a cup of tea, somewhere quiet, and have a look around the various social media platforms out there and decide which ones you think would work for you.

Go into those platforms, set up your accounts, get to work and see that you are NOW working on your PR!

Notes:

....

....

....

Blog It

If want to spread the word about your work so the world knows who you are, a blog is your new bestie. The word 'blog' comes from 'weblog', which pretty much translates as an online diary and is a great way to dip your toes into the world of self-promotion, show people what you do and let them know what they can expect if they work with you.

Media coverage is important, and we have already established that it adds to your credibility, but writing a blog can be incredibly empowering, very helpful and puts you in control. There are no red pens, no rules, nothing but your words, your images and your brand, told your way.

Designers, bakers, writers and artists can benefit from having a blog and, when you combine sharp content with impactful images and add in glowing customer testimonials, you're going to shine.

You might also be surprised to know that the media do look at blogs as a source for ideas and stories, which again shows that the Internet is a big place with massive potential, so tap into it and you never know who will find you.

Gemma Went, business mentor and mindset coach, confirms this and says, "*Members of the press often find me via my blog or social media feeds and tend to either ask for comments on online business or bigger pieces on strategy or mindset.*"

Chris Gower, founder and Editor of Dining Devon, has a great blog and some handy advice when it comes to getting started in the blogging world:

Find your niche
Simply put, what are you going to write about? Is it interesting? Who is it aimed at? And why are you even writing? Ask yourself a few questions first, even before you've created a snappy name. It is important to have some sort of strategy as you start, but remember it isn't set in stone especially at the beginning; you will be just finding your feet to begin with so don't be scared to change your mind and don't be afraid to change your blog's direction in the very early days, although once you're established with regular readers, a change in direction might mean that you lose followers.

Choose a platform
This is often an easy conversation starter with any blogger. Most bloggers will choose between Blogger.com or WordPress.com. I would recommend trying both to see what you feel comfortable with, but I personally use WordPress.com. Invest in a good domain name as well – it looks slick and professional, especially if you are looking to approach PR agencies.

Be consistent
So you've thought of a name, you've set up the blog with an 'About' page with all the relevant links and you've written your first post! Congratulations, you can now call yourself a blogger, but all bloggers know the importance of staying consistent. Post regularly and as often as you can, but don't sacrifice quality for quantity.

Use SEO
When you hear people talking about SEO – 'my blog has good SEO' – this roughly means that the words and the content are particularly attractive to search engines. Search Engine Optimisation has a whole industry built around making content and web pages appear high up in search-engine rankings. An easy way to start doing this is to make sure you use search-engine-friendly key words.

Think about social media

As social media has become more integral in daily life, it too plays its vital part in the world of PR and blogging. It is almost unheard of to see a successful blog that has absolutely no social media presence; most bloggers realise how important social media is at driving traffic to their blog. I would expect a blog to have at least an Instagram, Twitter and Facebook presence. Don't underestimate the power of Pinterest if your topic is visual too.

Creating content

When we talk about content in terms of a blog, this can mean everything from written posts to videos. Think about different ways that you can get your message across. There is a growing trend towards creating YouTube videos as well as a written blog.

The more you post, the more you promote those posts and spread the word, the more you form an audience who will come back to your blog again and again. This does take time, so be patient because the rewards will be awesome!

Working with PR agencies and blogger services

PR agencies love bloggers. Big ol' broad statement right there, but more and more agencies, naturally depending on the clients, will want to engage with bloggers. Sign up to PR agencies and services such as 'Bloggers Required' that specialise in working with bloggers on behalf of big companies who understand the power that bloggers now hold on opinion.

Have a press pack

I would definitely recommend creating a 'press pack' which is essentially a fact sheet detailing important information that PR companies can use in getting to know you and your blog. Included some statistics, add in some follower counts; it is always worth having one to hand!

One step beyond

Many bloggers use this as a valid way of becoming freelance writers and journalists. It is in itself a very valid route into publication – I myself have written a few pieces for local and national magazines on the back of my blogging work. With this, how about writing a book? Deliciously Ella is a prime example of a blogger who took it further – writing books and even opening her own restaurants, all on the back of her blog. Maybe, depending on the type of blog you want to write, you could hold workshops, or run a course on a service like Udemy.com.

Podcasts

Another way to be your own media maker is by hosting a podcast, which pretty much lets you create your own radio content. So, if you have ever fancied being a presenter, now's your chance.

Podcasts are becoming increasingly popular because they allow you to connect with your audiences, they are cost-effective and easy to create, and you can distribute the content on your website and on social media, thus sending your story out wider than ever.

Corrie Jones, CEO and founder of UNTAPPED, has a fantastic podcast called Self-Made Women, and she has some top tips on getting started when it comes to getting started on podcasts:

Pick a concept
Go for a concept or idea for the podcast that you're passionate about. Whether you'll be interviewing others or sharing stories or creating comedy, it needs to be something you're able to talk about enthusiastically for 30 minutes. Decide on a name, format, podcast artwork, and how often you'll be uploading new episodes.

Equipment
Research the equipment you'll need to get started. Read reviews on the kind of microphone and editing software that's best suited for your budget – remember that it doesn't have to be super expensive and some are available for free (Audacity is the editing programme I use). Spend some time playing around with the new equipment and becoming familiar with how to use it.

Start recording!

Doing your first episode can be scary, particularly if you've never hosted a show before. Don't be too worried about getting it perfect first time, your podcast will naturally progress and develop as you become more practised at recording the episodes. You can always listen to some radio or podcast hosts you admire to learn how they speak and interact with their guests. When do they pause for effect? Do they use filler words like 'um' and 'ah'? Think about what you can learn from this and bring into the cadence of your own voice.

Create an RSS feed

RSS stands for really simple syndication and it's a way for information to be delivered to someone, rather than them having to go and find it themselves – so you are making life easier for them. Create a feed for your podcast and submit it to the iTunes store and don't forget to submit your RSS feed to other podcast apps for Android listeners, such as Acast or SoundCloud.

Promotion

After all that hard work, promote your podcast! See if you can arrange any press attention for the launch of the podcast and use social media to spread the word. Encourage your listeners to leave reviews so that your podcast becomes more visible on iTunes and might even enter the charts.

The podcasts I really enjoy listening to are: Jenna Kutcher's Goal Digger podcast and Emma Gannon's Ctrl Alt Delete, and they're part of the inspiration for starting Self-Made Women.

Get Your Glow Back, Path to Success, School for Mothers, Table Manners and Prosperity Kitchen are just some of the podcasts I love and being a guest on someone else's podcast is a fabulous way to shine.

Be Part of the Conversation

Before you go out there and proactively tell your story, you can make a start on your PR journey by simply reacting to what is happening in the world. This is called newsjacking.

I don't want to add to your workload as I know you are super busy already, but if you know what is going on around you, you'll be on track to being a pro.

Being on the ball and responding to stories as they hit Twitter is a proactive way to turn on your PR machine. If you consistently step up, in time you can become the go-to person for the media and this in turn can help build your credibility and reputation as an expert in your field.

If you see a story about the sharp rise in stress at work, don't go to the gym as usual because by the time you get home, someone else will have already written a blog post, spoken to LBC or secured the 1pm slot on Sky News.

If you are serious about your PR, you need to make it an integral part of your business and a priority at times when it could help you to shine.

One example of this is from PR School member, Jenny Tschiesche, author and one of the UK's leading nutrition experts. She says, *"Right name, right time. The day I got national media coverage on* Sky News, BBC News, The Guardian, Channel 4 News, *was the day the government mentioned the idea of banning lunchboxes. Being known as the Lunchbox Doctor that day was quite handy."*

So, how do you do this?

Wake Up to the News

Whether it is on the radio or TV, I generally start my day by seeing what is going on in the world as I check my emails and drink my first coffee. I learned this in my early agency days when the receptionist would hand me the daily papers and I'd read them from cover to cover and look for opportunities for our clients before the morning meeting.

One of my most memorable media reactions was when Earthwatch's beloved Peter the Penguin was found alive and well in Antarctica. We sent out a press release straight away and this led to coverage on the BBC website and in print publications, which in turn raised awareness of the charity's projects and work.

You see, while you still have your story and brand at the heart of your PR activities, by turning what is happening in the world into something relevant too, you are creating new chances for your business to be seen by the right people.

If you want to get in on the action here, writing a timely blog post and sending this out over social media using relevant hashtags is a good starting point as people will look at what you have to say and want to find out more about you.

An email or phone call to your local news desk offering yourself up as an interviewee, a tweet to *Metro* or a post on your blog can put you at the heart of the debate.

Writing a quote and sending it to your contacts and the Press Association (PA) is another option. I love the PA as their information drops into the inbox of news desks around the UK and can lead to LOADS of coverage and exposure in a variety of places. This isn't an easy win, so make sure you follow them on social media, build a relationship with a relevant contact and things could get really busy, really quickly.

Read the Papers

Print media might be in decline, but newspapers are still popular and being featured in them can take you places. You don't have to read every single article, but it's always worth skimming through and not only noticing what's hitting the headlines and what the current trends are but also recognising the regular feature opportunities you could be tapping into and being part of.

Whether you buy a paper or flick through copies in the library or at your local coffee shop, taking a look could be really beneficial. Try to keep your news intake varied and if you usually read *The Guardian*, but your target audience reads the *Daily Mail*, swap things around. I love the reviews, interviews and product guides in the weekend papers, and often rip out the pages that interest me and stick them on my office walls as a reminder of where I want my clients to be seen next.

Online editions of newspapers are also worth looking at and paying attention to, but because the stories are turned around quickly, you need to be fast to get a shining win here.

Listen to the Radio

BBC Radio 4, LBC, talkRADIO and 5 Live all offer news and views and as I drive at least 30 miles a day, I often tune in and see what is happening around the world.

I'm not saying you are going to find gold dust on the air waves, but there might be a phone-in about school dinners on BBC Radio Berkshire that you could be a part of, or a debate about the future of grammar schools might interest you as a Governor. When you have stopped driving, follow the station on Twitter, look at their Facebook page, send an email to the studio and offer yourself as a guest.

Yes, other people will be doing the same thing, but if you don't try, you will never know if you are the right fit for them and it's amazing where opportunities like this can lead.

One person who found success from a radio appearance was Rebecca de Jager of Hugo's Workshop, who says, *"I was on a James O'Brien phone-in on LBC and my followers increased immediately and so did my sales!"*

Check Out Podcasts

Podcasts are becoming increasingly popular and they cover everything from business and parenting to mental health and fitness. An episode could spark an idea, lead you to being a guest or even inspire you to create your own podcast, and all of these are vehicles for PR and can open up many new opportunities.

Keep an Eye on Social Media

Never before have we been able to access breaking news in such an immediate, real-time manner and I encourage you to embrace this with your PR.

Dipping in and out of Twitter or Instagram can give you the heads-up on what is happening out there, and you never know when the moment for you to shine will strike.

One morning I woke up to news on my Facebook feed about swaddling babies safely, which was the perfect opportunity to talk about DDH. The result wasn't immediate, but a blog post and emails to various contacts eventually led to the story being covered in the *Daily Mail* and online.

#journorequest is used all the time by the media who are looking for quotes on anything from mindfulness and healthy eating, to stories of people who have retrained and forged successful new careers, so make sure you are seeing them and following the relevant ones up.

Alison Simpson confirms this when she says, *"#journorequest is something I use regularly and strongly encourage other people to use. #journorequest, and Twitter as a whole, is an amazing tool for connecting journalists with PRs and their clients. It allows you to reach out to people you perhaps wouldn't have access to otherwise and helps to build a relationship with them. It's a definite 'must-have' tool!"*

The key to success here is to be fast to respond, be sure to engage with the media if they do come back to you and always deliver what they want, and if you can't, let them know.

Laura Sweet, founder of Amamaya Clothing, had success with this: *"I answered a journorequest hashtag on Twitter from* The Telegraph *which led to an interview on how I combatted loneliness as an entrepreneur. There was a mention of my business and a link to my website as part of the feature[6] and from this I saw an increase in hits to the site which were visible in my web stats."*

Bear in mind there are millions of users on Twitter and this is becoming an increasingly popular way to source opportunities, so try not to rely on this as your main PR activity.

Create Google Alerts

Setting up Google Alerts for key terms and words that are relevant to you, your business and your industry, is a clever way to keep one step ahead of the pack. For example, if you campaign for less plastic to be used in supermarket packing, go to Google News and set up alerts for terms such as 'plastic', 'packaging', 'supermarket packaging', 'environment' etc., and you will be sent the news for those subjects as it comes in. You can react accordingly, be that in the form of a press release, a pitch to one of your contacts or a blog post you then send out via social media to glean interest from your followers.

PR School Homework: Google Alerts for My Business

Create three Google Alerts for your business and start to monitor those as they hit your inbox:

....

....

....

....

....

....

....

....

....

....

Subscribe to Media Enquiry Services

Services like ResponseSource and PressPlugs send media enquiries directly to your inbox with numerous categories to choose from. These aren't cheap, so do your research and work out if the cost is worth the potential gains for you.

From comment pieces in the *Sunday Express* and *Daily Mail* to full-page case studies in *Red*, not only have these services led to coverage for me and my clients, they have also been the start of great media relationships and ongoing successes.

Tap into Awareness-Raising Activities and Seasonal Events

Christmas, New Year, Mother's Day, Easter, Father's Day and Halloween are all prominent annual events and the media is always full of stories about them.

From interviews with famous mothers and daughters, to product round-ups and competitions, I bet that editorial opportunities you may not have noticed in the past will now start to catch your eye and you will want a piece of the action.

The key thing to remember here is to plan ahead – especially if you want to target the print media.

The monthly magazines tend to work three to four months ahead, so if you want your healthy turkey recipes for Christmas to be in *Good Housekeeping*, then contact them in July, or you could be too late and they'll be researching their Easter offerings.

The media planning ahead is referred to as 'lead times' in the industry, and it is a good idea to be aware of these early on. Weekly magazines generally work three to four weeks ahead of time, daily newspapers vary depending on the pages and sections, but front-page news has to be hot, and the weekend supplements and magazines will be working around six weeks ahead of themselves.

When it comes to websites and blogs, things are more fluid and people are responsive to breaking news, so if your story is strong, it could be used very quickly.

Big events such as elections, summits and anniversaries all offer the chance to be part of the bigger picture, so use them to your advantage.

As well as seasonal events, there's an ever-increasing number of awareness-raising days, weeks and events each year and being part of them can help you to shine.

From International Women's Day and Healthy Hips Awareness Month, to National Curry Week and World AIDS Day, you can start building a PR calendar today.

If you are going to use these events, be clever and creative in your approach and rather than just talking about the event, focus on what you are bringing to the table. For example, use World Book Day to launch your novel, World Animal Day could be a great hook for your conservation work and if you are a marvel with muffins, then World Baking Day could be your time to shine.

Keep an eye on what's coming up, be ready to jump in when you see an opportunity, use your blog and social media channels to be your own media maker and you will soon start to see ideas come to life. Remember, be brave and step out of your comfort zone and into the spotlight so you can shine just like you are meant to.

PR School Homework: Awareness Days and Events for My PR Plan

As you see them, use this space to create a list of awareness days and seasonal events that you could tap into, and you will be able to add these into your PR plan.

....

....

....

....

....

....

....

....

....

....

....

....

....

....

....

In the online PR School community, we constantly share resources and opportunities to help you make the most of awareness days and events, so come on over and check out what's on offer and going on.

Lesson Three

It's All About the Story

Let's face it, from a very young age stories are a part of our lives.

Fairy tales at bedtime.

Weekend news being written in exercise books at school on Monday morning.

Degree dissertations being completed as the sun rises and the deadline approaches.

Water-cooler conversations in the office.

Book clubs.

Dare I say it, gossip at the school gates.

All around us, stories are being told, written and shared and are very much a part of the fabric of life.

As a self-confessed introverted extrovert, stories have always been a huge part of my life. I read them, write them and I tell them. I would spend hours in the library as a child, racing from one book to another to win the summer reading scheme, then I pored over the set texts at school, soaking up stories like a sponge.

As an adult, I not only tell stories to my sons, I write them on my blog and share them for my clients because the media want stories they can tell their readers.

The story could be the devastation of the ivory trade, the fundraising efforts behind the opening of a new home for disabled children, the evolution of a clothing brand or the life-changing reason behind the writing of a book, and I have used all of these to secure media coverage.

People constantly make decisions based on emotions, and understanding this will allow you to find your story.

We all have something to say and share.

A picture to paint.

An image to create.

A talking point at a party that will make people take notice and remember you.

Something to be proud of.

What's Your Story?

Whether you file taxes, draw landscapes, bake cakes or teach sewing, there is a story behind every scenario, and it is this story that helps a customer make an informed decision about whether to buy from you or someone else.

The key is to focus on what makes you unique and this will form your story and the start of your PR journey.

A company launch will only be news if there is a story behind it and that is the same for a product launch, event, partnership or funding deal.

Laura Sweet told me, *"I set up Amamaya Clothing when my daughter was born. Spending time outside walking and climbing was great but stressful because I couldn't find the right clothing for my child. What was available was unsuitable or cheap and ineffective. I thought I could do better and the company was created. I secured a two-page spread in Somerset Life by utilising my local connections and how living and walking in Somerset had inspired me."*

Opening a gallery might not be news, but if you talk about leaving London and swapping city smog for the sea mist of St Ives and painting in your grandmother's studio, that gives you a hook for a story and a starting point for your PR.

Winning an award as an industry leader or for having an outstanding workplace culture can add clout to your reputation, and I have had this with several clients and seen impressive media results.

Chloe Leibowitz, adds, *"Being an award winner was completely amazing and has benefitted me in two ways. It has definitely added gravitas and authority to what I do, which means people take me more seriously. In terms of confidence, it's the ultimate boost. It really allows me to feel that what I am doing is being well received and is making an impact and that is a fantastic feeling."*

It could be that an accident led to your retraining as a therapist and now you work with ex-military personnel, giving them hope for the future, and it is this story that could get you an interview with a newspaper, especially if your clients are happy to talk too.

Maybe you had a tough divorce and while you don't want to go into the nitty-gritty of the settlement, it led you to opening an online shop that is a global success, something you would never have done when you were married.

After working in an office job you hated, you took voluntary redundancy and retrained as a hypnobirthing teacher who now works with pregnant celebrities.

With a wealth of experience in the City, you have founded a networking group that brings women together and helps them smash that glass ceiling.

These are the kind of stories behind the headlines, the kind of stories we hear all the time and the kind of stories you have to tell.

As you move forward, you will hear journalists ask about the 'angle' and this is your unique story and what I would ask you to think about before going any further, because these are your key messages.

Yes, you have a business to promote, a product to sell or a name to make for yourself, but if you look outside of that, delve into what makes you interesting, what connects you to people, then things get a whole lot more exciting and the world becomes your stage on which to tell your story and stand out.

PR School Homework: My Story

What is my story?

....

....

What are my key messages?

....

....

What makes my story interesting?

....

....

How Much of Your Story Do You Want to Tell?

Some people are happy to talk about everything. Maybe they work for a charity or promote a cause close to their heart, and it is those stories that can be so impactful because they are real, raw and true.

You will also read business interviews where company owners happily talk about staff retention rates and profits as well as how much they have invested in the company, what mistakes they have made and what their plans are for the future.

Kiss and tell stories are, in my opinion, short-sighted and cheap, but for some people it is a gateway to five minutes of fame and cash.

How much you tell is down to you and we all have our limits and know where to draw the line in the media sand.

My story is about how my professional career collided with my personal life when my son was diagnosed with DDH and how that led to me writing *Cast Life*, setting up DDH UK and now writing this book and founding PR School.

I started to campaign for more awareness around DDH when Lucas was first diagnosed. Fast forward seven years and our school took part in a one-mile walk to help raise money and awareness of DDH and the charity. The event was a massive success both in terms of money and exposure. We were interviewed by BBC Radio Devon, featured on the 6pm news and the story was covered by a number of local papers and magazines, before and after the event. Lucas was photographed with our Patron, the Paralympic swimmer, Gemma Almond, as well the mascot from the Exeter Chiefs rugby team who came along on the day and added a special local edge.

It really was brilliant and I felt that same old PR buzz in my blood, but as the media coverage came in and I kept seeing my son's photo in the press, I took a step back and wondered how much longer I could take this approach.

The reality was, I didn't want Lucas to become the poster boy for DDH and I didn't want his condition to define him and make him any different to any other kid in his class. It was at that point I decided to change course with the promotion of DDH UK and the work I did to put hip dysplasia on the global medical map. Today we look for stories, such as an increase in hip replacements in young people or Sir Andy Murray having a hip injury, that we can newsjack and comment on. By doing this we remain part of the conversation, but Lucas is no longer the centre of the PR or the face of campaigns, and that feels right to us.

Over time you may need to come up with more ideas, more content and more stories, and you may need to change direction, but having a clear, strong starting point will help you make the right decisions so you can shine like the bright star you deserve to be.

Have a think about what works for you and get a clear idea about what you are happy to do and happy to talk about.

PR School Homework: What Am I Happy to Share?

What are you happy to talk about with the media?

....

....

What you do not want to talk about?

....

....

Are your family happy to be discussed and have their photos used?

....

....

Are you happy to have your photo used in the media?

....

....

Who Are You Telling Your Story To?

When you start out on your PR journey, the temptation can be to tell everyone your story. The reality is that not everyone needs, or wants, to know about you and if you try to do that, you might not reach anyone and you may give up, and I don't want that to happen to you.

Knowing your target audience is at the heart of any PR strategy because they are the people who will buy your products and use your services, so you need to know what media they use.

You might like the idea of being in *The Sunday Times*, but if your customers generally read *The Sun*, you could be wasting your time contacting the broadsheets.

One of my clients is a life coach who predominantly works with women between the ages of 30 and 55 in the home counties who are interested in health and well-being and tend to read newspapers, monthly magazines and lifestyle websites. As a result of pinpointing her target audience and tailoring her PR accordingly, she has been seen in the local press, *Pick Me Up!*, *Daily Express* and *Natural Health* magazine. From this there has been an increase in traffic to her website, new client sign-ups and a regular slot on Marlow FM that has secured further potential projects and fantastic networking opportunities.

This is PR!

At this point I would say there is no reason to automatically assume that national coverage is better than being included in a restaurant review in a regional magazine.

If you're looking to target people in a specific location or industry, having a really great story in a local newspaper or on a blog might be far more effective than a couple of lines in *OK!*

The main target audience for *Cast Life* are mothers with a baby or infant who has recently been diagnosed with DDH. My secondary audience are dads in the same position, grandparents and medical staff, and while the book is sold all over the world, my main geographical focus was the UK.

With this information set out, I knew that parenting magazines and blogs as well as the lifestyle and health sections of national and regional newspapers and magazines were the best media for me to contact. Local papers and the medical trade press were on my radar for later in the campaign.

Today there is a steady flow of book sales and nearly 3,000 parents and patients use the DDH UK Facebook page to access 24/7 global support, and many of them reach that as a result of reading about us, and that is PR.

PR School Homework: My Ideal Client

How old are they?

....

Are they male or female?

....

What is their marital status?

....

Do they have children? If so, how old are they?

....

Where do they live?

....

What is their income level?

....

Are they employed, self-employed or retired?

....

How do they spend their spare time?

....

What are their shopping habits?

....

What products do they buy?

....

Where do they go on holiday?

....

Do they look for value for money or are they interested in luxury?

....

What magazines and newspapers do they read?

....

What websites and blogs do they visit and what social media do they use?

....

Do they listen to podcasts, the radio or watch TV?

....

My ideal client is:

....

....

Where Do You Want to Tell Your Story?

If you take anything from this book, please let it be to understand the media that your target audience use.

I am a total media junkie and buy the latest magazines the moment they hit the shelves. I read the papers on Sunday morning and as I drink my coffee, I scribble notes in the margins and rip out the pages to remind me of where I want to be seen or products I want to try.

In my office, kitchen, bedroom and living room there are stacks of magazines and newspaper supplements I've saved to read 'later' with Post-it Notes sticking out of the tops as reference points. I have websites I love, blogs I subscribe to and a growing list of podcasts to listen to.

I know this is my career, I know this is how I earn my money, but I want you to do this too, so you can be on those pages and dazzle.

Media Options

National Newspapers

As I write this, national newspapers like the *Daily Mail*, *The Sun* and *The Times* are alive and kicking and are where many people want to be seen because their clients read these publications and trust the Personal Recommendations being given by the journalists.

Between the print copies and online editions, national newspapers reach a lot of people, fast, which leads to raised awareness, increased sales, higher web traffic and partnership opportunities.

The overall focus is national and international stories, so a fund-raising event in your village hall wouldn't make the cut, but if Victoria Beckham was opening it and auctioning her clothes at the event, that's a whole different ball game, especially if David was attending too.

While there is fierce competition to get into the national press, if you have a strong story, with images, that is timely and relevant, go for it because you stand as good a chance as anyone else of getting it in there.

Many of the weekend papers, like *The Observer*, have multiple sections covering entertainment, lifestyle, TV, fashion, sports, travel, homes and cooking and, as I have said before, go through them and see where there are chances for you to appear.

Daily papers have tight deadlines and their lead times (the time they work ahead of schedule) could be 24 hours for a news item, but a feature that needs photos and interviews could be looked at up to a month in advance.

Regional Newspapers

These papers are in decline due to a change in the way people access their news and a lower advertising spend with them, but while they are still being printed, they remain an option for your story.

While they might not have the 'wow' factor of a national paper, some titles do have a strong circulation, so you have the potential to be seen by your target audience. For example, if you own a vegan restaurant in the Midlands, then a review in the *Birmingham Mail* could be priceless, so never rule this option out.

These papers do tend to have online sections, so as well as being familiar with the print versions, also look at their websites. It could be there are more opportunities to be online, but you still need to have a good story and be the right fit.

Local Newspapers

Local papers generally only cover the news of one town and maybe the surrounding villages.

Laura Sweet has had success in this area: *"I secured a quarter-page profile including headshot and product shot in my local paper, the* Wellington Weekly News, *which was duplicated online. This directly led to an increase in my social media stats and activity and I got more reactions, likes and shares than I did with coverage in a larger publication, and I think that was because of my local connection, as well as my products."*

It is getting harder to get into these titles, many want advertising spend, but there are ways to still be included and reach your target audience. The key to being considered is to have a really local angle. These papers stick to their patch, and being even slightly outside can make your story invalid.

Charity stories, local news and reviews as well as feel-good stories are all considered – think fundraising events, the opening of a new school or a village festival that brings people together.

Some local papers do have an online section, so do your homework and check them out and see what is on offer.

Consumer Magazines

Consumer magazines cover a wide range of areas from food and cars to weddings, fishing, music and travel, and while there is a shift to online as advertising and reading habits change, there is still scope out there to shine in print.

Cosmopolitan, Vegan Life, Country Living, National Geographic, Psychologies, Kindred Spirit, and *T3* are just some of the titles on shelves and you could be inside the pages if you put the work in.

These can be broken down into local, regional and national options and each one will have a mix of editorial opportunities including interviews, competitions and product placements, as well as adverts.

When you are looking at magazines, remember who is reading them. A magazine like *Vogue*, which targets female readers, would of course not be the first place I would suggest for promoting a new range of men's vitamins – these would be better suited to *GQ* or *Esquire*; which are specifically targeted at a male audience with an interest in health and lifestyle.

It is worth remembering that many of these magazines have an online edition, so you could get double the coverage if you are savvy and ask! Always ask and always look online to see where you could be featured.

Trade Publications

Trade magazines and websites cover specific professions and industries such as accounting, banking, finance, management, marketing and sales. They offer the latest news, reviews, interviews and trends and give readers an in-depth look at their areas of expertise.

Readerships may be smaller than nationals, but being featured can be beneficial and help position you as an expert in your field with your peers, something money cannot buy.

Journalists on these titles tend to be easy to approach and open to ideas for stories, something Emma-Jane Batey, a packaging writer, agrees with, *"As a trade press journalist, I look to build relationships with friendly, responsive brands and PRs that have a specialist area and stay close to their clients. There is a huge value in knowing that a certain PR or brand will always have something interesting to say and will respond quickly to a request."*

Yes, I'm going to say it again: check online offerings too. *PR Week*, *HR Magazine*, *Packaging News* and *Property Week* all have print and online offerings (when I wrote this in 2019) and it can be really valuable to be in both.

Journals

You may come across journals in your media searches. These tend to be academic publications aimed at a specific profession, e.g. doctors. They are more formal than a magazine and often home to research and papers. This could be something to consider if you are a physiotherapist with a specialism, but again, do look at who you want to talk to and be sure this is the right fit for you.

Radio and Television

Radio and television are still big business and securing coverage can be a game changer for many businesses. From *BBC Breakfast* and *Newsround* to the *Channel 4 News* and *The One Show*, there are opportunities out there to be had so you can be more visible.

Being aware of the news agenda is key if you want to be on news and current affairs shows. This is where knowing what is happening in the world around you can lead to you securing opportunities on lifestyle shows such as *This Morning*, so keep up to date with your media searches.

For example, the moment obesity in children is a hot topic researchers will be looking for GPs and nutritionists to speak to. A spike in skin cancer figures and dermatologists will be in demand, and when mortgage rates go up, financial advisors should show their cards.

Online Magazines

As a business owner, you might want to be seen on the pages of national newspapers and glossy magazines, but stop and think whether these are what your target audience read and use.

In this digital age, featuring on blogs and online magazines such as The Female CEO, British Style Society and Glamour are just as, or more effective, than being in a print publication. It is worth noting that trying to secure online coverage can be great when you are starting out and feeling a little nervous.

When it comes to online articles, they can be uploaded almost instantly and, with links to your website not only can your traffic increase but you may well find your sales rocketing and your credibility going up too.

The Duchess of Cambridge has been snapped by the press many times and the dresses, coats and shoes she has been wearing have sold out almost instantly and taken unknown names to the top of their game as a result. While it might not be a royal who is 'papped' wearing your products, if they do appear online be ready to react and track the impact the exposure has on enquiries and sales.

There are an increasing number of online magazines out there looking for great content and this can be a brilliant way to get your name out there and start to build relationships with the press.

Make a Decision

There is a huge amount of choice out there when it comes to the media, but as I have already said, it simply isn't possible to target everyone, so you need to fine-tune your options.

I would suggest creating a list of between five and ten key outlets where you really want to be seen and known. I am not saying these are the only places you can send information to, but it means you will be more targeted in your approach and you will then take a more measured approach to your activities.

PR School Homework: My Media Vision Board

A media vision board is your image of the future, a picture of what you are aiming for and by representing your goals with pictures and images you can strengthen your ambitions.

First of all, decide on your target media then collect the pages of these magazines, newspapers, trade papers and websites and put them onto your board – be this a large piece of bright card, your office wall or an art canvas.

You can add a photo of yourself, your business card, inspirational quotes, past pieces of media coverage and anything else that inspires you.

Once your vision board is complete, put it on the wall in your office, preferably near your desk so you can see it as you work and use it as a constant reference point of where you are going.

Where Does Your Story Fit?

Whether you are telling your story by means of a press release or email to a contact or writing a post on your blog and circulating it on your social media feeds, there are various ways that the information can be used by the media.

You can't dictate where you go in a publication – that is called advertising – but having an idea where you fit is wise and shows you are committed to your PR and have done your research.

Once again, it is important to remember that while you supply the story, once it has left the confines of your inbox, the journalist can use it or interpret it however they want.

You might think your story fits in one part of a newspaper, for example an interview, but the features editor might take a look at it and think you would be perfect for a three-person case study about women who have set up businesses from their kitchen tables.

There is also the chance they might simply press delete and move on. Sorry.

The next time you look though a newspaper or magazine, as well as reading it also have a think about where the following options appear and where you would fit.

'The News'

The big news of the day appears on the front, and early pages, of papers as this is what readers want to know about first. It is often on the home pages of websites too, but as we move through the day this will change as breaking news comes in. These tend to be the BIG stories like terrorist attacks, medical breakthroughs, political changes and natural disasters. It isn't impossible to feature in these parts of publications, but the news has to be big, really big, to seal the deal.

Trend Stories

I have been thinking about this area and wanted to include it because it's the snippets that appear in the lifestyle, fashion, cooking, tech and entertainment sections that can be so valuable to a small business. They look at what is going to be on-trend for the summer, which gadgets people will be adding to their Christmas lists and who the latest band is on the music scene. These really are the things that are new, fresh and exciting in the world of art, fashion, film, music, technology and cooking. The pieces are quick, easy to read and make you want to go out and buy the products featured, and if you can have a piece of the action they are great PR.

Personality Profiles and Interviews

A profile piece or interview lets the reader know more about someone, they include images and are a really effective way of telling your story. From *Breathe* to *Pick Me Up!* and *Coast* magazine, there are interview opportunities out there for the taking if you are brave enough to go for them. Make sure you have a relevant story that fits and remember, these slots aren't just for celebrities. One example I have is with *Devonshire* magazine who did an interview with me about my book and setting up DDH UK. It talked about our move out of London, my work, and included photos and website links. I didn't see a direct increase in sales, but quite a few people I knew saw it, which helped spread the word about my client work and led to several writing projects – evidence again to know your 'why'.

Features

Features tend to appear later in a publication and are longer articles that look at the issues of the day in greater depth. They usually tie into current events, issues or trends and are where you can comment as an expert, which is why I say make sure you monitor the media and know what is going on in the world.

The one thing to remember about a feature is that they don't just tell the reader what happened, they explain why it's important, who is affected and may also include a call to action, so be prepared to offer something more in these situations.

Human Interest Stories

Human interest stories are all about that strong emotional, heartfelt connection with the reader. Look in most weekend newspaper magazines and supplements and they will be full of stories about true love, adoption, family disputes, and they all tell a story. With these you need to go back and look at how much of your story you are happy to tell because you will need to be honest and prepared to bare your soul.

Letters to the Editor

When I worked in the charity sector, we would often write letters to the editors of newspapers, magazines and trade titles and I am sitting here wondering why I don't still do this as they are a great way to shine. If you do take this approach, use clear language, be concise and write your reply on the day you see the article you are replying to, otherwise it will be old news. You will often find the right email address in the 'Letters to Editor' section of the publication, so the next time you notice this in a target media outlet, take out the page and add it to your vision board.

How-To and Top-Tips Features

These are really popular on websites like Forbes. They are usually written by experts in their field and are a fantastic positioning tool. The person is passing on their knowledge to their audience on a trusted platform and that is really powerful. I have written for Talented Ladies Club and Family Friendly Working about how to do your own PR and have certainly seen an increase in traffic to my website and social media follower numbers, so I know they are worth doing.

Quizzes and Questionnaires

If you look in magazines such as *Psychologies*, there are often quizzes for readers to take to determine what career they should consider, what type of parenting skills would work for them or how stressful their lives are. As part of these features, there is usually an expert, say a life coach or HR consultant, who goes on to give advice, and this is certainly something you can use to get your name out there.

Product Round-Ups

Even when Christmas and Easter aren't knocking on the door, you will find endless product round-ups in newspapers, magazines, blogs and online. From the must-have swimwear for the summer and baby buggies to the best electric toothbrushes and the hottest sunglasses, these photo-led spreads are a brilliant way to get your products in front of a captive audience and drive sales. Twitter is a good place to find these opportunities, so look out for the #journorequest hashtag and see who is looking for what and where you could appear. Do remember, either images or actual products tend to be needed for these and you probably won't see the return of goods, so be sure it is worth the investment before you say yes.

Reviews

Reviews are a staple of the media, both on and offline. Pretty much anything can be reviewed, from clothes, shoes and jewellery to video games, books and restaurants. These contain honest feedback from the reviewer and can be really powerful and persuasive. Just think about a time when you have read a review for a new anti-ageing product and been so impressed with the results the reviewer has seen that you go out and buy it yourself the next day?

Recipes

For the bakers and chefs out there, you will find many media opportunities for your recipes and books to be mentioned. This can include a summary of who you are, images of you at work, and if you partner with certain titles they may try out your recipes and give their honest feedback.

Guest Blog Posts

If one of your aims for your PR is to drive traffic to your website, you might consider writing guest posts for other blogs. This is a fantastic way to share your knowledge and expertise as well as promote your business and build your reputation. Guest blogs have useful 'shareability' and can be a really good way to attract interest not only from other influencers and potential customers but also journalists looking for experts and stories.

Competitions

Competitions are another way to directly get in front of your target audience. Various costs are attached and range from a page placement fee in the bigger magazines to offering the prizes and images to smaller outlets and influencers. I have organised competitions for clients as diverse as Betty Crocker, Cartoon Network, and Crowne Plaza and they have all been successful in terms not only of engagement, but as part of an overall awareness raising campaign that has driven sales.

You can't do everything, so keep an eye out for something that would work for you.

What's On

Many newspapers, radio stations and magazines include a section that covers things like fetes, services and concerts, but often people don't realise these opportunities are out there for the taking. Just think how much money you would save by having your exhibition listed in *Cornwall Life* rather than printing and distributing thousands of flyers? I have seen with past clients that if you get it right, you can sell out a cookery workshop from one well-placed mention in the listings of a weekly magazine, so it has to be worth a go.

Opinion Pieces

This is one person's opinion or point of view and it can be a really powerful, effective and memorable way to get a message out or tell a story. These can be seen across the board and it might be worth trying your trade titles as a starting point.

Columns

Columns, which are a little bit like ongoing opinion pieces, represent the opinion of one writer on an issue of relevance that could be anything from fishing, cooking and sustainability to parenting, depending on the publication, and they generally follow a similar tone and format each time.

Photo Features

The Sunday Times Magazine is a great example of where photo features work. These tend to be a series of strong images that tell a story, embrace a culture or capture a community. Photo features have a really emotional impact and are an excellent way for photographers to showcase their work and shine. Hard to secure, there is no denying that, but worth the effort if you get a yes.

Product Placement

Product placement is another option for branded products to be included in print and online but also on TV. From Costa on the cobbles of *Coronation Street* to BlackBerry in the law offices of *Suits*, there are opportunities to be taken across the board and if you can secure one, I bet you will see the sales flood in.

PR School Homework: Where My Story Fits

Set aside an hour this week to sit down with your key magazines, newspapers and websites and really get to know them.

Go through each one, read the contents, work out the tone of voice and find the opportunities that could work for you, writing notes here to help you remember what you find.

Use Post-its to mark relevant pages and then create your own media library that you can refer to when you have a story and one you can add to as you progress with your PR journey.

This will play a key part in your success because knowledge is power, so invest some time and energy now, to benefit your business in the future.

If you get stuck and can't work out where your story fits on the page, don't struggle alone. The PR School online community can help you to piece your puzzle together, and you may make valuable connections and spot media opportunities in there too.

Lesson Four

Find Your Media Tribe

You now know your target audience, you know the papers they read for their news, the magazines they find their decorating inspiration in, and the websites they go to for health advice. You know what the potential editorial opportunities are, so now you need to know who writes for them so you can make them aware of you.

Now is the time to find your media tribe.

Deep breaths, you can do this!

Remember that first day at school where you looked around and wondered who would be your friend?

That first cup of coffee you made in the kitchen at a new job and hoped someone would speak.

How about the first parent and baby weigh-in you went to with your newborn and waited for just one of the other mums to say hello?

Of course, you made friends at school, everyone would gather in your room before going to the pub when you were at college and those mums who looked like they had it covered, well they're now your BFFs!

This is just the same when it comes to finding your media tribe.

At the moment, the idea of approaching members of the media might feel a bit scary and alien.

You aren't sure whether your emails are going to be answered.

You feel sick about sending your press release out there to be prodded and poked, and possibly rejected.

But, you have done it before in so many situations and you can do it again now.

The main thing to remember here is that they are human beings just like you, doing a job to pay the bills and not a scary fire-breathing dragon whose main mission in life is to scare people away and burn their stories to the ground.

Just as much as you need them to help build your brand, they need people like you to fill their pages and keep their readers coming back for more.

It's also important to understand that you aren't going to be right for every journalist and it is going to take time, but if you go for it, it will be worth it.

Gail Shortland, Editor of *Chat* and *Pick Me Up!* specials, adds to this sentiment: *"Don't assume your product and business will speak for itself as that's quite a naive take on things. Unless you are looking after David Beckham's pants, you should always work as hard as you can. Make sure you are 100% familiar with the title and know how it fits in the market, and that you know who you are pitching to. It's then a mutually beneficial relationship! And remember, this is a very small industry that is getting smaller (I have four mags when back in the day they would have had four editors). If you get a good contact, you never know where they will turn up and they will come to you for help. Treat them poorly, and they end up an editor, and you'll be kicking yourself."*

During my career, contacts really have come into play and often saved the day when a client is chasing world-class exposure with only the lightest of stories.

There are journalists out there who know me, like me and trust me to not only give them a story but also one that is right for their audience and publication.

This said, I'm no saint and there are people I've annoyed, who may have even blocked me from their emails and social media feeds, because I didn't deliver what they needed.

I don't want you to be in this situation, so let's look at how you can build positive relationships from the start and be the go-to person journalists know they can trust. While there is no guarantee that your contact will say yes to every story (the days of favours are kind of over, I'm afraid) you stand a far better chance of standing out in a crowded inbox if they know your name.

Who Is Who?

The bottom line is that while there are some really talented journalists out there and uber-cool bloggers, you need to identify and cultivate relationships with media contacts who have the ability to move your brand forward.

After years of doing this I sometimes assume, wrongly, that everyone knows who is who when it comes to jobs in the media, but this isn't always the case, so let's look at this now so it's a little clearer.

Print Media

The Editor

Newspaper and magazine editors decide what goes on the pages of their publications and they have the ultimate responsibility for everything that gets published. While they probably wouldn't be the right contact for you (especially the big titles) it is good to be aware of them.

If you are interested to know more about them, read their letter at the start of each issue. This tends to be an informal welcome to the magazine (less so in newspapers) and while it tells you about the content of that issue, it also gives you an insight into their interests and passions. I can remember someone talking about securing an interview in a magazine connected to their dog-walking business simply because they saw the editor was a huge dog lover and they pitched their idea at the right time, so never say never.

PA to the Editor

A PA helps with the day-to-day running of the publication and manages the editor's schedule so everything runs smoothly. These guys tend to be the editor's right-hand person, so can be a good contact for you to have.

Features Editor

The feature editors are more senior journalists who write those gripping interviews that inspire and empower readers. They know what works as a story, their writing is strong and engaging, which makes them the kind of people you want in your tribe.

Fashion Editor

Fashion editors decide what goes on the fashion pages of newspapers and magazines. As well as knowing what is hot, and what's not, they know where the latest trends are coming from and what will go from the catwalk to the high street. If you have a fashion brand, they need to be on your list.

Beauty Editor

A beauty editor's job is to know everything there is about the world of beauty. They will work on a range of projects from product testing to photo shoots to ensure readers are inspired and trust their publication implicitly.

Staff Writers

When I first started out in PR most of the journalists I worked with were on the payroll and based in the office. This has changed a lot, with people working remotely. While there are generally fewer 'staffers' out there, those who are involved are always looking for new ideas, conducting interviews and writing features as well as working with other members of the team.

Digital Writers

Digital writers tend to work on fast-paced daily content that is inspired by the breaking news like the results of *Love Island* or a high-profile couple getting together – things you could comment on if it is right for you.

Team Assistants

You might not get to know the editors, but team assistants are worth having on your side. They not only 'call in' products from businesses but they also help write and collate articles and are very much at the heart of the day-to-day running of publications. Get to know them now and, as their careers progress, they may well take you with them.

Sub-Editor

You probably won't have much, if any contact, with a sub-editor but they ensure copy is grammatically and factually correct. They could, however, get in touch to check your details, so it is worth knowing they exist and, if they ask you to get back to them, do it.

Picture Editor

From choosing which photographers to use and managing photo shoots, to sourcing stock photos from agencies, the picture editor brings words alive and may email you for your images, so get back to them fast if you want to keep your space on the page.

Freelance Journalists

I think that freelance journalists are some of the very best contacts you can have in your database. I work with a lot of freelancers who work with a number of publications on various stories. Most of them I have known for many years and are a great help to me and I try to be the same in return.

Broadcast Media

For those of you who want to be on TV, I would suggest you start with the researchers.

From *BBC London* to *Newsround* and *Top Gear*, there will be a team of researchers working in the background to find the best stories, news and products out there for their programmes.

While you might see the presenters on Twitter, they don't tend to put the shows together and while they know their stuff on air, they probably won't be involved with getting the programme in place and ready to view.

What Do They Want?

As well as at least one cup of hot coffee a day and no interruptions when they are on deadline, this is actually quite simple – the media want news they can tell, and content they can use.

Whether it's copy, stories, leads, images or video, if you are getting in touch with them, make sure you have easy-to-read content they can potentially make use of.

Stories

Breaking news, information no one else has, and exclusive stories are welcomed by the press, so if you have this to offer pick your contact wisely and let them know they are the only ones who have it.

People

Spokespeople and real-life stories (case studies) are important because they bring a story to life, add meaning and allow the audience to make a connection. One word of warning is to ensure case studies do actually want to speak to the press. There is nothing worse than having a feature set up only to be told at the last minute they have changed their mind or don't want to have their photo taken. It might not be your fault but the journalist won't be happy and may not come back to you again, so do your homework before making any promises.

Numbers
PR consultant at ASSISTED., Sofie Tooke, makes a good point: *"Journalists love numbers and statistics, so if you have a key fact that you can focus on then that should catch their attention."*

Products
If you are writing to the press about a product, please, please, please make sure you have it available for review. People won't always ask for your latest book or organic wine to be sent to them, but if they do, have it ready to go. In some cases, these will be returned to you, but at other times, they won't, so it makes sense to build these costs into your business plans and if you can't afford it, don't do it.

Relevance
I cannot stress enough how important it is to make sure your story is relevant to the publication you want to be featured in. If you have a story about fly fishing, don't offer it to *Cosmopolitan* because they will laugh in your face. Equally, a story about a new coffee shop opening in your village won't get into *The Observer*, but it could be perfect for your local paper if it is generating jobs and paying staff the living wage.

The Truth
In general, the media want the truth. If you can't offer it, leave it.

Speed
You might have to miss lunch, because if you're given a deadline to meet, you need to meet it. Get the information and images to the journalist on time and not only will you secure that media coverage, but you will also be remembered as someone who can deliver, and that can help you to shine. I remember one client having an amazing opportunity to talk about her book with a national newspaper. I sent the email over, and she responded in ten minutes, telling me that in the rush and excitement, she actually fell

off the treadmill in the gym. The journalist didn't know this, but it made me confident that she was serious about her PR and that if I was to put her forward for a media request, she would come through.

Answers
When a journalist asks how many products you stock, tell them. If they want images, send them, and if you can't help with a request yourself, suggest someone who might be able to. You want to make yourself as helpful and reliable as possible and you will be amazed at how people will start to trust you and come back for more.

Space
We all need space, and that includes the press. Give them time to look at what you have sent them, don't call them as soon as you send them an email and do not stalk them on social media.

Where to Find the Contact Details for Your Media Tribe
Like so many aspects of PR, finding contact details for the media isn't rocket science, but it is something people seem to find hard and often make more difficult than it needs to be.

You can subscribe to a media database, but to be honest with you, I don't think you need this right now. While they can be really useful, they are expensive, and I think you can use your resources in a far more effective way as you are going for a really targeted list at the moment.

Your starting point is to go back to your media vision board and dig out the hard copies of the papers and magazines you want to be featured in. By looking through these publications you will see certain journalists writing the travel pieces, others doing interviews and some covering product round-ups and reviews.

This is the first place to find their contact details. Often in the front there is a section (the masthead) where there will be, at the very least, phone numbers, and if you are lucky email addresses too.

If you need to, call the publications and ask for contact details – some publishers will be happier than others to give these out. If in doubt, ask to speak to the editorial assistant who may let you send them your press release or give you the name of someone who can help.

Telephone books are a thing of the past, but the Internet is a very effective replacement, so use it to seek out the contacts you want to talk to and you may come across new and niche titles at the same time.

Social media is a great place to find contacts. Follow them on Twitter and LinkedIn and use this as a starting point for a conversation.

Sometimes, as Laura Sweet found, it is simply the luck of the draw: "Trail *magazine was a huge win and that was down to having the courage to email them about my new brand. I hit the right editor at the right time – honestly this was more luck than judgement – but I have since maintained the relationship and secured further coverage in their Gear Guide and we are due to be featured again soon!"*

Remember, you aren't going out to conquer the world, you are predominantly aiming at a small number of titles that your target audience reads and, by being targeted, you will soon be able to find the right contacts and build up a rapport.

I am not going to say it will happen overnight but if you are persistent and send good-quality information and can support this with images and additional information, it will happen in time.

Create Your Media Database

See what I wrote there?

YOUR media database.

I bet when you read the introduction, you didn't think you would get to the point of having the contact details of influential people who know who you are, what your story is, and who could potentially write about you?

Life is full of surprises and, hey, this is one of them.

When I started out in PR, a bright red Rolodex sat on my desk in my Gloucester Road office and followed me from job to job, collecting more business cards. The Rolodex went in the bin years ago, and I now use an Excel document for keeping details safe, and you might want to do the same. In accordance with GDPR rules, and to comply with good business practice, keep this in a password-protected folder in the Cloud, rather than on your desktop, and do not share with anyone else.

As well as updating contact details (people move around a lot) I also add notes of when I have spoken to people, what the conversation was about, and I will record any resulting coverage they have produced for me or clients, always sending a thank you when it comes out.

One further note: if a journalist asks you not to contact them, then remove them from your lists, for good.

PR School Homework: My Media Tribe

Create a simple Excel spreadsheet for your contacts with columns for names, the outlet they work for, their job title, telephone number and email address.

I would then have one that records any communication you have with them and a second that details any coverage they have generated for you.

Try to keep this updated and, in time, you will have a database that will become as much of a PR bible as this book.

You'll find freelance journalists and influencers hanging out in the PR School community. This is where they go to look for stories, products and case studies, so make sure you're in the community if you want to build your media tribe and be seen by the right people.

Lesson Five

Bloggers, Vloggers and Influencers

Being endorsed, interviewed or reviewed by a blogger, vlogger, podcaster or influencer (let's call them 'social influencers' for the sake of this book and for ease) can do wonders for your exposure and is something I would suggest you consider.

At some point, social influencers will come together with mainstream media, or something new altogether might be created, and, while they are part of your media tribe, I felt that at this point in time it was worth creating a separate chapter to cover these gatekeepers.

Who They Are and What They Do

To break things down a little bit, bloggers specialise in the written word, vloggers create video, and influencers use social media feeds to add their content and spread their messages.

Influencing is a huge business in its own right, with the top bods earning thousands from their collaborations with brands, but smaller ones equally own their part of the Internet.

Covering a wide variety of areas and niches, including food, fashion, sports, mental health and parenting, many influencers are go-to sources for information, tips, and advice.

What I love about influencers is that they can help tell the human side to your business in a very authentic way. They don't just create content about you, they go on to engage with their followers through comments and shares on their social media channels, and so more connections are made.

They tell your story, their way, and while they might be reviewing your London print cushions, what they are saying to their followers is, "Hey, I really like these guys and think you will too, so check them out."

"I try and wind a review into something tangible. For example, I went on a gin tour but instead of writing a gin tour review I wrote about how the gin company uses stories and their history as part of their branding. Therefore, I was giving valuable tips to my readers but also reviewing the gin tour, which keeps the brand happy."

Joanne Dewberry, small business blogger

I believe some people still underestimate the power of social influencers and fail to see them as the path to audiences they might otherwise never reach.

Just as with any other member of the media, if you want to work with influencers, you need to take time to get to know them, become familiar with their writing and get a feeling for who they are and what they are about.

For many people, this is not a hobby, it is their livelihood, so they need to be treated with respect and please don't expect something for nothing just because they are online or work from home.

Each and every social influencer works in a different way and has different requirements, but as Stephanie Darkes, exploringexeter.co.uk, says, *"The biggest mistake people make when it comes to connecting with bloggers is assuming they work for free"*, and she isn't alone.

"Expecting the earth and wanting bloggers to do something for nothing is a mistake. We are people with lives and families. It might take us a bit longer sometimes and we might forget but we will get there in the end!"

Chelsea Williams, thatschelsea.com

"One of the biggest mistakes people make is assuming we are amateurs and will work for free on the promise of good content or exposure. Build a relationship with a blogger, offer recompense with product, a good event or cold hard cash and I for one certainly would consider posting occasionally for free as a goodwill gesture."

Afra Willmore, madmumof7.com

There is a lot of choice out there, so do your research, choose wisely, be strategic about where you put your efforts to maximise your results and work on building relationships that are going be long term.

What to Consider

When you undertake your influencer research, I would consider these key elements:

Do They Influence Your Target Audience?

It is really important to ask yourself, "Would this social influencer's followers buy my product?" If you are selling high-end homeware, working with a blogger who focuses on money saving won't be the best match, but an interiors blogger might be.

If you specialise in luxury breaks in the Cotswolds, collaborating with a travel blogger who loves backpacking probably isn't going to be as successful as joining forces with a vlogger who makes beautiful films of boutique hotels.

As Afra points out, "*Look beyond the follower figures. An Instagrammer with 50k followers and lots of pretty pictures of hat-wearing in sunflowers may well not reach your market if you are selling nit spray. Equally, a blogger who writes about the dating scene and reaches millions is maybe not the best person to promote an event at a theme park for under-fives.*"

How Often Do They Post?

It is a good idea to see how often someone posts new content. Is it once an hour, every day, twice a week? If it's only once a month or less, I would say this isn't going to be the best match and I would question how effective their reach and commitment is.

Do They Engage on Social Media?

The people who engage, interact, retweet and push their posts out there, are the ones you want to be working with, but remember you need to do the same.

Location, Location, Location

Are you a location-based business or do you sell products online around the world? What countries do you ship products to? Where do you get the most orders from? If you only deliver to a five-mile radius of Greenwich, then working with Helen from South London's Mummy's Gin Fund will be far more effective than a collaboration with a blogger from Manchester.

Do They Fit with Your Budget?

We have touched on this already, but influencers aren't a free way to shine. Some may charge £50 to feature your product, another may want £500, and a new kid on the block might be happy to do it for nothing more than the product itself. See what people are looking for, what the costs are and what you will get in return before going ahead.

"A clear idea of budget is useful. As a new blogger, I can feel a bit lost, so working with a brand to openly discuss what they are prepared to gift/pay is hugely helpful and reassuring."

Michelle Green, Fifty and Fab

Size Doesn't Always Matter

Remember it's not all about numbers in this game, it's about building relationships and engaging with people. Don't be afraid to ask for a screenshot of their Google Analytics as they should be happy to share that along with their media pack, which will give you the total low-down. So you know, Google Analytics is a service from Google that gives you information about how users find and use websites, including those of influencers.

Blogger Katie Upton agrees, *"Do not put a follower limit on working with people, because small bloggers may have a more loyal following than some of the larger creators. I feel like the number of followers you have doesn't say much about how well that person can promote a product, mainly because of all the algorithm changes. Someone with 100k followers may only receive 1,000 views, so the follower count doesn't say much about working with an individual. Plus, small and upcoming bloggers should have the same opportunities as larger ones in order to expand and grow in the industry."*

How to Find Them

Bloggers, vloggers and social influencers generally want to be found, and as Chelsea Williams suggests, *"Reach out and talk to people. Do your research or you will miss out on many little gems that would love to work with you!"*

Google Is Your Friend

These people are online, so it makes sense to start with Google when it comes to your social influencer search. Typing in terms such as 'UK travel bloggers' or 'fashion blogs UK' will pull up lots of results, with the highest-profile bloggers and vloggers coming out top. You then need to go through and spend time looking at the sites, the content, the tone of voice, the comments and finding the ones that work well for you.

Take to Twitter

Many social influencers will be on Twitter, so this is another place to seek them out. Searching hashtags like #bbloggers (beauty bloggers), #fbloggers (fashion bloggers), #mummybloggers and #techbloggers will lead you to some great people and again, go to their sites and work out if they are the right fit for you.

It is also worth looking for the #PRrequest hashtag as many bloggers who are searching for people to work with use this. The #bloggerswanted hashtag is a good one for researching people and could throw up all kinds of interesting results for you. I warn you, once you start looking, you could be lost in cyberspace for a while, so make a coffee and get your notebook out.

Blogger and Brand Networks

Bloggers Required, Joe Blogs Network, ShoutOut.ly, The Blogger Network, and Zeal Buzz can all be tapped into, but some come with a price tag, so be aware of that before going ahead.

Use Your Networks

Facebook groups, family, friends, clients and even mums at the school gate may know influencers (or be ones themselves) so don't be afraid to ask.

Ways to Work with Them

There are many ways you can work with social influencers, and Claire Hall, the award-winning blogger at Tin Box Traveller, says, *"I offer reviews of products, services and experiences, as well as competitions, which always prove popular and give brands extra exposure. I also put together product and event round-up posts. All of this is supported by my social media channels, which are now followed by nearly 20,000 accounts."*

Michelle Green adds, *"I offer reviews on Fifty and Fab and have recently done my first Instagram competition,"* and Vanessa Holburn at ahappyhealthymummy.com comments, *"I like reviews, interviews and using the brand or product in a wider feature."*

There are a variety of activities you can get involved in and consider:

Sponsored Posts

When a blogger is paid to write a post in their own style, which mentions and includes a link to the brand, this is called a 'sponsored post'. These posts may not be about things they've tried or tested themselves but could be based on a brief from your business, such as five cool ways to wear a wrap dress. Post costs vary depending on the influencer, their popularity, reach and social media following, as well as the amount of work they are doing for you.

Ana De-Jesus who blogs at fadedspring.co.uk tells me, *"I very rarely host competitions and interviews, so most of the time my posts in collaborations with brands are 'sponsored posts' or product reviews, but so that it feels more authentic and intrinsic to who I am as a person, my style of writing and photography aesthetic is 'personable' as I like to inject personality into my work, regardless of whether it is organic or sponsored content."*

Product Reviews

Having a social influencer review your products or services can be an effective way to generate digital content about your company and raise awareness. This is still PR and the social influencer will pride themselves on honesty, so be prepared for them to air their opinions – you cannot tell them what to write but if there is an issue or problem, try to work through it together and find a solution.

Social Media Campaigns

Brands do work with social influencers to support campaigns that are running across Twitter, Facebook, Instagram and YouTube. Each project is different but typically involves creating content to share on their platforms or asking them to take part in a hashtag campaign and roll it out across their main feeds.

Competitions

Competitions to win a product or opportunity from your company are a popular choice when working with social influencers. A blog post, video or social media posts on a particular theme can help promote your company and drive traffic to your website and feeds. Be creative and generous and ensure the social influencer states it is a competition, and not pure editorial.

Gift Guides

Many social influencers create gift guides for Christmas, Mother's Day, Easter, Father's Day, and Halloween might get a mention too. Typically, these will be round-up pieces including comments, images, prices and website details. Get the right influencer and this can be a good way to raise awareness and boost sales. I'd suggest looking at other guides they have done in the past to get a feel for their work, the number of comments they get and the budgets they work on. You'll often have to gift them the product – do factor these costs into your plans, and while many take their own images (and are good at it), make sure you have your own photos that can be sent out (we will talk about this later).

Events

From the launch of *Cast Life*, to wildlife events at London Zoo and documentary screenings in cinemas across Europe, I've organised many events as they are a fantastic way to tell a story to influencers and members of the media, as well as clients and investors.

Inviting social influencers to events where they can find out more about you and your products or services is a good way to get to know them and find out how they work and what they look for from a brand.

I recently worked with South West Holiday Parks and we held a blogger event at their flagship site. It was a lunchtime event at the park's stunning restaurant overlooking the Jurassic Coast and as coffee and cake were served there was a brief talk about the company, then a chance to try out the indoor pool and have lunch. The results included social media shares as well as blog posts, which helped to let local people know the park was there and they could use the facilities.

The main thing to remember is, if you are going to do this, you need to know WHY you are doing it and WHAT you want to achieve.

For example, Stephanie Darkes attended a PR School workshop last year and as a result of her tweeting about it and writing a post on Exploring Exeter, I secured bookings for future events and my social media following increased, which is exactly what I had hoped for. Thank you, Stephanie.

Events Organiser Sarah Brunning has some great hints and tips for getting events right:

Preparation

Date

Look at a good time and date for your event. If you want influencers to bring their children along to try a new pottery painting class, then a weekend would make sense; if it is a cocktail event, then an evening towards the end of the week might be more appropriate.

Always do a quick check on the date you are thinking of, as you don't want it to clash with a major football game, end-of-term presentations or the Olympics!

Budget

As soon as you start to plan any event, start a costing sheet. Whether it is on paper or in a simple Excel spreadsheet, make sure every penny you spend is recorded so you know where you are.

Venue

Do your homework. Do you want modern and chic or traditional? What fits best with what you are trying to promote and the ethos of your brand? Visit two or three venues to get a feel for each one. Envisage being a guest walking into the party, how does it feel? Is there somewhere to welcome people? Somewhere to hang coats. Ask what packages are available that include canapés, drinks and food. How helpful are the staff? Can you give a presentation?

Think about location and timings to maximise turnout. Is it in the city with a 6pm start time? Or a country retreat with lots of parking? Find out about parking/train times/buses, etc. Do remember that not everyone lives in London!

Branding and marketing

Order any banners, leaflets, marketing material in plenty of time, and don't forget to add it to the budget sheet. Use your social media channels and your blog to start creating a buzz about your event so people can see what it's all about and want to be invited.

Gifts

If you are planning to give gifts to attendees, try to make these in keeping with the event. For a book launch maybe give signed copies of the book and a pen; if you make beautiful pottery then maybe a mug and some lovely teabags would work well; and if you are a life coach then a free session or discount code could be the way to get more people to try your services.

Guests

Now, this is a time to look at your media tribe and decide who you want to come to the event. Is it just bloggers who you have a relationship with, or do you also want the Features Editor of your local paper and a photographer to come along? Like any party, asking doesn't mean someone will come, so once you have a date, send out a 'Save the Date' email and follow this up with an official invitation.

Ideally this should be fully branded, explaining exactly what the guest can expect (food, drink, entertainment) and include a map or 'how to get there' information. Ask for an RSVP so that you know roughly how many people will come. There will always be some that don't make it, so if you have press releases, information and gifts, maybe send them to those people so they know what your news is and how they could work with you.

Entertainment

What would be appropriate for this event, if anything? A comedian, a nutritionist or maybe a motivational speaker. Perhaps a short welcome speech from you would work well and can certainly be a good idea if you are launching a new book or exhibition of your work.

The Event

If you have prepared thoroughly, your event should go smoothly and help you to shine.

Arrive in plenty of time to arrange the room to suit your needs.

Team

Ensure you have enough people to help as the last thing you want is to see a guest standing awkwardly on their own looking at their watch.

Either ask members of your team to come along, or call on your wider network and you might be surprised at just how many people want to get involved. Always brief them fully on what the event is about, who is coming, what is happening, the timings of talks and what gifts and press packs are being handed out.

Name badges

Name badges may be suitable for your event as they can help break the ice and get people talking to each other. This also helps record who turned up and who you need to follow up with if they didn't make it.

Press packs

Press packs ensure people have all the details they need about who you are, what you do and why there has been an event. You can either print these out, offer the information on a branded pen drive or email documents and images to people after the event.

Photos

During the event, take photos and add to your social media feeds, using any suitable hashtags, and make sure people are happy to be pictured – if they are influencers and media they should be, but it is good practice to check. If you are going to be busy, maybe hire a photographer to come and take pictures, or if you don't have the budget, see if you have a friend who is good with a camera who is happy to help in return for a bottle of wine.

Feedback

You have done the hard work, so ask people what they thought. A quick email thanking them for attending, offering more information and including a link to a short survey (SurveyMonkey is a good one) can work well. Go back to those who didn't make it, too.

Remember, you are your own media maker, so write a blog post about the event, talk about who came and what the news was and share on your social media channels.

Good luck!

You will also want to let the world know about your event and this is where social media comes into play.

Claire Sparksman, says, "*It is a great idea to create a teaser campaign several weeks before your launch or event. Post regularly, reminding about the event, launch etc. Share the event/launch details but also the back story and behind the scenes: who's involved (tag them), what's involved, the journey behind the launch, why this event/book/launch has come about and what it means to you or the company personally.*

"*You can create a countdown to the big day. Share behind the scenes, getting ready (event space, self, the team) and then TA DA! LOADS of content about the event itself as well as awareness of what you are doing and why.*

"*People love a video, so take them during the event, inducing Boomerangs (short videos using Boomerang app) and share across your social media platforms, tagging people as appropriate. Collages are another great way to let people know about an event, but you might want to ensure people are happy to be included.*"

Brand Ambassadors
These tend to be long-term relationships with a small number of social influencers who represent your brand. They might create exclusive content for you, attend events or share your story on social media and if you are working with them over a long period of time a solid relationship can be built, making this a good way of working.

What to Remember

Know Your 'Why'
Working with social influencers is an investment of time and resources, therefore you want to be sure any collaboration is going to be beneficial to your business. Are you hoping to drive traffic to your site, maybe boost sales in the run-up to Mother's Day or build your social following?

Make It Personal
Yes, this again! Make sure your communication is based on each individual social influencer because nobody likes to receive an email

that's been sent out to the masses. Let them know what you like about their blog and why you'd like to work with them as that will show you are serious and if you take time to find out about them, they might be more inclined to work with you.

"I don't work with any PR or brands that send me generic press releases for things my own son can't use. A PR once sent me a press release for a toy which would be physically impossible for my son to use – it was a pull-along toy and the headline was something like 'your child will love running around the house with this' – my kid can't walk let alone run! So, for me it's really important that they've bothered to check out my blog and aren't just sending out press releases with no research."

Laura Moore, Mum on a Mission

Agree on a Plan

If you do work with a social influencer, agree on a plan of work. Maybe you'd like a written review on their blog, two photos on Instagram, two tweets and a Facebook post? This might seem like a lot but if you are sending them a pair of bespoke silver earrings you have made just for them, you want to be sure it is a fair swap – so get things signed off in writing before starting the project.

Set a Time Scale

Just as you agree on the content, you need to agree on dates too. If you are pushing products for Christmas, you don't want a post that comes out in January – you may laugh but this can happen, so put it in writing and chase them if need be, nicely of course.

It Works Both Ways

I know we are talking about YOU, but I believe that the best collaborations happen when both parties are going to benefit. Whether you're offering a product, cash, a competition prize or a trip, be clear about what is in it for them. Please do not offer 'exposure' as they already have that, and it's just insulting. It's fine if you don't have a massive budget but be upfront and honest and you will find the best fit for your brand and someone who will work with you again.

It's 'Their' Space

A blog, vlog, podcast or social media feed belongs to that person, they can do what they like (within reason) and I am afraid this is PR and they can write as they see fit. As a blogger, I would give a brand the right to reply before posting anything negative, so maybe a faulty product would be replaced, but you can't dictate what they write or how they take images. Again, do your research before you work with anyone to make sure you get the right fit for you and remember they are lovely people and will want to make sure you shine.

Sharing Is Caring

Once a post goes live, don't just let the influencer push the content. You can share on your social media feeds to ensure it is seen by as many people as possible.

Be Polite

You are contacting influencers because they can ultimately help you to stand out from the crowd, so always be polite and professional when you are working with them.

Think Long Term

The main thing to remember is that collaborations with social influencers shouldn't be seen as a one-off arrangement, but a long-term relationship that needs to be invested in and nurtured.

Smart businesses understand the value of building relationships and if someone does a great job of reviewing a product or hosting a giveaway for you, go back and say thank you and try to work with them again.

Also, ask them about their peers and see if they know anyone else who would be interested in working with you.

You might not realise this, but influencers can be your greatest advocates, so treat them well and not only will they talk about you, but their followers will too.

PR School Homework: My Social Influencers

Take some time out to research social influencers that could be a good fit for your brand.

Look at the content, style, other brands they have worked with as well as their social media followers, and engagement.

I would suggest adding a new sheet to your contacts database document where you can add the details of your top five influencers and include the name of the blog/vlog, the URL, the name of the contact, as well as their contact details, which should be easy to find on their sites or social media channels.

Lesson Six

Get Your PR Materials Ready

With your media database at the ready and a beautiful media vision board in front of you, you might think I am going to tell you to go out and get in touch, but you aren't quite ready yet.

Imagine the situation. You get an email from *The Guardian* after you send over a press release about your new range of silver cufflinks for men that have their kids' fingerprints embossed on them. The perfect Father's Day gift, you said, for the man who has everything. The paper is running a product round-up and wants images and a price. You get the journalist the details they need, they run the piece, the orders come in thick and fast and you simply cannot keep up with the demand.

Yes, it is great to be featured in the media and of course that is why you are reading this book, BUT don't get carried away with the excitement if you can't then fulfil your obligations.

Before you go any further, I want you to think about what materials you have in place RIGHT NOW that you think would ensure you are media ready.

I have gone into organisations and been asked to set up their Press Office function from scratch, which I love doing. Either they hadn't had a PR team before, or there had been a recruitment gap and things needed to be tidied up and re-established, and this was a challenge I always relished.

Now, I am not telling you that you need to create a corporate Press Office, but I wonder how much more confident you would feel if you knew that all your press materials were saved in one place and ready to go when that email you have been waiting for drops into your inbox?

Your Image Library

A lot of people think about PR and immediately assume it's all about words, which, to a certain extent it is. However, from the moment you look at the front page of a newspaper or magazine, it's the images that tend to catch your attention first.

Given that the human brain processes images 60,000 times faster than copy and 90% of information transmitted to the brain is visual[7], I think this shows why images are so important to your PR activities.

I learned this early in my agency days, when I had to take a single slide from my Soho office to a photo desk on the other side of London, after work, to guarantee coverage for a client the following month.

Today, when I take on new clients or during my coaching sessions or workshops, I always talk about the need to have media-friendly, brand-ready images for when that question is asked.

Before I send out anything to the media, I make sure we have good images, in JPEG formats that can be sent out on request. Gail Shortland, Editor of *Chat* and *Pick Me Up!* specials, reinforces why this is key to success: *"Don't pitch unless you're ready to provide everything I will need to cover the story. I will email back in a second and say, 'Can I have images for this product', and sometimes the PR or business won't even answer or say that they aren't ready yet. So why send it out?"*

Heidi Scrimgeour, a freelance journalist, adds, *"I spend hours of my life chasing images and I love the PRs who use WeTransfer. I scan to see which pics I want, download the good ones instantly and come back to them in my Dropbox folder as and when I need them, whereas attaching them to emails means I need to remember where I put that email and go back and save the attachment."*

As images are such a key element to your storytelling and PR activities, award-winning photographer Antonina Mamzenko, has the low-down on getting your snaps PR ready:

How important are images when it comes to representing your brand?
It's a cliché, but a picture is really worth a thousand words. In this digital age, attention spans are very short, and you have just a few seconds to make a positive first impression. Great images, that are on-brand, can do that faster than any bio or blurb you've written about your business.

What kind of images best showcase a business?

What you need are images that are full of life and personality, and ones that communicate your brand promise clearly and instantly.

Bog-standard studio headshots against a white background are old news, and most people expect more lifestyle imagery that really lets them into your world. While headshots still have their place (hello, LinkedIn and tiny profile photos everywhere), you'll make more impact with lifestyle photographs that relate to your business and your personality.

Those can range from great environmental portraits (think photos of Holly Tucker inside her Holly & Co shop or an artist posing in her studio with a backdrop of canvases and paints) to more action shots like you walking on the beach, playing with your dogs, drinking tea, digging up the garden – or whatever is it you do that lets your personality shine (just how personal you want to go depends entirely on you and your business, but do remember people buy from people).

Similarly, lifestyle product pictures that show the product being used by people or photographed with a backdrop of an actual location, be it a kitchen or a beach, whatever is appropriate for what you're selling, will make way more impact than any cut-outs on white background ever could.

What do you need to look for in a photographer?

Finding a great photographer that's the right fit for your brand is really important, so take your time and look not only at how much they charge, but also practical things like whether their style is right for you, if they specialise in what you need them to photograph, and also if you get on with them.

If your brand is light and airy, but the photographer mainly shoots dark, moody images, they will not be able to deliver photographs that are on-brand for you. Similarly, if they mainly take photos of buildings, the action shots of you teaching a yoga class might lack inspiration and movement.

Get on the phone with them, too. When you talk to them, do they sound excited and fired up and full of ideas, or does it feel like it's just another job for them? Do they feel passionate about working with businesses like yours? Do they sound trustworthy and like they know what they are doing? Are they asking you the right questions?

For example, when I talk with a potential client I will not just ask them about what they *think* they want out of a photo shoot but will try to take it further, asking them about their business and them as a person and see if it sparks more ideas on how we can capture their brand's essence in the best possible way.

Does the photographer sound like someone you wouldn't mind having around for several hours? Are they easy to talk to, can you relate to them? For best results, you need to be comfortable around your photographer, so really make sure you're a good fit for each other.

Also remember that a photographer that's right for your friend might not necessarily be the right fit for you. So, welcome all recommendations but do your own research.

What makes a great photo?

Just like good PR, a great photo tells a story and is emotionally engaging in some way. Maybe it's a relaxed headshot of you smiling, shot in great light, that showcases your friendly and approachable character. It tells a story of you and invites your potential clients to work with you. A great portrait could actually be the deciding factor in someone hiring you – or moving on!

A great photo of a product that you offer would be something which the viewer can almost place themselves into – they could see themselves running across the beach in that flowing dress that sold out on your website or cosying up on the sofa in front of the fire with a glass of wine from your vineyard or feeling confident and empowered following a coaching session with you.

What if you can't pay for a pro?

First of all, I would say try to find a way to pay. Photography is a marketing expense and if you're running a business this is something you should totally budget for. Photography could cost anywhere from £100–£200 for a handful of great headshots to £2,000 and more for a full-blown, custom commercial shoot.

If your budget is low, it's worth finding a local photographer who is running a headshot day, where they get several people together and photograph them in one location in 15–20-minute slots, therefore allowing them to keep the individual fee quite low.

Please don't ask photographers to work for free (no one should work for free, we all have bills to pay and photography is not a cheap business to run), but if someone is just starting out, or is in need of your services, could you offer to barter? Maybe you're a life coach and could exchange a couple of coaching sessions for a personal branding photo shoot? Or provide them with a pass to your yoga classes if you're a yoga teacher?

Just make sure it's mutually beneficial, it's a fair pound-for-pound exchange, and you're not asking someone to work 'for exposure' (because let's face it, that one never pays off).

Can you do it yourself?

Yes, there's always the option of learning to take pictures yourself! You can't really take your own portrait (so at the very least go get that professional headshot done), and not everyone can be a great photographer (just like not everyone is technical enough to be their own web designer), but you can learn to produce good, strong, simple images, often using just your smartphone, which have become really, really good in the past couple of years.

For best results you'll need to know how to use available light and understand the rules of composition; no camera can do that for you. There are some great tutorials and online courses out there, so I would look at these and then practise, practise and practise some more. Remember, the first 10,000 photographs you take will be your worst! It gets better from there!

PR School Homework: My PR Image Library

Carry out an audit of the images you have right now and save the ones that are good enough to use with the media.

Which ones do I need to bin?

....

What images do I need to add to my resources?

....

Do I have the budget to get some good professional images taken?

....

Can I tap into my professional network and find a photographer to work with?

....

What are my next steps?

....

Creating a Press Pack

Members of the media are busy people and when they want something, they want it NOW.

If you have to spend ages trying to find your logo or a photo of yourself that you like, you could be missing out not only on this opportunity, but others in the future, because if you don't send the goods, someone else will.

Your press pack won't actually 'get' you coverage, but it will help you be efficient in your PR activities, it will help ensure you're using consistent materials and messages when you talk to the press and it will remind you of your 'why'.

Things have changed since the days when I would stand at a photo-copier and collate Betty Crocker press releases and documents, putting them into shiny folders and adding bright red measuring spoons and boxes of cookie mix.

Today, people want things sent by email, or to be downloadable from websites. Materials need to be easy to read, free of jargon and they need to get to the point, so it's easy for the journalist to see where your story fits and why you should be included in their work.

Hazel Davis, copywriter and media trainer, says, *"In your press materials, does the language reflect the language of your audience? Are you using expressions and references that you understand but they won't? Are you paying too much attention to what your hipster competitors are writing to the detriment of your own customers who might be with you because they like the way you do things? Think about your customer every step of the writing process just as you would when you're designing the product or packaging.*

"Make sure everything is spelt right and always the same way. This isn't as obvious as it sounds, and you might be surprised at how often this isn't observed. Is your company name two words stuck together? Does it have a hyphen? Does your company name have an and in the middle or an ampersand? Consistency matters. This not only makes it easier for people to cut and paste but also helps consolidate the brand."

As a starting point for your press pack, I would include the following elements:

A Company Background Document (Backgrounder)

While this is a factual round-up of your business, you can still make it interesting and stand out by the language you use, the ambitions you share and the details you give away. From your starting date and location, to staff numbers, CSR policies and turnover, add it into the backgrounder to give a full summary of the business.

Product Information

Maybe you sell gorgeous children's clothing, bake delicious cakes or have a line of hand-painted greetings cards; whatever it is, add clear descriptions to your press pack and include ingredients, materials used, allergy information (if relevant) as well as prices, delivery costs and stockists (if appropriate) with links.

Logos

Now seems like the right time to touch upon branding. This is not only an integral part of your business but also your PR, because it is connected to how people see you and talk about you.

Jen Pringle, creative designer and founder of Pen&Pringle really knows her stuff, and has some wise words to help you shine: *"Getting your branding right is so important and is often underestimated. A logo isn't just a graphic. It's a* reflection of you and your business. When developing your brand, it's important to find someone who will work hard with you to deliver your vision and where you want to see your business. A good logo is like a shop window. Neglect your window and people will walk on by. Invest in it, and people will be drawn to you. It's as simple as that. Good design really does matter.

"If you can't afford a designer right now, do some research and use a programme like Canva to create a logo and brand identity you are happy with and when the time comes, look for a professional who can take things to the next level."

When your logo is ready, add it to your website and social media channels so people start to associate it with you. Also make sure you save it as a JPEG with your other press materials so it is ready to go out should a member of the press request it.

Testimonials

PR is what people say about you, so make sure you include feedback from your clients, suppliers and even social influencers you have collaborated with.

If people are going to work with me, I know they will go and look at my website, and my analytics show that they go and see what other clients and the press have said about me on my testimonials page.

Save these comments in a Word document and also add to your website or blog so that the world can see just how brilliant you are.

Awards

In a similar vein, if you have won an award make sure it is not only on your website (the organisers will often give you the logo and copy) but also on your press page and mentioned in your press materials. This gives you added clout and you should be shouting about it from the rooftops whenever you can.

Biography

Now, don't confuse this with your story. A biography is factual and covers areas such as education, work experience, previous roles, membership to industry bodies, qualifications and awards. Keep it clear, concise and 100% truthful. If you have members of staff, you may want to add them and think about having a 'Team' page on your website with their title, a brief biography and a headshot.

Media Coverage to Date

If you have been successful in securing coverage, you can mention this in your press packs. You need to adhere to the rules of sharing and be mindful of copyright laws, but simply saying 'as seen in' can give you credibility and send people searching for more, because that is what they do in our digital age.

Frequently Asked Questions

This might be overkill for some businesses, especially if you are really small, but a 'Frequently Asked Questions' section can be really helpful for journalists if they are on a deadline and your mobile is out of juice. Please note: always make sure you have a charger with you and that you're around if you have sent out a press release to take calls or pick up emails.

Make a list of all of the possible questions people ask you and offer truthful answers.

Contact Details

Make it easy for people to find you and get hold of you. As well as a phone number, email address and website, I would also suggest sharing your social media details, with Twitter being a great people finder. The media will sometimes check you out on Twitter or similar, so do be mindful of what you post as once it's out there, it is out there.

Where to Keep All of This

First of all, save all of this information in one place on your business computer, or better still, in the Cloud, so it can be sent as soon as it is requested.

Secondly, as I am sure you have guessed, I would suggest you create a 'Press Page' on your website or blog. As well as making it even easier for people to find information about you and your brand, it can also add kudos, shows you mean business and sets you on the path to shining.

Heidi Scrimgeour says, "*I adore the PRs and brands who have really slick press sites set up where I can download the salient details and images myself without having to email them requests and then wait for them to reply or worry about keeping a mental note of the need to chase them if they don't come back to me. THAT is the future.*"

You have been told!

PR School Homework: Create Your Press Pack

I hope you can now see the value of having a press pack and would ask you to go away and create this for your business.

Tick off the items below as you work through the requirements and do share your press pack, media page or ask any questions you have over on the PR School Facebook page.

My Press Pack

ITEM	YES	NOTES
Company backgrounder		
Product information		
Logos		
Images		
Testimonials		
Awards		
Biography		
Frequently asked questions		
Contact details		

Lesson Seven

Writing a Winning Press Release

If you aren't quite sure what a press release is, it is quite simply a written statement for communicating 'news' to the media.

As a writer and blogger, I receive hundreds of press releases a week and whilst some impress me, I am increasingly disillusioned by the standard of copy, lack of news and inability to get to the point – fast.

While working for TV channels, IT companies, fashion houses, supermarkets, charities, start-ups and many more organisations, I have written more press releases than I can remember and while there is an ongoing debate about the future of press releases, they are still being written and sent out and I'm not sure if this is going to change any time soon.

Kelly Rose Bradford, a freelance journalist, says, "*I think press releases can be hugely useful. The angle might not be for me, but the product could be.*"

Heidi Scrimgeour, however, says, "*I hate press releases with a passion. I know they're a necessary evil, but I always prefer a friendly one or two lines in a personal email about an event or product, that gives me all the details I need without all the PR-y extra waffle that I won't use!*"

Heather Lowrie, Deputy News Editor/Travel Editor at *The Scottish Sun*, further comments, "*Keep press releases short and sweet. Make sure you know which journalist to target and address them personally and they will get in touch if they need anything else.*"

"*I don't think the press release is dead. It's extremely useful. However, I would stress that I like to receive a press release as a Word document rather than a PDF, which is much harder to use,*" is the advice of Jenny Itzcovitz, the Editor of Sixtyplusurfers.

The reality is that the press release is still part of the PR world, but if you want yours to be read, and more importantly used, you need to get it right, which means it has to be newsworthy and relevant.

You can pay a consultant or agency to write them for you, but what is stopping you from doing this yourself?

Time? Well, if you pay someone else you will have to earn that cash, so that isn't a reason.

Inspiration? Look at your business and the news you have to tell, and this should give you all the inspiration you need to write a winning press release.

Motivation? Go back to your vision board and look at the magazines you want to be featured in and right there is your motivation to sit down and get it done.

Know-how? Maybe you don't know how to do this right now, but by the end of this chapter all that will have changed.

What's It All About?

If written well and targeted properly, your press release will give your contact the whole story at a glance, make everyone's lives easier and increase your chances of getting those all-important column inches.

Forget fluffy, overly exuberant words and a host of exclamation marks. What the press want is news, real stories, hard facts and ultimately something their readers will want to read, and their editors will want to publish.

Hazel Davis adds to this: *"Don't fall into the trap of thinking your language needs to be flowery and complicated. The best writing is writing that's clear and concise and jargon-free. Try and avoid clichés. Journalists and readers are so used to seeing the words 'state-of-the-art' and 'world-leading' to describe things that they've become meaningless. Use language that accurately describes your brand and its offer rather than what you think will make you look clever.*

"The important thing is to make sure all the information is there. Can journalists read it and use it without having to trawl around the Internet for more information? Can it be easily repurposed in an article? Does it convey everything you need to convey? Don't think you need to spend three pages doing this either. If you can do it in as few words as possible, all the better."

It is vital to understand that whilst you might send a journalist a press release, there is no rule to say they have to read, use or like it. Once it's in the public domain, the press can delete it, laugh at it, demand you take them off your database and even block you from their Twitter account (yes, really).

The best way to ensure this doesn't happen to you is to send them press releases that contain news, are relevant, well written and of potential use to them – who can ask for more?

What Do You Write in a Press Release?

That's easy – news.

Sounds obvious, but if it's gone, it's too late. Write about what's happening now or what's about to happen in the future.

News can include:

A new fundraising campaign but one that has a story to go with it, people to talk about it and a reason to be of interest.

A new app that is solving a problem, filling a gap, making a difference.

A new website that has a story behind it. The DDH UK website launching wasn't a story but the fact that it meant there was going to be a comprehensive online resource available and a support network too, made it a news story for my media tribe.

A new product, shop, service or a store closure can all be in a press release as long as the story is strong enough.

The announcement of company profits, or losses – again, this is happening across the board at the moment and, the bigger the loss, the bigger the news.

The appointment of a celebrity supporter or ambassador can be newsworthy, so if Harry Kane is going to do some coaching with your son's football team in North London then that IS news and that is a story you will want to shout about (if his PR team says it's OK).

Human-interest stories, with a news element, are popular with local and consumer media as are stories with a charity or fundraising angle.

Controversy and scandal are always of interest but it is a good idea to have a crisis management plan in place, just in case things backfire.

Unusual or unexpected events and activities can be newsworthy and can often work for the regional and local press. One example was a story about plastic being washed up on beaches being recycled and made into kayaks, which struck a chord with BBC Devon and because it was very visual, it was even more successful.

If you think you have a story just stop and ask yourself if there really is anything 'new' about what you are planning to say.

Is there anything different about what you are doing that others might want to do too and so need to know about it? Maybe you are paying all your staff the living wage in an area where it just doesn't happen and you could be setting a precedent?

I know this might sound mean, but just because you are proud of your new coaching package for women on a career break, will anyone care on the news desk of *The Times* or is it better suited to a mummy blogger who writes about flexible working?

If you're not sure whether the story is newsworthy, go back to your vision board and your key publications and see whether your story fits.

If it doesn't have a strong enough news angle, maybe think about offering it as an interview or running a competition with an influencer so you still tell your story and shine, but just don't send the idea out as a press release as it probably won't get the attention you are hoping for.

Planning Your Press Release

Once you have all your information in place, it's a good idea to use the 'five Ws and one H' process to write your press release. This method has been used forever, it works and it is pretty much expected by the media.

What is the news and call to action?

Why is this news?

Who are the key people? Who is affected by your news? Who does it benefit? Who is your target audience?

Where is this happening?

When is this happening?

How did this come about?

Writing Style

When writing a press release think tight and bright and use as few words as possible to make your point.

Remember to use the third person – don't write, "We did this" or "I think that", unless it is as part of an approved quote.

Use the name of the company, and remember these are always written as singular.

The first sentence, or paragraph, should give the journalist the essence of the story, which means don't waffle, and avoid wordy, unnecessary explanations.

Try and keep all sentences to around 25 words so each one delivers a 'punch' and keeps the journalist interested.

Remember you are not writing an advert, so ensure that what you write is not overly promotional but instead remains factual and objective.

How to Lay Out a Press Release

Format and Style

Ensure you have 'Press Release' at the top of the document.

Add the distribution date for the press release at the top of the release so people can see when it came out, wherever it is in their ever-growing inbox.

Use your company house style font throughout in 11 point.

To double space or not to double space? Views are mixed but with email and computer editing it's probably not necessary as long as your release is easy to read. Short paragraphs with a space between each and slightly wider than normal margins are helpful.

Length

A press release should ideally be one side of A4, two at a push, or around 300 to 400 words.

If you reach three pages this would indicate that you either haven't got to the point or you have written a feature, so go back to the drawing board and decide if this really is a press release or more of a blog post, feature or a case study.

Strong Headline

A strong headline is a MUST as this will help to catch the journalist's eye. Go bold with this if you dare!

Paragraph One

The first paragraph is the most important as it tells the story in a nutshell. The test of success is whether the full story can be understood if the first paragraph was reproduced in print.

Paragraph Two

The second paragraph expands on information in the first, giving a bit more detail and adds depth.

Paragraph Three/Quotes

Often, the third paragraph provides a quote from a designated spokesperson, which has been signed off. Keep quotes upbeat and to the point but true and transparent.

Depending on what the story is, you may have two people offering quotes. This could be an investor, celebrity, service user or an MP, but this should add to the story and make it more newsworthy and credible.

Paragraph Four

The fourth and final paragraph outlines any additional information including calls to action such as visiting a website, downloading an app, donating or signing up for an e-course.

Ends marks the end of the press release so use the word 'ENDS' and ensure it is in bold and centred. I also put this in capitals, but it's your call.

Notes to Editors

Sometimes it's necessary to include extra information and rather than clutter your release, the best option is a section at the end of the release entitled 'Notes to Editors'.

This can be as long as required and can include:

- Your company backgrounder (as discussed in the press pack section)

- Facts and figures
- Full research and survey details
- Sales figures
- Biographies
- Company website details
- Notes about the availability of images, samples and press trips.

Contact Details

It's really important to include contact details and ensure that someone is available to take calls on the day that the release goes out.

Press Release Template

Press Release

Headline

Date

Paragraph 1

Paragraph 2

Paragraph 3/Quotes

Paragraph 4

- ENDS -

Notes to Editors

Contact Details

How to Send Out a Press Release

We will look at pitching in Lesson Eight, but in today's fast-paced, instant world, the best way to send out a press release is via email.

You will have your target press list, so there is no need to blind copy out blanket emails to hundreds of journalists. Ensure each email is sent personally, with the right name, using the press release title as the header of your email to catch the reader's attention and prevent the delete button being pressed.

Do not send as an attachment; instead, under your personalised note, copy and paste the press release in the body of your email.

PR School Press Release Checklist

I have put together a checklist of tips that will not only make your press release shine out in a cluttered inbox, but also make your company look professional, your story interesting and ensure your call to action is obvious.

- ☐ Is this REAL news?

- ☐ Have you checked you have answered who, what, why, where, when and how?

- ☐ Does your heading have the wow factor?

- ☐ Do you tell the story in the first paragraph?

- ☐ Have you gone over one page?

- ☐ Have the quotes been signed off?

- ☐ Do you have images?

- ☐ Is the language easy to read and free from fluff and jargon?

- ☐ Are your facts and figures correct?

- ☐ Have you double-checked the spelling and grammar?

- ☐ Have you included contact details?

PR School Homework: Write a Press Release

Using your story or newsjacking something in the press, write a press release...

Headline

....

Who?

....

Where?

....

What?

....

Why?

....

When?

....

How?

....

Quotes

....

Lesson Eight
Pitch Perfect

Now things are getting exciting.

You have a story that the world needs to hear, you know your audience and your vision board is on your office wall inspiring you to get out there and shine. You have your contacts book open, your press page looks amazing, you smile every time you see your gorgeous logo and you are confident your press release is newsworthy and relevant to your media tribe.

People, it's time to pitch!

At the start of your PR journey, pitching (that is telling your story) to the press can be a bit scary, but the biggest thing holding you back is you.

We talk ourselves into thinking that the media won't be interested in our business or want to listen to our story, which can make us nervous about approaching them, so we put it off.

Don't!

Yes, they are busy and have many deadlines, but they also need stories, so they do want to hear from you if you have something that is right for them and their readers.

As Chloe Leibowitz says, *"At the end of the day journalists are people who want to feature stories that their readers will be interested in. I would suggest contacting a journalist as an opportunity to get your message across to the readers and listeners who want exactly what you do. Show them your passion and enthusiasm, which will jump out and be appealing.*

"This definitely comes down to mindset – if you're apologetic and lacking confidence, that can be felt. Whereas, if you see it as the chance to shine in print or on the TV in a way which will positively impact your business, then what do you have to lose?! If you believe, and can give a clear, precise message, then it will be received positively. It's also about building relationships – so even if it doesn't come off the first time, or first ten times, you are now on the journalist's radar for future reference."

There are three main ways to do it, and that is by email, phone or social media.

Pitching by Email

From my experience and research, I know that the majority of press prefer initial contact to be made via email.

Kelly Kemp, at It's a Tink Thing, says, "*I, and many other bloggers, prefer initial contact to be made via email; it's more convenient and easier to check back through emails for details than trying to find notes scribbled during a phone call.*"

Gail Shortland further comments, "*I never answer my phone. I don't have the time unless it's a contact I know well. If you can't provide all you need these days through email efficiently, then you're struggling somewhere. But people like a chat on some titles! If you're going to end the call with 'I'll email you all the details' then perhaps that's what you should have done...*"

Finally, a contact once told me, "*Always, ALWAYS email unless I have phoned you and you're calling me back*", and I always stick to that rule with her.

There isn't a 'one size fits all' approach to email pitching, because what and how you write to the BBC will be different to the details you send to the *Mirror*, even if it is the same story.

I am afraid I can't make your dream team come back to you and snap you up for the evening news, but I will share what has worked for me with the likes of the *Daily Mail*, *Good Housekeeping* and *National Geographic*.

Make It Personal

No one wants to feel like just another number on a faceless database, so get their name right. For example, I often get emails to 'Dear Nathalie', which is rude and shows a lack of interest and attention to detail, 'Dear Editor' is even worse.

Each pitch should be unique, so add a personal touch, for example if you read something by that blogger last week, mention it. This is a two-way relationship, so give a little back, don't just take all the time.

As Stephanie Darkes says, "*I am more likely to open an email if there is a strong title and if it is personalised, so use my name and maybe add a comment about my work so I know you have taken the time to look at my blog and understand what I write about.*"

Do NOT copy and paste without changing names because this doesn't look good and if it is your first pitch to someone, it could also be your last.

Time Is Money

Don't waste a journalist's time: it is precious. Heidi Scrimgeour explains, *"I literally get hundreds of emails a day and I'd say 90% of those aren't relevant to the work I do. A good proportion of my day is spent deleting these and trying to weed the rare good ones from the overwhelming influx of irrelevant ones. I have a daily sense of inbox pressure because if I don't stay on top of the PR junk, my inbox can become totally unmanageable within a day."*

Headline Happy

Start with the headline as this will be the first thing the recipient sees and it needs to be thoughtfully crafted. Anything beginning with 'FW' will probably be deleted as they will know it has been sent out before and no one wants to be your back-up plan. 'Press Release' and 'Interview Opportunity' will get lost in the noise of a busy inbox so find something that is attention-grabbing and explanatory – but using no more than seven words!

Get to the Point

When writing your email, Nicola Brown, accredited MCIPR (Dip CIPR), freelance Director of PR and Communications at NB Thinks, suggests, *"Journalists often look at the preview of an email rather than opening it up – so make those first few words count. Don't waste them with 'Hello and how are you today', instead try, 'I've got a case study about X which I think you'll be interested in.' Keep the email short and to the point."*

Step Away from Emojis

Yes, you might think a smiley face will make a journalist warm to you – it won't! You are a professional, they are a professional, so step away from emojis!

You OK Hun?

Another no-no! Unless the journalist is also a real-life friend, hun, doll, darling and lovely are totally off limits and will do you no favours, but might get you mentioned on a freelance Facebook page for all the wrong reasons.

Kiss, Kiss, Kiss

You are not sending an email to your sister, so sign off with kind regards or best wishes and leave the kisses for loved ones.

Keep Large Files to Yourself

Yes, we know the media want images but sending over your entire library isn't a good plan. Either offer images in your email or send a link for downloading them. You don't want to fail at the first hurdle, so keep things light.

Be Realistic

I know Selfridges gets double-page spreads all the time and Brad Pitt has had miles of coverage during his career, but you are new to this and need to keep things in perspective so try not to be disappointed if a long call with a journalist only results in a two-line mention in their feature, and do send a thank you.

What Happens Next?

This is the million-dollar question. Once you've pressed 'send' I will be honest and say that, in the main, if someone wants to use the information they have received they will either go straight ahead and use it (especially if it is a blog or online magazine) or contact you for more details and images – so, again, make sure you have your press materials ready to go.

Many journalists find it annoying when a PR calls up asking if they got their press release, and that includes Kelly Rose Bradford, who says, *"Resending an email is fine – phoning to ask if I have got it is not. It is just an irritation and really is my biggest bugbear as I think it's such a waste of PR resources to do this."*

Heidi Scrimgeour adds, *"If I haven't replied to a press release you can safely assume it's not of interest so phoning me about it won't endear you to me, sorry to say! I realise how uppity and unkind that sounds and I am hugely admiring of the many excellent PRs I work with, but those ones never phone unless they've got something they know I'm going to want to hear. They've earned my trust to get to that place, too!"*

It's also a yes from Emma-Jane Batey, *"I'm happy for PRs or brands to follow up press releases, as long as they are prepared for either a 'not at the moment' or a 'yes, quick, send me more!' response. I also appreciate it when I say, 'I have something suitable in the pipeline for x date' and they keep in touch. Do remember to follow up press releases by email, phoning is so noughties!"*

That said, people are busy, and things do get missed so, if you do call to follow up, try and have something extra to offer like a case study or expert who can give additional insight, and it could be what is required to get that much-needed yes!

If a journalist comes back to you for images, comments, product or an interview, get it to them. The early bird catches the worm and if you decide that going for a coffee with your friend is more important than sending images to *The Times*, then you may well lose that opportunity, and that contact. If they ask – DELIVER!

Say Thank You

You've spent days, even weeks, working with a journalist on an interview in *Good Housekeeping*, images have been sent, copy edited and a photo shoot on the other side of the country attended. The day the magazine comes out, you go and buy it, you smile with pride as you see yourself on the glossy pages (it is amazing how those make-up and wardrobe teams work) and before you share it on social media, please email your contact and say thank you. It is so, so, so important to do this. It doesn't matter whether it's the Editor of *Vogue*, the reporter on a local newspaper or a new blogger on the block: if they have taken the time to write about you, then please take the time to say thank you. They will remember you did so and it could just be why they work with you again.

PR School Homework: Write an Email Pitch

Write a simple email pitch using the template overleaf and use your story or look at the news and find something to comment on.

Email Pitch Template

Hi [ADD NAME]

My name is _____ and I'm getting in touch in regard to [ADD DETAILS OF YOUR BUSINESS].

[PARAGRAPH INTRODUCING YOUR STORY AND KEY POINTS]

I would love to know if this is something of interest and can send over more details, images and products if needed.

Kind regards,

[YOUR NAME]

Name
Position
Company
Telephone number
Website
Social media details

Pick Up the Phone

I know email feels safer, but there might be times when you might have to make a few calls if you want to shine.

When I started out in PR, the fax machine was about as advanced as it got, so I spent a lot of time on the phone and soon realised that journalists are busy people and you have to go with the flow. Some were abrupt, some were nice and some put the phone down on me, but calls are part of the job and you have to take the rough with the smooth.

One of the first lessons I learned was to only pick up the phone if I 100% knew the story, knew the publication and had an idea where the client could potentially fit in that publication.

I remember working in an open-plan office and, while I was very good at my job, I was super shy so the thought of calling the tech press in front of the MD made me feel sick.

My tactic was to book a meeting room for between 10.30 and 12 or from 3 and 4.30pm then take my papers (no laptops for Account Executives in 1998) in and make my calls in the quiet away from glaring eyes and open ears.

I would rehearse what I was going to say and I was confident when I was talking because I knew I was telling them something they would be interested in, and that their readers would be keen to read about, so they were, in the main, happy to listen. Over time I became the 'IT girl' (computers not parties) and my contacts would take my calls because they knew I knew my stuff and that I would bike images to their offices if they were on deadline, because I was hungry for the coverage and wanted to progress up the career ladder.

Know that saying, 'Fake it 'til you make it'? Yes, I used it then and I use it now if I am dealing with a project that is out of my comfort zone or the pressure is really on to deliver.

Although you may feel nervous about phoning a journalist, the reality is that it can sometimes be the best way to get them to notice you and the worst that can happen is they say no.

So, how do you do it?

Know Who You Are Calling

As you've carefully picked your contacts, you should know about the people you are calling. If for any reason this is someone totally new, maybe there is a breaking story about a rise in National Insurance and you want to talk to the Money Editor at the *Daily Mail*, then just do a little research first. Find the right person, try to get their direct line, or do a quick online search to see what they have written about recently to give you as much background detail as possible. Why not also check their tweets, as this can be helpful and their biog may have their email address in it.

I would suggest printing out what you are going to say and practising before making that call. This makes you more confident and can stop you from mumbling or getting nervous and talking about your dog or the school run.

Do You Have Time?

When you call, say hi, tell them who you are, and ask them if they have time to talk, rather than just blurting out a load of information about your new puppy training classes only to realise you are speaking to the receptionist and have to go through it all again. If they don't have time, ask if you can send the details in an email and get their address – if they say no, don't!

Get to the Point

Why should they care? Yes harsh, but these are busy people, especially if a news story has just broken, so get to the point right away, use clear, simple language and avoid jargon.

Remember Your 'Why'

I know this is a lot for one call, but do not lose sight of why you are telling them your story and what you want to achieve from the call.

Be Enthusiastic and Friendly

Don't let a less-than-cheery hello put you off. Be polite, be professional and never underestimate how much your enthusiasm can rub off on someone else. Worst case, they will remember you as the happy one!

If more details are requested, send that information as soon as you can.

Also record the conversation in your media database and make any notes in your diary on following up with them or when they plan to cover the story, if this information was given to you.

PR School Homework: Practise Your Phone Voice

No, I am not going to make you call the Features Editor of *Country Life* right now, but I am going to suggest you have a rehearsal conversation in your office so you get used to the sound of your own voice and can fine-tune your pitch.

When They Call You

Imagine, it's 6.30pm, you have a baby on your hip and a toddler throwing fish fingers at the dog and just as the smoke alarm goes off your phone

rings and you get a call from the journalist working at the *Daily Mail*.
Yes, that was me.

Calls aren't always scheduled and freelancers work unusual hours, but if you want to shine, make sure you are prepared to take a call at any time.

Make a Note

Always make a note of who the journalist is, what they are calling about and take down the publication/programme as well as contact details in case you are cut off (I live in Devon and this is a real thing).

Be Helpful

While you are speaking, be helpful, don't talk too fast and if there is something you aren't sure about, don't try to wing it; instead let them know you will get back to them later with the details.

Follow Up

After the call, send them an email thanking them for getting in touch, recapping what you discussed and send any additional details as well as requested images. If the story goes out, email the journalist to say thank you and share links of the coverage as appropriate and within the copyright rules.

When They Say No

Easy to say, but if a journalist says no, by email or on the phone, you can't take it personally or you would never send another pitch again.

There will have been a good reason for declining your story and that won't be because they don't like you! It could have been the wrong time, too left field for that contact, a busy news day or something similar may have been covered recently.

If you can, try to get some feedback about what the problem was, and you can use this to move ahead for the future and with your next pitch.

As with most things in life, you aren't always going to get a yes and a page in *Elle* every time you send out a story, it's just not how it works, unless you are Kate Moss, and even she might have off days.

If you don't get the answer you want, don't stamp your feet or take to Twitter to rant, and don't give up but instead reflect, learn and move on.

As Nicola Brown says: *"Say thanks for their time. Also, check with them what kinds of things they might like in the future, and say you'll be in touch as and when you have news or feature ideas that match what they say."*

When a Yes Becomes a No

This is another PR occupational hazard that we have all had to deal with and it can happen after you have put in all the hard work of writing emails, sending photos, doing filming or taking part an interview – the piece simply doesn't run.

I remember the first time an eagerly anticipated piece of coverage didn't come out. I was at the newsagent bright and early one Wednesday morning, I bought my copy of the *Daily Express* and went through it five times looking for the piece on the supermarket I was working with. It wasn't there. My heart sank, and I may have cried. What would my boss say? What would the client say? Well, neither were happy, but when I called my contact they said they were sorry but it had been pulled at the last minute due to a breaking news story. I was gutted but it taught me a valuable lesson to never count on coverage until I am looking at it.

As Kelly Rose Bradford wisely says: *"Accept that lead times can be very long, and that even if you have done a really long interview, provided pics, or even had yourself or your client attend a photo shoot, there are NO GUARANTEES you/your product will make it in – things can be pulled/ dropped at the last minute. Always remember that this is as frustrating and embarrassing for the writer as it is for the PR."*

What I don't want you to do is take the first no as a sign to stop; instead treat these situations as learning curves and accept that if you want to reach great heights, and you want to shine, then you can't give up, and as someone said at a recent event, "A no means it is time to look for the next yes."

PR School Homework: Reflection Exercise – When It's a No

What was the story?

....

131

Why didn't it work for this journalist?

....

Did I get any specific feedback?

....

What changes could I make next time?

....

What other media outlets could this work for?

....

What have I learned?

....

Have I written up these details in my contacts database?

....

When You Need to Say No

I know that when it comes to PR, the temptation is to say yes to everything, but sometimes you need to say no.

We have instincts because they guide us and that is why we need to listen to them.

Remember that girl at school who you didn't quite trust, who then ran off with your boyfriend?

How about the colleague who would claim your ideas at team meetings or sneakily send your reports to clients as if they had written them?

The PT you didn't quite click with on day one, and who really didn't help you get fit at all.

These are all examples of listening to your instincts and when you are doing your own PR, you need to trust them or things can go very wrong.

Maybe your products aren't right for *The Sunday Sun*, you don't feel comfortable talking in the *Daily Mail* about your earnings, or you aren't keen on the requests of an influencer: this is fine.

Saying no is OK, and it could be the best decision you make.

TV Appearances

TV appearances are the dream scenario for many people because this kind of exposure can open up many opportunities, which personal stylist Lisa Talbot confirms: "*I presented on QVC and it certainly drove traffic to my website.*"

Ruth Kudzi explains, "*I was on* Good Morning Britain *and nothing directly came to me as a result BUT people now see me as an expert.*"

It is one thing sending a pitch to *This Morning*'s research team about a health diagnosis (and well done you if you do), but quite another to talk about it live in front of millions of people, but you can do it.

For Lynsey Sizer, a PR consultant, TV was a success but she says it wasn't all plain sailing: "*I was working at a well-known toy company and secured a spot for our remote-controlled dog on* The Big Breakfast. *Of course, the dog didn't work first time on live TV but Johnny and Denise had a laugh with me and we tried it again. That dog then secured a spot on the top ten toys list and sold out three weeks before Christmas.*"

When you get the email that the *BBC Breakfast* sofa has your name on it, once you have said yes, my advice is to be prepared before showtime.

What's It All About?

Once you have agreed to take part in any interview, it is vital to ask the journalist or researcher for the main questions or topics they will cover.

How long will the interview be?

How early do you need to get there and where do you need to go?

Will it be a live show or a recorded interview?

Are you going to be interviewed alone or as part of a group discussion? If it's a group interview, then it can be helpful to know who else is involved so you can do your research on them as well.

What Do You Want to Say?

I would write down the key things you want to communicate when you are in the spotlight. If you have a clothes range, it could be how your business was created while you were on maternity leave, the fact you only work with British suppliers, and the pieces you sell are 100% organic.

Maybe you're a coach who retrained after a health scare and now work with women who work in the city but want to have a more balanced approach to life.

Go back to your 'why' and look at your story and this will help you be totally clear on what you are going to say, and if it helps, write it down and rehearse it in front of a mirror or even do a Facebook live, and this can help you prepare and build your confidence.

Anticipate Difficult Questions

The press aren't trying to catch you out, but if you know they could ask challenging questions, be ready with your answers.

Maybe you are a sleep nanny who advocates controlled crying, or you are going on TV to talk about a vegan lifestyle together with the owner of a farm – things could get heated, so know your stuff, stick to your messages and believe in your story. It might not always be easy, but it should be worth it.

What to Wear on TV

Unconsciously we make judgements about people almost instantaneously based on how they look, therefore it's crucial to think about what you want your TV appearance to say about you when you are on the TV. Shelley Kelly is a top personal stylist and has some helpful advice:

What do I want people to think about me before I even open my mouth? What three words do I want people to use to describe me? These become your brand's "style words".

When you are selecting an outfit take a good look at yourself in the mirror, or even better ask a trusted friend. Does this say (for example) professional, trustworthy, fun? Does the outfit go with your style words?

Does this fit the context of the broadcast – wearing a suit on kids' TV might not work but as an expert on a news channel, it might be the way to go.

On a practical level, always wear something you feel incredible in. We should all have at least one outfit which makes us feel invincible – when we put it on we stand taller, we smile more, we are more sociable. In short, we become the best version of ourselves.

Look in your wardrobe. What is your outfit? Think about the last time you felt motivated, strong, productive and that you could take on anything. What were you wearing? It matters less what it was, what really matters is how it made you feel. That's the outfit. Bottle that feeling. Use that.

If that outfit isn't there, start looking out for someone in the public eye whose style you admire and whose visual brand sits well with your own. How could you go about recreating that look to work for your lifestyle? Investing in that outfit is investing in yourself, your brand and your business.

Whether it's photography or TV work, the same principles hold true, but TV has some additional potential pitfalls you should be aware of:

Interviews tend to be from the waist up so focus on working out the best shades and tones for your colouring. Make sure you get your best colours near your face – you should always look healthier in what you wear!

Avoid stripes, busy patterns, noisy jewellery as well as beige and other skin tones – you'll end up looking topless, and never wear green as you'll disappear against The Green Screen.

Think about your hair and make-up too. Keep it simple but for TV always wear more make-up than you think you need; you might find the team will do your make-up for you and it might be heavier than usual, but you will thank them when you watch back.

Lights, Camera, Action

Just like your wedding day or birthday party, interviews fly by really quickly, so try to get your key messages in as early as you can, making sure they fit naturally in the conversation!

Be passionate about your story as this will allow you to connect with the presenter and the audience, but don't give a lecture or become defensive, as people will switch off.

Look at the presenter and other guests when you are speaking, not at the camera.

Stay calm and believe you can do this, because you can.

Enjoy it, this is your time to shine and a TV appearance can be an absolute game changer for your business.

When It's Over

Before you know it, the presenter will be saying thank you and the programme will be heading for a commercial break, so give yourself a pat on the back because being on TV isn't easy.

When you get back to the office always send a follow-up email to the team to say thank you, and offer your services again – you would be surprised how often this doesn't happen and you lose the brownie points you could score by doing this one simple thing.

Also, make sure you put a post on social media, before and after your TV appearance, and write and share a blog post, as this can help you shine even more and allow you to reach even more people.

Nothing Is Off the Record!

I am pretty sure you've heard the term 'off the record', but my advice is if you don't want something published, don't say it in the first place.

In the past I've pulled up staff members who have spoken off the record to local papers or have had cosy chats during press events when the wine has taken over, and this just isn't on and should be avoided. Yes, be friendly, but also remember that PR is part of your business and you need to maintain a professional approach at all times.

I don't want this to make you nervous, but I do want you to be aware that if you don't want something to be shared in the public domain, then don't say it.

PR School Homework : What Is Off the Record for Me?

....

....

....

Lesson Nine

Have a Plan

You have secured your first couple of pieces of media coverage – congratulations, this is a brilliant achievement.

Maybe it was a story in your local paper about the opening of your new shop where £500 was raised for charity, you took part in an interview about your innovative business in the *New York Times* (go you) or you secured a five-star book review in *Woman* magazine.

Whatever it was, be proud that you are shining but also see that you need to keep the momentum going for long-term gains, and that is where a plan comes into play.

While the media agenda changes by the minute and online platforms mean things happen now, I believe there is still a place for a PR plan and I am not alone.

"The pace of change means it's more important than ever to have a plan. If your PR is purely reactive you're not giving yourself a chance to maximise the opportunities that come your way or develop your own."

Gemma Pettman, PR consultant

"You always need to have a plan, even if it's just as a fall-back option. PR shouldn't stop and start, it should be a constant stream of stories building the profile of a brand, product or business – if you just rely on outside influences to shape your PR, you'll be busy trying to keep that stream going."

Sarah Learoyd, Director, GLRPR

"Start with a plan. Know what it is you want to achieve, know your audience and work out how best to reach them. Having a strategy

will help you measure your success and achieve your goals much more effectively than scatter-gunning your efforts."

Claire Hall, PR consultant and blogger

I love a plan and actually really enjoy writing them, implementing them and seeing the results come in. At one point, I was managing ten PR agencies across Europe and the Middle East and my 12-month plan was a multipage Excel document masterpiece that took weeks to complete and covered four channels in multiple languages.

I am not saying that you need something as comprehensive or complicated as that, but I would advise having a PR plan in place and combining planned activities with the newsjacking, reactive opportunities we have looked at.

Jocasta Tribe has many years of experience of creating plans, and says, *"Naturally the news agenda changes and can provide opportunities to showcase your thoughts, products and messages that can't be predicted. Therefore, it is important to have both a planned and reactive approach to your PR strategy. If you know, for example, specific events are happening in different months or there are certain weeks where topics are likely to be discussed in the press e.g. International Women's Day, the Budget, the* MasterChef *final, there may be things that you can proactively plan communications activities around that will enable you to tell your story at a time that has the greatest chance of being used by the media.*

"Equally it is good to keep a lookout for ongoing journalist requests that may come up that will allow you to contribute to topical debates or keep an eye on breaking news to position yourself as having interesting insight on the topic making the headlines."

Not only will a plan help keep you on track and motivated, it will help remind you of what you want to achieve and how you will do that.

What to Include in Your PR Plan

You don't need to go into massive detail with your PR plan, so aim for three to four sides of A4, making the information easy to read, manageable to execute and detailed enough to work.

What's the Story?

Having a summary of your story can keep you on track with your PR and remind you of what you want people to know. Remember to think about what you don't want to talk about too.

Your 'Why'

Try to be as specific as possible with this, so rather than saying you want to increase your sales, you could say you want to increase your sales by 50% in the next year or you would like to see 100 people attend your Christmas event.

Who Is Your Target Audience?

Write down your target audience and go back to your notes earlier in this book if you need a reminder of the finer details.

Who Are in Your Media Tribe?

You have worked on the media outlets you want to appear in, so look at your vision board and contacts book for this one.

How Will You Tell Your Story?

Are you going to use a press release, host a competition, write a blog or post on social media or is it going to be a combination of all of these things, with some newsjacking too?

Budget

Work out what you want to do and when, and if there are any costs, for example competition prizes, photography or review products, then add these in and ensure you have the ability to cover these.

Timeline

Create a timeline, maybe one that covers six months or a year, and write down what you are going to work on proactively week by week, then add in a reminder about jumping on the news agenda too.

Measuring Success

You need to decide how you will measure your PR success. For this try to identify specific goals, for example your PR will help boost your sales in the next year by 30% and you will secure two speaking opportunities in London. It could be that you want to sell 1,000 copies of your first novel and use this to help you secure a number of literary festival appearances. It could be that you want local people to know you offer dog walking and day care so that you can give up your part-time job and work with the animals full time.

PR School Homework: Write Your PR Plan

Below is a simple template to help you plan your journey. Take time to really get this right and over time, as the successes come in and you start to shine, you can make changes, but do have a plan and do start it now.

My PR Plan

What's the story?	
Why am I telling the story?	
Who is my target audience?	
Who are my media tribe?	
How will I tell my story?	
What actions do I need to take?	
When do I need to do this?	
How will I know if I have been successful?	

Lesson Ten

Celebrate Your Successes

"We saw you in the *Daily Mail*."

"Oh wow, you have 12,478 followers on Twitter."

"I saw your book in Waterstones."

"You are EVERYWHERE."

These are just some of the comments people might make when you are working hard on your PR and the results start to come in.

You have done really well to get to this point, so please be your own cheerleader when this happens. You'll want to let people know you've been in the press, but do this the right way. Make sure you have permission to share coverage from the outlets you've been featured in (or get a license), but as a rule of thumb don't just take a photo of it and share away, as that could lead to copyright issues. Take those compliments on board rather than shaking them off as nothing, say thank you and smile because you are out there shining as you deserve to be.

As Joanna, a PR consultant, rightly says, *"When it comes to PR enjoy it but be aware that it's not all glamorous parties and long lunches. It's hard and sometimes the work can be thankless but it's totally worth it – I still get a buzz seeing the daily cuttings!"*

Over the past few years I have appeared in titles across the media and people are used to seeing me in the press. I won't lie, I still love getting those PR wins and might do a small dance around my office when I see them, but I don't do this for vanity reasons. These wins help to raise awareness of hip dysplasia, drive sales of my books and secure clients, as well as giving me credibility amongst peers, the media and even the medical world when it comes to DDH.

It is something I am used to doing and feel comfortable about and I hope that you will start to feel that way, too.

As your story gets out there you will want to not just celebrate success, but measure it too.

Helen Dewdney, founder of The Complaining Cow, has seen direct success with her PR efforts: "*I have been on* Rip Off Britain, BBC Breakfast, *in all the major newspapers as well as magazines and I've also been interviewed on various BBC Radio programmes. I would say that all of these PR opportunities have resulted in varying degrees of profile raising, increased traffic to my blog and there have been extra book sales. But, without doubt, my first stint on* Jeremy Vine *saw me sell five times the average daily book sales and was the first time I went to number one in consumer guides on Amazon!*"

Darren Blackstock, founder of PedalTalk, has been impressed with the results of his PR efforts: "*In response to an interview in the* Swindon Advertiser, *we had a few enquiries from local business people who cycle and wanted to know more about my idea, which was great. We have also been invited to attend a cycling festival in Swindon where we can put up stands and banners, run competitions and give out flyers, and with a couple of thousand visitors expected at the event, that's a mega potential audience for us. Finally, the article helped me connect with an X Pro Racer who runs his own sportive company and we're joining up to take private corporate events into several industries. These are exciting times and shows just what PR can help you achieve, and I don't think an advert would have generated the same results.*"

If you are putting the time and effort into your PR activities then you need to ensure they tie into your overall business objectives, otherwise it's time to revise what you are doing.

When I first worked in PR, I would live in fear of the moment when I'd be asked to calculate the advertising equivalent of a client's coverage for the month. The cuttings book and calculator would come out, along with scissors, a ruler and strong coffee and I'd spend an eternity trying to work out what the PR would be worth had it been paid for as advertising.

We would get very excited at all the zeros that came out for a piece in *The Guardian* or for a case study write-up in *PC Pro*, but for some reason no one really questioned what it was actually worth, they just loved pound signs and pages of press exposure.

The thing is, while having your bespoke wallpaper on the pages of *Prima* and *Livingetc* is great, what is it doing for your bottom line? You need to look at whether it led to a spike in traffic to your website or if you took the most orders ever when the magazine came out and this will show whether you are converting your efforts into sales, awareness raising, web traffic or increased donations.

Measure Your PR Successes

There are, of course, academic metrics in place to measure the outcomes of PR activities, but I think if I start to explain the Barcelona Principles you're going to move on to the next chapter and lose interest and I don't want you to do that.

I've put down some ideas so you can see how far you travel with your PR and what impact investing your time and resources in PR has.

How Many People Have Seen You Shine?

If you look at the number of features that mention you and your business, that can help tell you about the pickup of your story. It will illustrate how many journalists have read what you have sent them and covered it. If you look at the circulation of who they write for, or the number of people that visit their blog or listen to their podcast, you will start to see just how many people have potentially now heard about you.

Look at Your Web Traffic

You can use a tool like Google Analytics to measure the traffic to your website, and track where most of that has come from.

Say your leather bags were mentioned in the HuffPost Christmas gift guide, you can look at how many visitors came to you from that feature and how many made a purchase and that will show the return on your investment of giving one journalist one bag to review.

Maybe you wrote a guest post for an influential parenting blogger about your new baby-weaning book which then sold out on Amazon – that is PR success.

Also look at your newsletter sign-ups as these can happen because someone has read a guest blog post you wrote, they heard you on the radio or saw your chocolate brownie recipe in *You* magazine.

Have You Seen an Increase in Sales?

Many of us do PR because we want to see an increase in our profit margins.

Maybe you have had mammoth orders for birthday cakes, sold more coffees than ever in your city centre deli or now have a waiting list for your yoga classes as places have been flying off the shelf.

Yes, it could just be good luck, or it could be that the newspaper and magazine features you have secured over the past year have really helped you to shine and in turn boosted your sales.

One thing you can do is ask your customers where they heard about you and if time and again it's your column in *Families* magazine, the interview in mindbodygreen or the competitions you have run with bloggers, then you know you are doing your PR the right way.

Do You Have More Volunteers?

If you are a charity and you have seen a direct increase in volunteers or fundraisers, well done as that is often the way PR can put you on the map.

When they sign up to help, make sure you check how they know about you and go back to any media outlets they talk about because if this is helping you to shine, you want to see if you can do it more often.

Charities can also see if they've had more people sign up to their newsletters or received donations as these can all come from PR efforts.

Are You Becoming an Expert?

Many businesses, especially small businesses, want to get their name out in their crowded market.

Whether you're an artist, novelist, Pilates teacher or book coach, there will be increasing competition in your marketplace and if you want to get ahead, your roar needs to be louder than anyone else's so that your light shines brighter.

A speaking opportunity at a big HR conference is a massive ego boost and if that resulted in being asked back the following year and being contacted by a journalist from *People Management* asking for you to be interviewed in a feature, you could certainly call that success.

The more media coverage you secure, the more your brand will stand out, so if your waiting list is growing, you can be pretty certain that some of those names are due to your PR efforts.

I hope this has shown you that while your return on investment (ROI) is important, there are more ways to measure it than just financial returns.

If you are working hard on keeping in the spotlight, that is amazing, and I want you to carry on that way.

Celebrate All Your Wins

It is really important to focus on what you have accomplished with your PR efforts, because it shows you have been brave, taken a huge step out of your comfort zone and are not only succeeding, but also shining.

Chloe Leibowitz agrees and says, *"We are far too good at noticing what went wrong, or what we didn't get done, or things we consider have 'failed'. In order to have a more positive, confident mindset, it is essential to celebrate every little win, and to notice more and more what we did do, what went well, and how great we are!! I think it's best to actually write down at the end of the day, week, month what was a win – there will be far more than you realise, and the ultimate effect is that we get where we want to go much quicker, because we believe we can do it."*

If you celebrate every success, no matter how small, this can help build your confidence and a positive mindset, which is what you need when you are not only running your business, but also your PR.

By telling yourself, "I am successful" or "I can succeed because I've succeeded before", when you send that pitch to *Stella* or call up the Health Editor at the *Daily Mail*, you feel confident about doing so and feel positive that they will come back to you and say yes.

You will start to see that when you notice and celebrate your successes, you see yourself as someone who is successful and winning at their PR efforts rather than someone who's trying to become successful and not quite there.

PR School Homework: Celebrate Your Successes

Find a pretty glass jar and EVERY time you get a win, whether it's huge or tiny, write it down and put it in there for safe keeping.

If you ever have a wobble or an 'I can't do this' moment, pick out one of your wins and remember how amazing you are, how far you have come and why you are doing this!

Lesson Eleven

Go Pro

If you have read this book, followed each of the lessons, carried out the homework and are now starting to reap the rewards, congratulations!

This means you now have a better understanding of PR, you've seen how it has started to take your business to the next level and how the increased exposure means you are attracting attention, achieving your goals and shining.

Knowing what you do now, being clear about which media you are talking to and owning your PR will hopefully have helped to ease those early feelings of uncertainty, so you now feel confident when you publish blog posts, send out press releases and offer products for review.

What you will probably have also realised is just how much time, work and energy goes into creating and sustaining your PR efforts.

You might have time to continue fitting your PR into your day, but you may get to the point where because of the increased media exposure you are busier than ever with clients (AMAZING!) and new business, and now need some extra support.

You might, on the other hand, think that doing PR yourself isn't for you, and that is fine. Sometimes we simply need to outsource and invest money in a professional who can keep the ball rolling and get you seen in all the right places on an ongoing basis.

Whether you take on a member of staff and have them trained, use an independent PR consultant, or go for a PR agency, this next level of investment could help you reach new heights and shine brighter than ever.

This isn't something to jump into quickly, believe me. In my corporate days, I made snap decisions and while I had regrets, I certainly learned from my mistakes, and that is important.

What Are Your Options?

The next step is to decide what kind of PR support will work best for you, and there are several options to consider.

You can go with a full-service agency and your PR team will be able to offer a range of services from media relations and content creation to event planning and crisis management. While Coca-Cola and Topshop might need this set-up, do stop and ask if this is for you and also, can you afford it, as they do come in at top dollar?

A smaller, boutique agency will give you more one-to-one support and hit the ground running when it comes to ideas, contacts and, hopefully, results.

You can go with an independent PR consultant who will be able to offer you their time, energy, dedication and expertise as well as the shining results you are after.

There are some excellent virtual assistants out there who can help with PR, marketing and social media, and this is a good option when you are starting out and want to get a feel for the water and find out where you really sit in the media landscape.

Whatever you go for, one of the key things about finding the right PR support for you is that they will become a seamless part of your business. They will understand who you are, what you do, what you stand for and be as close to the brand as you, and this will make them perfect for telling your story.

Your support should work with you to lead your PR strategy and also your content if that is what you need. I believe this is very much a collaborative and creative process and partnership, and if you want it to work, there needs to be not only experience but also enthusiasm, trust and integration.

I've hired many PR firms over the course of my career and while they were equally qualified, some I was drawn to more because they were hungry for the work, they got it, they had great ideas, were creative and wanted to work with me.

This was certainly the case when I carried out a PR review in Scandinavia for one company. While we saw some amazing people, and visited some pretty funky offices in some stunning cities, it was the most creative agency with the best ideas and solid contacts that we worked with and they really did deliver.

Remember those instincts we talked about earlier? Follow them when it comes to outsourcing your PR and you will be glad you did.

What Do You Need from a Professional?

If you think you need, or want, to work with a PR professional, then it is a good idea to decide what you need doing and create a brief before you go any further.

It is really easy to meet with experts and get carried away with their enthusiasm and experience, and while it is great to be inspired, you need to know what you want and go with that, to start with at least.

Is it writing press releases and sending them out, or do you just need the copy and you can do the rest?

If social media is taking over your life, do you need someone to take that on and ensure people keep seeing you?

Are you missing a trick with the trends and seasonal events that could get you more proactive opportunities but you just don't have the time to do it all?

Do you want to be speaking at conferences, but need someone who has their finger on the pulse of events to help get you on that stage, so you can shine?

Be clear about what support you need, make a list, work out your budget and stick to it.

PR School Homework: My PR Support

What do I need help with in terms of my PR efforts?

....

....

Why do I need that help?

....

....

When do I need that help?

....

....

What kind of person or company would I feel happy working with?

....

....

How would I measure their value and success?

....

....

What budget do I have for this?

....

Find the Right PR Professional for You

I know I've got the most out of my PR agencies or assistants when I've really loved working with them and the chemistry was right. There is nothing more soul-destroying than working with people who are on a different wavelength, who don't get you or go off and do their own thing regardless of the brief and the fact you are paying them. Believe me, I have been there and got burnt when it came to letting them go!

One of the best ways to find 'the one' is to ask around! Family, friends, Facebook groups, mums at the school gates are all well connected, and you might be surprised at who knows someone, and someone good! This goes back to that **P**ersonal **R**ecommendation and you will be surprised how many times it comes into play when it's on your radar.

A Google search will throw up various ideas, and this can be good if you are looking for a very specific skill set, for example a PR who has experience of working with artists in Cornwall or you want a defined location like Manchester because regional media are your bread and butter.

Like the perfect pair of jeans, the right lipstick and a favourite mug, only you will know what is right for you and who is going to be the best fit for your work.

Finding names is one thing, but to get the best out of your PR investment, you need to really gel with the person you work with, so meeting them face to face, or via Skype or Zoom and having an initial chat is your first port of call.

This is like any interview situation, and while they are offering you their experience, contacts, creativity and insight, you are offering them a contract and the chance to be a part of something amazing – your business – so you want to get it right.

I would start by getting a better idea about their background and what PR means to them, and move on to questions such as:

- How much do you know about my business?
- Where do you think you could add value?
- What are your main skills when it comes PR?
- If your media tribe were to describe you in three words, what would they say?
- How do you measure success?
- How do you see PR fitting in with social media?
- What are your reporting methods?
- Can you give me an example of a newsjacking success you have had for one of your clients?
- If I were to work with you, what do you think your priorities for me would be in the first three months?
- Why do you want to work with me?

Please don't ask them to write you a PR plan before taking them on – this is part of a paid project or retainer fee once there is a signed contract in place.

The same goes for contacts. If you don't want to be offended by a no, then don't ask for media details as this isn't good business or GDPR practice, and I never share journalist information with clients.

Getting Started
Be it an Independent PR consultant, virtual assistant (VA) or an agency, if you decide to work with them, draw up a contract and confidentiality

agreement, get them signed, agree a start date and you are good to go.

I would suggest you provide a handover document, so they can see what you have done to date, where your successes have been and where you have fallen down. You never know, they may have a great contact at *The Guardian Society* supplement who would love your charity story even though the News Editor on the same title said no.

Also send them your press pack collateral and images (using Dropbox or Google Drive might be easier than email if you have big files) and maybe get them to review these as part of their first project for you. A fresh pair of eyes can be really helpful, and they might be able to suggest changes, updates and improvements.

Share your PR plan as it stands today. You might have taken them on board to revamp this and give it a shake-up, but at least they have a starting point and you can then sign off additions and changes.

This is a good time to let them know of any other marketing or social media activities, as they can be weaved into the new PR plan to maximise results.

If you are asking them to help with your blog or website, it is up to you whether you give them passwords and access, but if you trust them to help build your business, this shouldn't be an issue and I certainly have this kind of relationship with my clients, but we are all different.

I would suggest you set timescales and budgets from the start as well as scheduling weekly updates and monthly calls which are added into diaries and help you stay on track.

Keep Shining

You want to ensure you are getting value for money and results, so you need to assess how well objectives are being met and what results are being generated. This could be the number of features in a list of top-tier publications, the execution of an event, working with more bloggers and seeing the results in your bottom line. Set these in the contract from the start and evaluate on a regular basis, with monthly calls and reports.

Don't forget to congratulate yourself on reaching this point.

Just look back and see how far you have come since you picked this book up for the first time and put this in your success jar, which by now I hope is overflowing with positive achievements.

Lesson Twelve

Stay in Your Lane

At this point I hope PR is no longer something you are intimidated by and that you are ready to start putting your hard work into action so that your business grows and you shine.

It is important to remember that PR is a marathon, where you are collecting media contacts and coverage mile by mile, rather than going for one big hit during a sprint.

This chapter looks at how to maintain your activities and keep your confidence high, even when your pitches don't go as planned and you feel like giving up and going back to those easier, but maybe less effective, adverts from the past.

Do Something Small Every Day

When it comes to PR, doing something small every day will make you feel like you are making progress. Writing a blog post, reading the latest copy of *National Geographic* or sending a follow-up email to a blogger who is reviewing your latest book is what it takes to make the progress that leads to success.

Make a list of the small things you can do each day that could add up and help you to take your PR forward.

Believe You Belong Here

"I have absolutely no idea what I'm doing with my PR and journalists are going to realise that very soon." Ever thought this as you have been writing a press release or picking up the phone to talk to a podcaster you met at an event?

I will let you into a secret – you're not the only one!

Many people feel like frauds when they are talking about themselves to the press and think that their accomplishments and successes are the result of luck rather than hard work and talent.

Come on, you are better than that and I won't let you scupper your own chances of success by thinking otherwise.

Let's be clear here: if you bake amazing cakes for your local deli and they always sell out, or you take stunning wedding photographs that couples cherish forever, then you deserve your place at the PR table.

We all get that odd moment when we just don't think we are good enough, but when it keeps happening, and that monkey on your shoulder is telling you that you are a fake, you may well be suffering from the worldwide phenomenon of 'impostor syndrome'.

Serena Edwards, CEO and counsellor of Calm Waters Counselling Ltd, often comes across this and says, *"When you choose to do PR, you truly are putting yourself out there. This is a really big step and one which can sow seeds of doubt and make you question if you really are who you say you are in your press releases and blog posts. These thoughts often aren't the reality of your situation, but part of the anxiety-driven impostor syndrome, that makes you feel that you're not good enough when that is usually far from the truth. It can make the most talented artists, writers and musicians think no one is going to like their music or buy their paintings, and I bet even J. K. Rowling didn't think her books would be this popular.*

"While there are many reasons why you think you can't sell yourself or say you are amazing, you need to look at why you can do exactly that. So, rather than think you can't have a launch party because your book is going to be rubbish, why not think you have worked hard and it's going to be amazing? Decide that your craft business is going to be successful because you have an excellent website and create gorgeous products your clients love. If you can believe and focus on your true, positive achievements and the evidence that supports them, you are halfway towards kicking out those bad thoughts.

"The other side of impostor syndrome is your own self-belief, your self-esteem and confidence. Try focusing on what you do, what you have done and what's great about you."

PR School Homework: This Is Me

Write a list of the things you know you are good at and add quotes and comments from other people. Refer back to this list when that pesky impostor syndrome makes an appearance, and this could help stop it in its tracks.

....

....

....

....

....

....

....

....

....

Stop the Comparisons

Just as social media gives, it can also take away and this is very much the nature of the digital-age beast.

Watching what other people are doing, where they are securing coverage and how many interviews they get can become an obsession and turn into toxic 21st-century 'comparisonitis'.

As a small business owner, it is really easy to be side-tracked by what other people are doing and to look at what your competitors 'seem' to be achieving.

I say 'seem' because while it might look like everyone else is winning and you are lagging behind, what you have to remember is that we generally only tell people what we want them to know.

Yes, another yoga teacher might write a post about her great success at an event, but I bet she won't mention the panic attack she had before she went on stage because she was so nervous.

A high-profile nutritionist might be in all the glossy magazines talking about the benefits of clean eating, but it could well be that she struggles to keep on top of her love of ice cream when she sits down after yet another exhausting 18-hour day.

I love social media and I love seeing other people succeeding, but I know that you can focus on what other people are doing, and this can get out of hand.

Eve Menezes Cunningham, author and online integrative supervisor, therapist and coach at Self Care Coaching, is pretty smart when it comes to not comparing ourselves to others: *"I love Gabrielle Bernstein's mindful approach with added closure where, in* May Cause Miracles, *she suggests, when we catch ourselves thinking such thoughts, we say, 'I forgive myself for that fearful projection, attack thought, making myself special, making them special' – the last two are especially helpful when we either think we're not worthy or if we get a bit big-headed. Attempting to simply stop ourselves from comparing ourselves to others is challenging to do as we all do it. By learning to notice this, take the charge away and then consider what we might learn from someone else's approach rather than begrudging anyone else's seeming success – seeing everyone as human and doing their best (including ourselves), it helps shift the energy around it."*

Why not stop right now and take a step back and look at you and your successes.

Don't follow the pack and please don't believe the hype. Instead, stay in your lane, do what works for YOU and makes you feel good, so you can shine the way only you can.

Dress for Success

One thing that I find really helps me to keep on top of my game, whether I am writing blog posts, coaching clients or putting together a workshop, is to look the part. I might be working in my home office, but I feel so much more professional if I'm wearing a dress and have make-up on, rather than sitting in my yoga pants and a dog-walking hoodie.

Shelley Kelly says, *"There is a well-recognised link between what you wear and how you feel, and vice versa. Dressing like you mean business can have a direct effect on how productive and successful you are. Working on your own business, often alone, at home, can be a huge motivational challenge. There are so many things you know you want to do and many more things you feel you should be doing but you just can't get going with them. I've been there, thinking how lucky I am to wear PJs and work from under the duvet. Only I can't. It doesn't work for me. I need to be well dressed, in keeping with my brand, stick some basic make-up on and style my hair a bit. And then, there I am, the productive, go-getting version of me.*

"It really pays to have your 'game face' on. You want to be a confident, professional, interesting business person. Unless you're selling insomnia remedies, PJs just aren't going to do it. Comfort, yes, that's fine. But those comfy clothes should still be in some kind of shape that means business – no holes, no stains, nothing misshapen – in short nothing which no longer deserves a place in your wardrobe. You deserve better. Your business deserves better."

So, from today I want you to pledge to yourself that you will kick off the trackie bottoms and wear the clothes that make you feel good and want to shine!

Create a Network

One of the most important things that can help you stay in your lane is having a support network who can celebrate your wins, pick you up when you hit a quiet spell and generally act as the water-cooler gang to share the journey of being a small business owner.

Whether this is with other local entrepreneurs, within a Facebook group or via a weekly Zoom call with like-minded people, it all helps to ensure you keep believing and keep shining.

Networking might feel a little stifled and even old-fashioned in the digital age, but this often-neglected activity is a great way to get your face known, it can help to grow your knowledge, allow you to meet influential people in your industry and put you front of mind for a whole host of new people and potential opportunities.

When I moved to Devon, I went from being well known locally to being totally unknown, and as I launched PR School there was the feeling in the back of my mind that had we not moved, my workshops would be booked out for months because I knew so many people. So, I got out there and made new connections and while I still have moments when I think 'What am I doing?', I carry on because I know I can do this and today my business is busier than ever before.

If you do your research, you will find various networking events and meetings that could work for you. From early-morning breakfast sessions to informal coffee meet-ups, lunches and evening drinks, the choice is big and there is something for everyone.

Networking isn't about going to one meeting and landing you a load of new clients, it is about finding something that works for you, talking to people and building long-term relationships based on trust and respect.

Remember, people buy from people and this is what networking can help with.

Along with meeting up face to face, I have found that online networking can be really effective. As well as being a source of support and collaborations, it also opens up local, regional, national and international opportunities. Facebook groups, Instagram pods, LinkedIn pages and Twitter parties are all ways to network and build a support network that can be really helpful for you and those around you.

Sue Tappenden, business and executive coach at Headspace for Change, has some good advice: *"I think it's really easy to go wrong with business networks and so it's important to choose carefully and be selective. In terms of support, I have a couple of favourite closed Facebook groups (arising from various programmes) of like-minded fabulous people (mostly women!) where the collective support is immeasurable and priceless. Not sure where I'd be without them."*

Another idea is to team up and create a collective. Do you have a friend who's a chiropractor? A massage therapist? Acupuncturist? Pilates teacher? Marketing consultant? Coming together can be really valuable to not only build your business but also means you are there to support one another in the good times, and the maybe not so great periods too.

Joanne Dewberry comments, *"It's really important, especially when you work from home, alone, to have a support network behind you. Think of your networking group as your cheer squad when things go right, your mentor when you hit a brick wall, the people who will always know someone you need at any given moment. The people who ease the loneliness and the people you can have a jolly good laugh with."*

Let Criticism Make You, Not Break You

I hate to break this to you, but if you put yourself out there and start to shine, there might be times when people will criticise you. This can be hard to deal with, upsetting and sometimes unfair, but it is the nature of the beast I am afraid.

Hillary Clinton was reported to have said[8], *"It is important to learn how to take criticism seriously but not personally,"* during a speech at NYU, and then added, *"Critics can be your best friends if you listen to them, and learn from them, but don't get dragged down by them."*

I think this is a really good way to think about the dark side of success and it can prevent comments from leading you to self-doubt, or worse, giving up on your PR, which is what we don't want.

People, be that the media, clients or even family and friends, can judge you and what you are doing, but you have the power to think about how you respond.

If a journalist tells you that your press release doesn't have a news hook, look at it again and see what it is missing.

If a blogger doesn't like the organic body lotion you sent them, try to find out why rather than blasting them online. It could be they just don't like the smell of lavender, which means you could send them something else that they do like and you could get a great **P**ersonal **R**ecommendation from them, rather than a lawsuit for defamation.

If you get a bad book review on Amazon, look at all the five-star comments you do have and maybe see that the odd three stars won't really damage your sales or your reputation and it could just make things look a bit more real.

While it is of course nice to have people say good things about you, that isn't life and if you can step back and look at what has been said and where you can learn, you will be the one winning, and shining.

I know some people don't like my charity work. Some think that I shouldn't share my experiences with Lucas and DDH and I know that my story isn't going to get the thumbs up from everyone. That doesn't mean I agree with them, but it does mean that I am still trying to get on *This Morning* to talk about DDH and I won't give that dream up, which doesn't sit well with other people.

So, don't you give up on your dream to shine, either.

Kick Back

No one is super-human, however much we like to think we are, and while the news agenda is working 24/7, it doesn't mean you have to be.

You can't pour from an empty cup, so switch off from looking for #journorequests and opportunities to speak to the press in the evenings and at the weekend. Press releases can be written tomorrow, you can research awareness days next week and offers of interviews and guest posts can sometimes wait an hour, but your well-being and mental health cannot.

Eve Menezes Cunningham agrees with this and says, "*Doing some yoga, going for a bike ride or seeing a friend helps me to leave everything and switch off. Swimming especially helps me go from that sense of feeling as overwhelmed as an amoeba to a fully functioning human, able to handle whatever I need to do.*"

Whether you go for a run, play netball, meet friends for a coffee or read a book, find something that helps you chill out and relax, and when you come back to that PR to-do list you will feel revived, refreshed and ready to shine again.

Have a Little Patience

As the saying goes, 'good things come to those who wait' and that is very true when it comes to PR. If you think that after telling your story once you will be a household name, then you'll be disappointed.

Like many aspects of business (and life in general), the more you put in, the more you will get out of PR. The stronger the relationships you build, the more chance you will have of shining in the media.

You are in this for the long haul and it is going to take time but I promise it will be worth it, so hang on in there and you will shine just as you are meant to.

PR School Homework: Positive Affirmations

I love positive affirmations and inspirational memes because I find they work when it comes to my approach to PR as well as my life in general.

Affirmations are simple messages which are repeated over and over, slowly changing both your thinking and releasing you from anxiety, negativity and fear.

Examples that might work for you include:

- My PR goals are worth accomplishing.
- I trust that my PR journey is leading me to success.

- In my PR activities, I stay true to my core values and authentic self.
- I'm building a supportive network that encourages and motivates me.
- PR will help me to shine.

Have a think about what works for you, then choose a positive affirmation and write it on a number of Post-its. Stick these on your fridge, on your monitor, on your bathroom mirror, in the car and basically anywhere that will remind you of just why you are on your PR journey and that you CAN do this and shine.

Each day say your positive affirmation out loud and reflect on the words you are using to maximise their effectiveness.

Be prepared to feel a bit daft at first but believe me that in time, you will do this as naturally as you make a cup of tea or read the paper and you will soon start to feel those emotions of confidence, energy and success.

If you're feeling out of your depth, need some feedback on a press release, are looking for people to collaborate with, or want to share your wins – the PR School community is the place for you. Join us today, and you'll never feel alone on your PR journey again.

The PR School Resource Centre

We have covered a lot of ground in this book, and I wanted to ensure you had somewhere to go and find the resources I have mentioned.

Blogging

Where do we start with this? There is so much you could talk about, but here we go with a selection of goodies that might get you started:

123 Reg for registering and buying domain names – this is also a great place to see if a business name you are thinking of has any domain names available – I was lucky with 'PR School' as no one had taken it.

bestbritishbloggers.co.uk connects brands with bloggers, vloggers and influencers in the UK and around the world and **joeblogsnetwork.com** is a network of bloggers from the UK that is worth looking at.

bloggersrequired.com is by bloggers, for bloggers, and is a way of working with brands on collaborations.

Blogosphere magazine is written by bloggers for the blogging and social media community and is a pretty good read. Find out more at **blogosphere.biz**.

thebloglancer.co.uk is a site all about the art of blogging, and worth checking out as Jenna really knows her stuff.

BloggingTips.com offers advice on blogging and is worth a look.

Moz.com contains tips on how to optimise your blog so it performs well, and is the place to go to learn about SEO, social media, marketing, link building and more.

ShoutOut.ly connects bloggers to brands and could be of interest to you.

The UK Blog Awards recognises bloggers, influencers, organisations and individuals in their multi-industry awards. You might also be interested in the **Vuelio Blog Awards** which can be seen at **vuelio.com**.

WordPress.com is the free (and more limited) version of this blogging platform and **WordPress.org** is the one for self-hosted blogs and gives you the power to do your own thing.

Books to Inspire You

These are just some of the books I love, and that friends have recommended. If you can, buy from your local bookshop, and you never know, if you make friends with the staff, they may stock your book if you're an author and hold an event for you which could generate more PR.

Big Magic, Creative Living Beyond Fear by Elizabeth Gilbert was a present from a friend when my first book came out and it was a moment of clarity for me.

Vicki Psarias is the Mumboss and her first book, *The Honest Mum's Guide to Surviving and Thriving at Work and at Home*, is worth a read. She tells it like it is and gives some delicious food for thought for getting the balance right.

Feel the Fear and Do It Anyway by Susan Jeffers has been on my bookcase forever and every time I think I can't do something, I pick it up, read it again and go out and do it.

How to Style Your Brand and *Brand Brilliance* are by Fiona Humberstone and are excellent for inspiration.

Ruth Kudzi is the author of *Is This It?* and if you are at a crossroads and wondering what to do with your life next, buy it today and clarity will follow.

The Little Black Book by Otegha Uwagba is a bite-sized read that is packed with tips on making business work for you.

Make Your Mark by Margie Warrell is my self-help bible; think inspiration on every single page.

The Million Dollar Blog by Natasha Courtenay-Smith has everything you need to know about creating, yes you have guessed it, a million-dollar blog.

Miracles Now by Gabrielle Bernstein was a turning point in my reading as she really does know how to put thoughts into your head and fire in your belly.

The Happiness Planner® sells a diary and planner that embraces the power of positive thinking, mindfulness, gratitude and self-development. Buy one and let me know what you think.

The Writers' and Artists' Yearbook is a PR must-have and is far more cost-effective than an online database subscription and you can see more at writersandartists.co.uk

The Life Plan by Shannah Kennedy is not only beautifully and mindfully written, it also has some really good ideas in it that are easy to implement and do work.

My sister told me to read *You Are a Badass* by Jen Sincero, and I did, in one coffee-fuelled sitting, and have never felt the same way again.

You Are Awesome was given to me by a friend who knew I would love the words of Matthew Syed, and this book now sits on my desk ALL THE TIME.

Business Admin and Assistance

Acuity Scheduling is an online booking calendar and scheduling tool; a friend told me how good it was along with **Dubsado**, which is useful for client management, accounting and invoicing.

Google Drive offers free tools for writing documents, creating spreadsheets and creating presentations and is a brilliant place to keep your press pack and PR plans as well as images.

Gmail (Google Mail) allows you to create your own email addresses and you can use the **Google Calendar** for keeping track of everything that is going on in your business, including those press calls and networking events.

If you want to set up online courses, **LearnDash** has your name all over it.

Dropbox is a much-loved and well-used online storage solution that automatically syncs with your computer and is free to a certain limit.

Evernote is a popular way to organise your life and syncs across multiple devices, as is **Trello**.

Mailchimp is an easy way to set up beautiful email campaigns and is pretty much a small business must-have.

Pomodoro timers help you to work in focused segments of time, and as I charge clients by the minute, it keeps me on track and could be good for you too.

Slack is the go-to for running a virtual team and **Skype** for online calls is a winner.

SurveyMonkey is good for carrying out – yes, you have guessed it – surveys, and there's a free option too.

The Freelance Lifestyle is a great resource for working as a freelance consultant and Emma Ward has a brilliant Facebook group too. Check out **freelancelifestyle.co.uk**.

Wave is used for accounting; give it a go.

Zoom is a video conferencing tool and works really well for training sessions, workshops and coaching, and participants all over the world can dial in.

Business Information Sources

There is a lot of information out there for small business owners, but these are some of the most authoritative:

- Advertising Standards Authority (ASA) – asa.org.uk
- British Chamber of Commerce – britishchambers.org.uk
- Federation of Small Businesses – fsb.org.uk
- Start Up Donut – startupdonut.co.uk
- Your local library is a hive of information, so make use of it.

Images and Design Resources

If you have the cash, you can hire a graphic designer but if not, **Canva** is your bestie when it comes to creating professional-looking social media banners, press packs and loads more.

Moo.com is brilliant for business cards and stationery that doesn't cost the earth but looks first class.

PicTapGo is an iPhone app for editing photos so they are Insta ready in seconds.

Try to use your own images where you can, but if this isn't possible, there are some fantastic royalty-free sites out there where you can download stunning photos for your projects:

- Pexels – pexels.com
- Pixabay – pixabay.com
- Unsplash – unsplash.com

Go to **Vistaprint** for car magnets, banners, branded books, pens and T-shirts at good prices and they can help with event gifts and promo products too.

Wordswag is an app for adding text to images and making things look your own.

Media Opportunities and Resources

As I have said in various chapters in this book, there are many ways to find media opportunities, and below are some of the resources that can help, but do look for the costs:

Ace Media is aimed at getting you into product round-ups and you can see more at **ace.media**.

AskCharity is a free service that connects the press with charities so they can find case studies and information for features. Go to **askcharity. charitycomms.org.uk** for the lowdown.

Cision has a paid-for media enquiry service that sends you requests from journalists looking for case studies, experts etc. Full details can be seen at **cision.com**.

Help a Reporter Out (HARO) is an American service which provides journalists with a database of sources for stories and opportunities – **helpareporter.com**.

JournoLink helps you manage your own PR and with this your stories can be sent to journalists, broadcasters and bloggers; costs vary with the different options on the site.

#journorequest on Twitter is free to use, easy to find and I hope you have seen in this book that it works.

PressPlugs is an online service that is for members of the media who are looking for quotes, expert opinions and people to interview. With a free trial and cost-effective packages available, **pressplugs.co.uk** is a good choice whatever stage of your PR journey you are on.

ResponseSource lets the press send out requests for information and while it is expensive, in my opinion, it's worth it – **responsesource.com**.

SourceBottle is an Australian media enquiry service and can be used by anyone looking for opportunities to get publicity for themselves and their business – **sourcebottle.com**.

Press Release Distribution

You can use a press release distribution service to send out your news. Doing this can help you reach a huge number of people in one hit, but I am not sure how effective it is for building those key media contacts you are looking for.

For a fee, **ResponseSource** will send press releases to journalists, bloggers and influencers and details can be seen at **responsesource.com/pr/releasewire/**.

PressGo will deliver your press release to thousands of opted-in email recipients; tweet your message to the @pressrelease followers; and share it with professionals on LinkedIn. More details can be seen on **journalism. co.uk**.

You can also try **Pressat** where you can create, manage and distribute press releases in minutes, via **pressat.co.uk**.

The Press Association is the UK's leading provider of content and you can send out your stories via their newswire service.

You can send your press releases out via **Vuelio** by email, phone, mail, website and wires – **vuelio.com**.

Media Databases

If you do want to subscribe to a paid-for database service, these are some of the best out there:

- cision.co.uk
- muckrack.com
- prmax.co.uk
- roxhillmedia.com
- vuelio.com

Media Reads

To keep up with industry news, as well as setting Google alerts, these are some of the best resources out there and many have newsletters which help you keep ahead of the competition:

- Campaign – campaignlive.co.uk
- Digiday – digiday.com
- Digital Marketing Magazine – digitalmarketingmagazine. co.uk
- The Drum – thedrum.com
- PR Moment – prmoment.com
- PRWeek – prweek.com/uk
- Marketing Week – marketingweek.com
- The Guardian Media – theguardian.com/media

Professional Bodies

For all things professional PR check out:

- PRCA – prca.org.uk
- Chartered Institute of Public Relations – cipr.co.uk
- Media Trust – mediatrust.org
- Women in PR – womeninpr.org.uk

Media Coverage Options

Keeping your media coverage together in one place is important because it not only tracks where you have been seen, but also shows you just how far you have come, which can be exactly what you need to see from time to time when you are wondering if this is worth it.

Coverage Book is an online service that allows you to create simple, cost-effective media reports that look good and demonstrate campaign results. Check out **coveragebook.com** and there is a free trial that's worth a go.

Social Media Resources

With **Buffer** you can set the times you want your posts to go out, add your tweets or Facebook updates, and it will do it for you. Scheduled content can be forgotten so if you do use this method, remember to interact and engage with your followers – some of whom might be the press.

Hootsuite is a social media management tool that schedules posts, monitors social media and with free and paid-for options, there is something for everyone.

Planoly is an Instagram planner desktop and app; the paid-for version will schedule too.

You can use **Later** to schedule Instagram posts and to manage multiple accounts, plus much more.

SmarterQueue is for creating, scheduling and 'recycling' content for social media while **Tailwind** is for scheduling pins and increasing engagement on Pinterest.

PR School Contributors and Experts

Thank you to each and every one of these amazing experts who have helped me with this book.

Emma-Jane Batey, packaging writer, I Can Do Better, icandobetter. co.uk.

Darren Blackstock, founder of Pedal Talk, pedaltalk.co.uk.

Kelly Rose Bradford, freelance journalist, krbradford.co.uk.

Nicola Brown, accredited MCIPR (Dip CIPR), freelance Director of PR and Communications at NB Thinks, nbthinks.com.

Eve Menezes Cunningham, author and online integrative supervisor, therapist and coach at Self Care Coaching, selfcarecoaching.net.

Hazel Davis, copywriter and media trainer, co-founder, Muse Flash Media, hazeldavis.co.uk.

Ana De-Jesus, multi-award-winning blogger, Faded Spring, fadedspring. co.uk.

Helen Dewdney, author and blogger, The Complaining Cow, thecomplainingcow.co.uk.

Serena Edwards, CEO and counsellor, Calm Waters Counselling, calmwaterscounselling.co.uk.

Joanne Dewberry, author, blogger and business owner, JoanneDewberry.co.uk.

Rebecca Ffrancon, personal stylist and colour consultant, rebeccaffrancon.com.

Chris Gower, founder and Editor of Dining Devon, diningdevon.com.

Michelle Green, blogger, Fifty and Fab, fiftyandfab.co.uk.

Claire Hall, accredited freelance PR and social media manager and family travel blogger at Tin Box Traveller, tinboxtraveller.co.uk.

Vanessa Holburn, writer and blogger, A Happy Healthy Mum, ahappyhealthymummy.com.

Jenny Itzcovitz, Editor, Sixtyplusurfers, sixtyplusurfers.co.uk.

Corrie Jones, CEO and founder of UNTAPPED and the host of Self-Made Women, corriejones.co.

Shelley Kelly, personal stylist, shelleykelly.co.uk.

Kelly Kemp, blogger, It's A Tink Thing, itsatinkthing.com.

Jessica Killingley, book writing coach, JessicaKillingley.com.

Ruth Kudzi, author and business coach, Ruth Kudzi Coaching, ruthkudzicoaching.com.

Sarah Learoyd, Director of GLR Public Relations, glrpr.co.uk.

Chloe Leibowitz, award-winning life coach, chloeleibowitz.com.

Heather Lowrie, Deputy News Editor/Travel Editor, The Scottish Sun.

Antonina Mamzenko, award-winning photographer, mamzenko.com.

Laura Moore, Mum on a Mission, mumoam.co.uk.

Gemma Pettman, PR consultant, Gemma Pettman PR, gemmapettmanpr.co.uk.

Jen Pringle, creative designer and founder, Pen&Pringle, penandpringle.co.uk.

Nicola Scoon, online marketing specialist, nicolascoon.com.

Heidi Scrimgeour, freelance journalist, heidiscrimgeour.contently.com.

Tamara Stringer, social media consultant and owner of Incredibly Social, incrediblysocial.co.uk.

Laura Sweet, founder of Amamaya Clothing, amamaya.co.uk.

Sue Tappenden, business and executive coach, Headspace for Change, headspaceforchange.com.

Alison Simpson, Digital Content Editor, WeAreTheCity, wearethecity.com.

Claire Sparksman, social media marketing expert, and founder at Be Social London, besociallondon.com.

Jenny Tschiesche, author, leading nutrition expert and founder of The Lunchbox Doctor, jennytschiesche.com.

Sofie Tooke, Head of Content Creation and PR, ASSISTED., assisted.co.uk.

Jocasta Tribe, founder of Marketing for Mums, marketingformums. co.uk.

Katie Upton, beauty, fashion and lifestyle blogger, Katie Summer's Fashion, katiesummersfashion.blogspot.co.uk.

Natalie Weaving, Director, The Typeface Group Ltd, thetypefacegroup. co.uk.

Emma Wyatt, social media consultant – LinkedIn and Instagram specialist, Social Conversations by Emma, socialemma.co.uk.

Gemma Went, business mentor and mindset coach, for small business owners, gemmawent.co.uk.

Chelsea Williams, lifestyle blogger, That's Chelsea, thatschelsea.com.

Afra Willmore, award-winning journalist and news editor-turned blogger, Madmumof7.com.

Glossary of Essential PR Terms

Advertising is paying for space in the media to say exactly what you want about you, and your business.

An **advertorial** is part paid-for advertising and part editorial but is not an unbiased **P**ersonal **R**ecommendation as you are in control of what is said.

A **backgrounder** is a document that summarises a business and can be used as a quick reference point for the media.

Backlinks are used in blog posts and the idea is that they can help increase traffic to your website.

When we talk about something being in the **body** of an email, this is the written text and details, nothing to do with arms and legs.

A **boilerplate** is the information that gives a brief description of a company and will often appear at the end of press releases and on websites.

A **brief** is written to explain to someone what needs to be done as part of a job or a project, and you might write a brief for a PR consultant, photographer or web designer.

B2B PR is Business to Business PR, which provides information between businesses, so think accountants, computers and HR.

B2C PR is Business to Consumer PR, which is the communication between a business and the consumer and this is more likely to be for things like beauty products, spa resorts, hotels and clothing.

A **byline** credits the writer of a feature or interview in a newspaper, magazine or online site. If you write something, ask for this to be added because it is your work and you need to be recognised, and your business name and website would be good to mention too.

Collateral is information such as the biographies, backgrounders and press releases you send to the media to let them know who you are and what you do.

Consultancy is a formal term for an external company that carries out activities (including PR) for other businesses, and is also known as a PR agency.

Copy is the written material used to create press releases, websites, brochures, blog posts and features (also copywriting or copywriter).

Your **corporate identity** includes things like logos, house style and fonts and it is the way you communicate your brand and image.

Coverage refers to being featured in the media, be that in a newspaper or magazine, on a social media feed or as a guest on a podcast. Do remember, you need to have permission to share so always check this before simply taking a photo and pasting it online.

Crisis management is the plan you have in place when things go wrong and how you deal with those issues.

Earned media isn't a term I really use, but it refers to media coverage that is generated from relationship building and story pitching rather than paid-for advertising.

An **embargo** is a request added to information or press releases that asks the media not to publish those details until a specified date. These are used and do very much rely on trusted relationships.

Exclusives are when you send your media information to one publication or journalist, so they can use it before anyone else, and I often use these with my very best contacts who I have worked with in the past.

E-PR/Digital PR is online PR, so think a feature in the HuffPost, mindbodygreen and Business Insider.

Evaluation is measuring the impact of PR, something I encourage you to do so you see what you are getting back from your efforts.

GDPR (The General Data Protection Regulation) is a set of rules designed to give EU citizens greater control over their personal data. This came into force in May 2018 and you need to comply with these rules when it comes to the data you hold for the media – so no spamming.

Hashtags are the symbols (#) used in social media, especially Twitter. This is the combination of the word hash from hash mark and the word tag, a way to mark something as belonging to a specific category that could be your PR secret weapon.

Headlines are crucial when it comes to emails to the media, as well as the start of press releases. These are intended to catch the attention of the reader, so make those four or five words stand out and count.

In-house is when PR is carried out by a business themselves, so exactly what you are doing.

Lead times refer to how far ahead publications and journalists work and these can be monthly, weekly, daily and even hourly.

Media relations refer the work carried out between businesses and the media and the building of relationships between you and them so you can shine.

Media training helps you feel confident about TV and radio interviews.

Owned media isn't a term I use much, but it is the content you create and includes copy on your website, blog posts, guest blog posts, video and social messages.

A **pitch** is the initial targeted message you send to a journalist to gauge their interest in your business.

PR is what people say about you and your brand, and remember to think about it as a **P**ersonal **R**ecommendation if you ever get stuck.

A **PR consultant** may work for an agency or as an independent person.

PR School is where you learn to shine.

Press packs contain the materials you create to send out to the media if they are writing about you. These can include images, press releases, logos, backgrounders, price lists and logos. They are also known as press kits or media packs.

A **press release** is a written document containing a news announcement that is sent to the media from a business and can be the starting point of a conversation.

Quotes are the words a person has said and these will be in speech marks and need to be approved by that person before being sent out to the media.

Round-ups are collections of items like lipsticks, shoes or reusable cups that are grouped together in one feature in glossy magazines, newspapers and on blogs. These give consumers an idea of what they can buy for Mother's Day, Easter and Christmas, and they can be a brilliant way to shine.

Shine is what you do when you are featured in the media.

A **spokesperson** is someone who talks directly to the media. This might be you, your business partner or it could be your PR consultant.

Your **target audience** refers to the people you want to reach and you can do this via the media and your PR efforts.

References

1. Chartered Institute of Public Relations
    cipr.co.uk/content/policy/careers-advice/what-pr

2. Simon Sinek, TED Talk
    ted.com/talks/
    simon_sinek_how_great_leaders_inspire_action?language=en

3. Muckrack 2018 survey statistic about Twitter
    muckrack.com/blog/2018/05/22/2018-muck-rack-survey-results

4. Pinterest statistic
    blog.hootsuite.com/pinterest-statistics-for-business/

5. Jo Tribe's Pinterest statistic
    business.pinterest.com/sub/business/business-infographic-
    download/2017-11-07-millennial-report-final.pdf

6. Laura Sweet media coverage
    telegraph.co.uk/connect/small-business/
    ways-entrepreneurs-can-combat-loneliness/amp/

7. Brain processing statistic
    visme.co/blog/common-myths-visual-brain/

8. Hillary Clinton NYU speech
    theguardian.com/world/2014/feb/13/
    hillary-clinton-melinda-gates-women-criticism

Index

Thank You

I would like to say thank you for buying this book and taking the time to read it.

I hope you have found it helpful and that my experiences and words have taken you on a journey you hadn't imagined possible.

For many entrepreneurs and small businesses, especially in the early days, confidence, the right attitude and a desire for success makes doing your PR yourself totally plausible and I hope you have recognised this as you have read this book.

PR isn't rocket science and it isn't a sprint. It is a marathon and one that might test and challenge you, but it's one that can bring rewards and success, so please keep going.

PR has brought many opportunities into my life and I sincerely hope it will do the same for you.

I wish you all the very best with your business and your PR efforts and look forward to seeing you shine as I know you are meant to.

Oh, and if you could please leave a review of this book on Amazon, that would be amazing, and it might help me to shine a little more too!

Natalie x

PR School Investors

Thank you to each and every investor who bought the beta copy of *PR School* and helped me to make this the best book it could be.

Francesca Aaen
Lesley Anderson
Lynsay Anne
Debs Aspland
Amanda Ayres
Helen Baggott
Rachel Barker
Judy Bartkowiak
Dawn Beth Baxter
Darren Blackstock
Melanie Bullivant
Nicola Cawood
Alison Chown
Lucy Clarke
Leisha Clarke
Clare Cogan
Jennifer Corcoran
Emma Cottam
Julie Cramer
Sarah Currer
Charlotte Daley
Marsha Daniel
Rebecca Daniel
Cass Davis

Joanne Dewberry
Rebecca de Jager
Jay-Anne Dingwall
Jenni Donato
Kris Drago
Emma Duke
Gillian Edwards
Claire Elbrow
Ingrid Fernandez
Nicola Fossey
Melanie Gow
Rachel Goldsack
Michelle Green
Haulwen Ltd
Helen Hamston
Elizabeth Hancock
Eveleen Hatch
Rachel Healy
Jo Halton
Louise Jenner
Amanda Johnson
Chris Johnston
Polly Jukes
Andrew Kings

Priya's Kitchen
Carly Keighley
Kelly Kemp
Jessica Killingley
Ruth Kudzi
Y Lam
Chloe Leibowitz
Emily Macdonald
Clare Mackenney
Beaullah Madziwa
Antonina Mamzenko
Boudicca Malone
Emma Maslin
Victoria Mason
Mind to Win
Karina Montagni
Suzanne Mountain
My Wellbeing
Pal
Ingrid Ngu
Tracey Norman
Ocean Coaching
Alexandra Owen
Nicola Parkin

Susan Quance
Angela Quinon
Clare Roebuck
Angela Shaki
SP Digital Assist
Grannie Sherry
Jessica Silva
Ilze-Lee Sinfield
Pamela Spence
Amy Stammers
Lucie Steyn
Gretta Solomon
Denise Spragg
Debbie Summerell,
Sue Tappenden
Caroline Thompson
Jo Tribe
Oliver Trice
Eleanor Tweddell
Rosy Tydeman
Hannah Upton
Esther Wane
Karen Washer
Serena Waters
Janice Watson
Claire Winters
Tracy Wood
The Working Mum Association

Where Next?

If you've enjoyed your PR journey so far and would like to get more training, accountability and expert support, then the PR School Academy is the place to be.

As a member you'll have access to an exclusive resource vault that's packed with blog posts, checklists, features, interviews, templates, training and videos.

The online community offers help and support as well as hot off the press PR opportunities, challenges, feedback, motivation, training, and Q&A sessions that will help you to shine even brighter. Plus, I'll be there as your PR guru and greatest cheerleader.

What are you waiting for?

Head over to www.pr-school.co.uk, take a look around and as a thank you from me to you, add the discount code PRSCHOOLBOOK at the checkout and you'll get 20% off your membership fee.

I promise that joining will be one of the best business decisions you make this year.

Natalie x

Connect with Natalie on social media:

[facebook icon] facebook.com/prschoolyourtimetoshinebook/

[twitter icon] @natalietrice

[instagram icon] @natalieprschool

www.pr-school.co.uk

Lightning Source UK Ltd.
Milton Keynes UK
UKHW040632091219
355034UK00001B/152/P

,085 Books

are available to read at

www.ForgottenBooks.com

Forgotten Books' App
Available for mobile, tablet & eReader

ISBN 978-1-334-66939-2
PIBN 10753020

This book is a reproduction of an important historical work. Forgotten Books uses
state-of-the-art technology to digitally reconstruct the work, preserving the original format
whilst repairing imperfections present in the aged copy. In rare cases, an imperfection in
the original, such as a blemish or missing page, may be replicated in our edition. We do,
however, repair the vast majority of imperfections successfully; any imperfections that
remain are intentionally left to preserve the state of such historical works.

Forgotten Books is a registered trademark of FB &c Ltd.
Copyright © 2017 FB &c Ltd.
FB &c Ltd, Dalton House, 60 Windsor Avenue, London, SW19 2RR.
Company number 08720141. Registered in England and Wales.

For support please visit www.forgottenbooks.com

1 MONTH OF
FREE
READING

at

www.ForgottenBooks.com

By purchasing this book you are eligible for one month membership to ForgottenBooks.com, giving you unlimited access to our entire collection of over 700,000 titles via our web site and mobile apps.

To claim your free month visit:

www.forgottenbooks.com/free753020

* Offer is valid for 45 days from date of purchase. Terms and conditions apply.

English
Français
Deutsche
Italiano
Español
Português

www.forgottenbooks.com

Mythology Photography **Fiction**
Fishing Christianity **Art** Cooking
Essays Buddhism Freemasonry
Medicine **Biology** Music **Ancient**
Egypt Evolution Carpentry Physics
Dance Geology **Mathematics** Fitness
Shakespeare **Folklore** Yoga Marketing
Confidence Immortality Biographies
Poetry **Psychology** Witchcraft
Electronics Chemistry History **Law**
Accounting **Philosophy** Anthropology
Alchemy Drama Quantum Mechanics
Atheism Sexual Health **Ancient History**
Entrepreneurship Languages Sport
Paleontology Needlework Islam
Metaphysics Investment Archaeology
Parenting Statistics Criminology
Motivational

BITTER SWEETS:

A LOVE STORY.

BY

JOSEPH HATTON.

THE web of our life is a mingled yarn, good and ill together our virtues would
be proud if our faults whipped them not; and our crimes would despair, if they
were not cherished by our virtues —SHAKESPEARE.

> There is a comfort in the strength of love:
> 'Twill make a thing endurable, which else
> Would overset the brain, or break the heart.
> WORDSWORTH.

IN THREE VOLUMES.

VOL. II.

LONDON:

TINSLEY BROTHERS, 18, CATHERINE ST., STRAND.
1865.

[*The right of translation is reserved.*]

JOHN CHILDS AND SON, PRINTERS.

823
H28b
v. 2

CONTENTS

OF

THE SECOND VOLUME.

BITTER SWEETS:

A LOVE STORY.

CHAPTER I.

BEHIND THE MASK.

In the supreme happiness of her married life, in the fond devotion of her husband, in her motherly love for the child which had blessed her union with Paul, five years had nearly wiped out the sorrows which, at the outset, had been coupled with Anna's joys.

There were times when sad memories would crowd into her heart and claim sorrow's customary tribute; but the brief shadows only heightened the sunshine of her settled happiness. She could talk about her uncle, with that loving familiarity with which lapse of time enables us to speak of loved ones who are gone. But the mention of Harry Thornhill always brought such a cloud upon Paul's brow that she seldom mentioned the old, old friend whose ring she still wore.

Sometimes she wondered at the change which marriage appeared to have wrought in Paul, and she often told him that she wondered at it. Not that the change was a subject for complaint. On the contrary, never had wife more affectionate husband. Paul's high spirits, his love of novelty, his delight in adventure, all appeared to have gone. His every thought seemed to be of Anna and her child, and Anna often said he would spoil them both.

When the silver bells at Helswick rang for morning and evening service, none responded to them more punctually than Paul Massey and his charming wife. There was not an object of benevolence in the district to which Paul did not contribute, lavishly; there was not a scheme which had for its purpose the improvement of the poorer classes that he did not aid.

In good truth, from the day that Paul Massey married Anna Lee, he had given himself up to a life of devotion to her and all that was good. And yet Winford Barns was a frequent visitor at Denby Rise, and would startle the servants with oaths, and coarse jests. Mrs Massey had once, in her affectionately frank manner, asked her husband why he did not give up the acquaintance of a man who seemed so wicked and so vulgar. This question was the only one that had ever elicited from her husband anything like a command.

"You must not ask that question again, Anna dear," said Paul very seriously; "I am under great obligations to him, and he must come here when he pleases."

Anna bent her head, and then looked up at her husband, with a sorrowful inquiring glance.

"Don't think me unkind, Anna," Paul went on; "Barns was a different man once, and I can never be out of his debt."

"I don't think you unkind, Paul, and I will do whatever you wish, dear; but would it not be better to pay all you owe to him, and—"

"I cannot, Anna; do not ask it: I will relieve you of his society as much as possible. There, there! Let us take a walk on the beach, and don't think any more about my grim cigar-smoking friend."

Paul kissed his wife, chucked her under the chin, and suddenly became so gay, that Anna speedily forgot that such a person as Winford Barns was in existence.

But Paul's forced smiles were gone when he was alone, and a settled melancholy put a seal upon his features. His was a dreadful state of existence; it was only his strength of mind, and his determination to make some atonement for his crime, that enabled him to support it. His terrible secret tortured him at all hours.

The memory of the thing seemed to burn into his heart, as the scarlet letter scorched and sered those bursting hearts in New England, of which Nathaniel Hawthorne hath told us. His wild nature was subdued with it, though the old spirit which, in his youthful days, had prompted him to travel, would, in lonely moments, when his wife was not with him, frequently take fierce possession of him. But it was the restlessness of the soul which seeks to flee from itself; the longing for some lonesome spot where memory should be overthrown. And now a new misery, a new dread, a new peril was before him. With the acuteness that seemed to come, chiefly from his big secret, he knew that Winford Barns would betray him: he felt that through him would come his punishment. The day of retribution appeared to draw nearer with every fresh sum of money which the voracity of his " friend " drew from him. He knew that this was the price of Winford's secrecy, and that some day, when he could no longer pay the price, Winford's malicious tongue would babble.

Had it not been for Anna's sake, he could almost have prayed for the relief of this great exposure. Like many a male-factor, who has found it impossible to carry his load of guilt about with him, he would fain have given himself up to justice. But when he remembered that dying request of old Mountford's, " Be kind to her—love her always," and when Anna put her arm in his, and her child came clinging about his knees, some of the old defiance kindled in his eye against Winford Barns. For Paul Massey loved those two beings, with all the fervour of his ardent nature. And it galled him to the quick to think that he was robbing them to buy the silence of his arch-enemy, — robbing them to cover up a dead body with gold, to hide the ghost of the companion of his youth.

Already his estate on the Wear had gone to buy Winford's silence. Mrs Massey was easily reconciled to the sale, when Paul told her that his object was to settle the amount upon their child in such a way that it would be more beneficial to him than it could otherwise be. Lie upon lie did Paul tell his wife, in order to put off the dreadful day which he knew *would* come. No moral nor religious compunction stood in the way of these falsehoods. Paul had no hope of salvation. He was a castaway, a wretch, who could not expect it; but he had repented of his great sin; nevertheless, he loved Anna, his wife, and he prayed that her life, and her child's future, might not be blighted through him. He prayed; but hope gave him no encouragement. He felt that his fight was a battle with Fate, and he knew that in the end he would be worsted.

In order to counteract Winford's attacks upon his purse he had speculated in various ways, but he had always been unsuccessful; and even such a contingency as poverty dawned upon him, to make his torments the greater.

"Let me buy your silence with a final sum," he said to Winford one day, when Barns had solicited a further loan, with more than ordinary insolence. "Name your price."

"How business-like we are to-day," Winford mockingly replied, "we were not wont to be so matter-of-fact."

"There need be no longer any disguise about our positions," said Paul. "The manner of your asking for money has been too peremptory, too arrogant, to make any other than one impression."

"And that impression?" said Winford coolly, lighting a cigar.

"Is that I am paying for my safety; that were I to refuse, you would carry out the threat which you have more than once made, howsoever vaguely."

"You were not always such a good interpreter of other men's intentions, Paul; you have read mine rightly."

"Coward! miserable coward!" exclaimed Paul. "Have you no compassion, no feeling, no gratitude, no humanity ?"

"Ah, ah, ah," laughed his tormentor, "that's devilish good. You are abundantly blessed with all those virtues, I suppose."

"I! I am more despicable than yourself, and ready to bend to the most terrible punishment: but there are others, Winford. You cannot be all stone: think of them. For myself, I ask nothing, but for them, I say, name the sum at which your silence is to be purchased, and I couple with it but one condition."

"Well, I don't wish to be hard," said the heartless spendthrift; "but I helped you into your new estates; I advised you to make up to the girl, you know."

Paul's love for Anna Lee had been no sordid one, and he bore this assumed partnership in her fortune with a heart ready to burst, and with fingers hitching to seize his tormentor and hurl him to the earth.

"It was a pleasant sitting down, for

you, as they say northwards, and it's only fair that you should deal handsomely with me," and Winford knocked a long ash from his cigar, and commenced a calculation. "Let me see, I owe £500 in a little matter of *roulet*, another instalment of £5000 towards the composition with those attentive creditors on the Tyne, certain fair ladies of Maryport must have £200 this week, and —but what condition is this you speak of?"

"The condition is that you write and sign a document which I shall dictate, describing Harry Thornhill's accidental death, and confessing therein that you were once wicked enough to try and make capital out of me, by basely and maliciously charging me with murder; all of which you now regret, pronouncing the truth of this declaration, which you make on condition that I do not prosecute you for slander; and that you leave England for ever, or permit me to do so. This will save the name I bear from a terrible blot; it will save my wife and child from a greater

misery than poverty. I ask a great thing
—I will pay a great price for it."

" Is that all ?" inquired Winford, with
a grim mocking smile.

" That is all."

" And how much will you pay for
that ? "

" Perhaps all you may have the conscience to ask. And I will also, in writing, agree to take no advantage whatever
of the document, and never to use it in
any way, unless to produce it in a Court
of Justice to which I may be summoned
on any charge relative to Harry Thornhill."

" But you want me to commit perjury.
No, no, I can't consent to that. I, Winford
Barns, perjure myself, stain my fair reputation with crime ! No, no, Paul Massey,
that I cannot do," said Winford in a ban-
tering, jeering way. " But if we can agree
as to the amount, and you will accept my
word of honour ; why, then I am open to
negociate."

Paul made other propositions in which he endeavoured to secure himself against his tormentor; but Winford Barns was too keenly alive to his power over his old friend to accept any terms which did not leave him a free agent.

"No," he said at length, "I *may* come to that pass, Mr Massey; the time *may* arrive when a pile of gold will tempt me even to a worse crime than perjury, but it is not yet, my friend. So, for the present, if you will just let me have, say ten thousand pounds—at five per cent., you know—a simple loan,—I'll trouble you no more this two years, at any rate, and if I'm in luck, I'll trouble you no more for ten years, perhaps. There! Now can you say I'm selfish and sordid?"

Paul felt that it was useless to struggle further with his fate, just then; so he consented to this twentieth loan.

"If you leave here to-night I will order the money to be placed to your credit, at Maryport, by the next post."

"It's unkind in a host to give his guest notice to quit," said Winford, emptying the brandy-bottle into his tumbler and tossing off the contents, "but I'll not oppose you in that: so we'll part at once."

If Paul had taken particular note of the unhealthy, besotted, and generally dissipated appearance of his unwelcome guest, he might have seen a cause for hope in Winford's trembling hand and glaring eyes. He looked like a man who would some morning be found dead in a gutter, or who would go off raving in a fit of *delirium tremens*. He had utterly sunk into the depths of debauchery, and his extravagance had gathered around him, in Maryport, depraved men and women who gladly encouraged his wicked orgies. But Paul received no hope from Winford's debauchery: once, for two days, when the news reached Denby that he was nearly killed, Paul had hoped that his wife and child would be rescued from the pitfall to which he was leading them.

It was little that Bessie Martin could tell Richard Grey about Denby Rise. Mrs Massey often came to Beachstone's to buy books, and was a beautiful kind lady, and wore lovely dresses, and real diamonds. Mr Massey often came with her, and he was a very kind gentleman. They had a little girl with bright curly hair, and a very impudent groom, named Wittle, who had assurance enough to joke her, though she had not disliked him half so much since he had said that Richard Grey was a fine fellow. It was impudence, however, Bessie went on to say, for the man to tell her that Richard was rather fast; but she hoped soon to be away from Helswick. She had met Mr Massey on the beach once or twice, and although people said he was so happy, she thought he looked miserable: he would stand staring at the sea, as if he should like to be far away upon it. So she thought, however, when she saw him; but when he was with Mrs Massey he was so kind, so good, so attentive. Oh, how delightful it must be, when people loved each other, to be always together! " Not to be separated as we are, dear Richard," Bessie continued. " But you will soon come, won't you, and fetch your poor Bessie? I am sure one of your letters has been lost; for I have only had this short one. Do write often to me, and be sure to come soon."

Bessie's was a true description of Paul's occasional solitary rambles; but how incomplete! Paul had thought all sorts of wild things in those reveries. Once it seemed as if a voice whispered to him that rest could only come through the death of Winford Barns, and then the prompter advised the forcible removal of his tormentor. Paul checked the murderous thought, and shuddered at the horrible suggestion. But the whisper came again, and seemed to ask what was the death of a worthless wretch such as Barns, compared with the happiness and safety of

Anna and her child. "Crush him out of your path—trample upon him," the tempter seemed to say, until Paul went home, in a frenzy of fear and dread, and lay seriously ill for many long weary days.

CHAPTER II.

JOE WITTLE DISCOVERS THAT " THINGS IS NOT
EXACTLY AS THINGS OUGHTER BE."

"SUPPOSING I were to turn out to be
a very bad man, Anna," said Paul, after
he had sufficiently recovered to be enabled
to take exercise; "supposing you should
discover that you had married a man of
infamous character?"

"You alarm me, dear," said Anna,
bending her clear bright eyes upon her
husband, half fearful that the delirium of
fever might be returning.

"Don't be alarmed, my love. Suppose, I say, you should discover, or it
should be discovered, that I, Paul Massey,
your husband, had been guilty of a great
crime?"

Anna, who was standing by Paul's chair, before the bright fire which blazed up the library chimney, laid her arm fondly upon his, and nodded for him to proceed with his question.

"Should you love me then, as dearly as you do now?"

"I shall always love you, Paul; but the supposition you put to me is altogether out of my power to imagine, much more to accept as a probability;" said Anna, her open countenance, full of confidence and love, endorsing every word she said.

"But I wish you to try and realize it," said Paul, looking into the fire.

"Don't frighten me, dear," Anna said gravely.

"Suppose it, Anna. Just suppose it, for the sake of supposition, love," said Paul, taking her hand in his.

"Well, then, if I must humour you, Paul, I should love you more than I love you now; I should pity you so much, knowing that if you had done anything wicked, your hot fervent nature had been to blame, and not your kind loving heart."

"God bless you, Anna!" said Paul, taking her face between his two hands and kissing it.

"Why did you put such a strange question, my pet?" Anna asked, looking up at the pale, handsome face of her husband.

"You say I said such strange things when I was delirious, Anna; that I prayed so earnestly for forgiveness, for your sake; that I—that I—"

The remembrance of what Anna had said, with regard to his ravings during the fever, overcame him: he covered his face with his hands and threw himself back into his chair.

"You are weak, my love; you should not excite yourself in this way. I am very, very sorry I told you about what you said; but you were so anxious to know, Paul—so anxious. Don't think of

it, dear. Surely you do not imagine that
I believed you had done anything wicked.
Dear Paul, I have heard that when the
mind of a man is burthened with some
dreadful weight of guilt—which is not
your case, my love," said Anna, smiling
lovingly upon him—" I have heard that,
when such is the case, a man does not
disclose it in delirium. Oh, Paul, Paul,
dear Paul, I know your soul to be un-
sullied, and your love to be the truest,
the best, the fondest."

Paul removed his hands, and looked
up at his wife, as though he had just
awakened from a dream.

"How foolish I am, Anna dear; I
have been asking some silly question—I
am not quite well yet, love, and my
thoughts are a little wandering. How
the wind blows! It must be a stormy
night at sea."

Anna had knelt down and laid her
head upon her husband's knee, and Paul
stroked her fair brown hair.

"However foolish I may be, Anna, and even if I were very wicked, I love you truly, do I not?"

Anna turned her face towards him, and kissed the hand that caressed her.

A few minutes afterwards they went, arm in arm, to the drawing-room, and Anna lulled Paul's unhappy thoughts to rest with that exquisite melody, the sprite's song, from "Oberon," which rose and fell, like the gentle murmur of an inland lake, when a summer breeze moves it with lullaby-ripples. Through many a subdued variation Anna's dear fingers seemed to charm out the soothing melody, until Paul dozed before the fire, in blissful forgetfulness.

It was just at this time that Joe Wittle unlocked the door of Harkaway's stable, and entered, shutting out the wind that made an effort to follow him.

A candle was burning, in a sconce, on the wall, and Harkaway had been duly

" suppered up," as Joe designated the last offices which the favourite mare required at his hands.

" Yes, old gal, I'm come to think just ten minutes, and then we'll put out the light, as they says in the play, and go to bed."

Joe perched himself upon an old corn bin, and kicked it with the heels of his short legs.

" 'Suppose I should turn out to be a werry bad man; suppose your husband had committed a werry great crime!' Them was the werry words," said Joe, looking straight at the flame of the candle.

Harkaway turned her head, and stamped her off foreleg, as though she wished to attract Joe's attention.

" All right, old gal; for you are agettin' aged, my pet; I'm just a talking to myself."

Harkaway turned to her oats again, and was silent.

" 'Supposing I had committed a werry

great crime!' Them's werry queer words,
master, werry queer words. It's not for
me to know as you've said 'em, of course;
and I'm as hinfernal a spy and eavesdrop-
per, as Mat Dunkum says, perhaps, to have
heard 'em; but the hintention being good,
the act ain't so bad. All right, my
beauty."

This latter expression to Harkaway,
who stamped her foot again.

" Two and two don't make five," went
on Joe, thrusting his hands into his waistcoat pockets, "and five and two don't
make six;" with which arithmetical observ-
ation he dropped his legs upon the stable
floor and dropped his little body after
them, and the twain went to Harkaway, who rubbed her nose against Joe's
cheek.

" Yes, old gal, things is not exactly as
things oughter to be; but your heart's in
the right place yet, and your nose too,"
and Joe patted the sleek neck so vigorous-
ly, that his patting roused up, in the next

stable, a fast-trotting cob, which plunging
violently in its jealous rage, Joe was
obliged to go to it and say "So-ho," and
"Gently, my sweet," and "So-ho," until
the cob was quiet again; and then he
turned up the stable bucket, and appeared
to be mentally examining the hay-loft, as
we saw him on that night, long ago, when
he drove Mrs Grey to the Denby caverns.

"If I could circumwent that ere fire-
eating friend of master's, as has got him in
his clutches somehow, I should say, Richard Grey, I'm werry much obliged to you
for being the cause of my getting a taste
for acting the spy."

It may seem absurd to some of our
readers that Joe should have talked aloud
to himself of matters evidently so important; but he had so long been in the
habit of talking to his horses, that the
stable had become his "thought-box," as
he called it, and it was an assistance to
him to speak his thoughts.

"It helps me to arrange 'em," he said

to Harkaway, who occasionally seemed to put in a protest against these thinking talks, "it helps me to dot my ideas down and put 'em straight, and look at 'em, old gal; and as they are werry important ideas just now, I must beg to be excused for arranging 'em so often in your presence; so jest go on with yer supper, and don't mind Joseph."

"Master's afraid of that ere Barns; that's Idea I.," Joe continued after a pause, during which he provided himself with a piece of chalk. "Barns is a ruining master, in consequence—I've heered some of their private confabs; that's Idea II. Barns has threatened to split—I've heered him; that's Idea III. The last time Master Barns came the heavy money dodge to the tune of a good many thousands, master was so overcome he took, and had a fever; that's Idea IIII. Master said queer things in that ere fever; Idea IIIII. He has just now asked missus (God bless her!) suppose he had done a great crime; Idea IIIIII.

That's enough ideas to bother a fellow, and quite enough for to-night;" with which after-thought Joe rose from the bucket, patted Harkaway, abstractedly, blew out the light, and went out himself.

CHAPTER III.

PAUL MASSEY AT BAY.

A FEW days after Joe had chalked up these ideas, a letter arrived at Denby Rise which sorely troubled Mr Massey. The hand that had directed it had trembled whilst doing so, and the envelope was blotted, and badly sealed. Paul had grown very much excited after reading it, and had told his wife that he had received some bad news. He feared they would have to reduce their establishment, and live more economically. He was most unfortunate, he said, in his investments.

Mrs Massey looked becomingly grave about the matter, though she was only troubled to see Paul troubled. But when their child came into the room to show

mamma the little whip which Joe Wittle
had been commissioned to purchase, with a
new set of pony harness and a side-saddle,
at Maryport, Paul's continual losses touched her, for a moment, through her daughter. For her own part, she could bear and
endure anything, but Paul's unsuccessful
speculations might interfere with Katy's
prospects in life; so she asked Paul what
these losses were, and how they were
produced. A vague statement about
the fluctuations in the price of money,
Stock Exchange panics, the failure of a
bank, and the mistake of an agent in the
matter of some railway debentures, did not
make affairs at all clear, in her estimation;
but what should she know about such
things? She asked Paul whether it was
necessary that he should have anything to
do with the Stock Exchange, or with railways.

Paul, with a sigh, said money must
be invested, must be put to account, and
he only wished he had better luck, or a

wider financial knowledge. It was useless, however, to repine—his losses, one way and another, had been very great, and they must reduce their expenditure accordingly. They might, perhaps, have to leave Denby Rise.

Anna's heart beat quickly, and the tears came into her eyes at the thought of this; and an observer might easily have noticed what a severe struggle Paul had had with himself, before he had summoned up sufficient courage to indicate so much of the reverse of fortune which threatened them. But he was evidently bent on preparing his household and his friends for a great change. When his doctor came that morning, he told him he had received very bad tidings of serious monetary losses. The rector of Helswick and his wife, who dined with them that day, received a similar intimation just before their carriage was called for their return home. And the next day Mrs Massey, following the instructions of her husband, told her maid that they would be compelled to reduce their establishment.

Thus it speedily got abroad that the Masseys were in difficulties in consequence of losses by railways, and losses in a bank, and losses on the Stock Exchange, and that nobody knew what the end of it might be. Mrs Massey had said to her maid, who told the housekeeper, who had informed the grocer's wife at Helswick, who had mentioned it to. the post-office, which had alluded to it at a private party, that, perhaps, they might leave Denby Rise for several years.

The news did not come so suddenly to Joe Wittle as to the rest of the household; but it worried Joe Wittle more than any other member of the domestic staff. . He went with it to his thought-box, and sat on his bucket, for a full half-hour, without speaking. Harkaway had gone out with the master, which enabled Joe to take un-interrupted walks about the stable, when he was tired. of sitting. He contemplated the marks which he had made a few days before, and which he had several times endeavoured to add up, and divide, and subtract, to his satisfaction, but always without success.

" It's a aggrawaitin thing when you've got the ideas and can't make nothin' of them, after you've made so much, to speak contradictory like," said Joe, his little eyes looking inquiringly up at the hay-rack.

" There's something werry wrong somehow, and Winford Barns is at the bottom of it; but how it's to be set right, blessed if I know. Joseph, Joseph, if you'd only a wife of your buzzum to argue the pint with! But then she might go a hargifying of it to somebody else's wife, and that wouldn't do. Perhaps it's better as it is. It's quite certin as master's done something wrong, and that's my difficulty. It would be a werry hard thing if I were to go on a meddlin' until I brought *that* to light. Them as lives long enough will see something, no doubt; but what I shall do, is jest to see if

I can't get something out of that ere Dunkum, though he do swear he'll be the death
of me if I don't mind my eye. There's
no doubt that letter, which was from that
devil Barns, as I see the well-known
carricters, when the post-office was a putting it in the bag—there is no doubt that
ere letter is the cause of all the trouble
just now, and Mat being Mr Barns's head
man, which office he must ha' got the
Lord knows how, and which he keeps in
the same way, considering how he talks to
the Commodore, as he calls him.

"Yes! I'm getting all abroad in my
ideas; my thoughts is bolting awfully,"
Joe went on, after a pause, finally giving
himself up to the bucket and a careful examination of his boots.

Paul Massey's energies seemed, for a
time, to strengthen with his difficulties.
The fact that he was being punished for
his crime, might have had its good influence, even though it were coupled with

the punishment of those who had not deserved to suffer.

"We will get away, love, to some distant place, where no one will know us; a few years of careful economy may bring my affairs round again," he said to Anna, raising his head, and looking like a man at bay with obstacles which he was determined to overcome.

"It makes me happy, Paul, to see you so cheerful. I have not seen so much light in your eye, and such a hopeful expression in your face, since your illness. I am ready to go wherever you wish, and at any moment."

Then Paul sat down, with his child between his knees, and husband and wife talked together about the future, as happily and hopefully as though they were only just going to be married and begin the world anew. For Anna felt her love increase, if that were possible, towards Paul, now that they were no longer very rich. There seemed to her to be new life in her affec-

tion, fresh reasons for its budding anew
and striking out more tendrils that should
cling about her husband and their child.

Paul felt that it would be a relief to
leave Denby for ever, to leave it far behind him, with its dark associations which
overshadowed its brighter ones. He
thought that he could now make such an
arrangement with Barns as would satisfy
his tormentor, and leave himself at peace
to continue his atonement, and administer
to the happiness of the woman to whom
he had devoted himself.

The first shock of Barns's letter, in
which another sacrifice was demanded,
had been depressing; but when it began
to dawn upon Paul that this might be the
last shock, that this might be the last sacrifice, his old determination to make his
wife's days happy, and to carry out her
uncle's dying request, revived strongly
within him; and imagination began to
picture a quiet, happy home in some rural
spot, within sound of the bells of a village

church, where he could devote himself to Anna, and to works of religion and charity.

If Paul had pictured himself in some busy, throbbing town, ministering to the weak and weary in narrow streets and close alleys, he would better have fulfilled the notion of a self-sacrificing life; but Anna was his first consideration, and he thought he saw, through the gloom, bright lights falling upon her path.

The next day he went to Maryport to make these final arrangements with Winford Barns,—who was not likely to live long to trouble anybody. Barns had conveyed as much to Paul in the letter, but had coupled with it his intention of leading a jolly life while it lasted, for which purpose he wanted more funds. He further intimated that it was his intention to visit Denby, with sundry friends of his, and to spend a month there. Paul Massey, Esquire, need be in no hurry to prepare, for he did not intend to come until the weather was warmer.

Paul had at once conceived the idea of letting Denby Rise, or selling it, and leaving the locality altogether; and, full of this plan, he went to see Barns, to settle the terms.

He found Barns magnificently lodged at Hightown, an aristocratic suburb of Maryport, and he found him craving for money. Paul, in firm tones, which somewhat startled the battered *roué*, said this must be their last meeting. If Barns did not agree to his terms upon this occasion, he would go to the nearest police station, give himself up to justice, and denounce Winford Barns as an accessory to the murder.

"You'll not do that," said Barns in a husky voice, and coughing between each word. "Shut that confounded door, —— it; I shall die of draughts," though the atmosphere of the room was almost stifling.

"I shall do it, you infamous rascal," said Paul, clenching his fist.

"Keep off, keep off, —— you, or I'll call out and give you up myself," said Winford, coughing again, and drawing his soft-cushioned chair nearer the fire.

"That you will not, so long as I have this," and Paul drew from his pocket a roll of bank notes.

"The *roué* raised his red eyelids with a pleased expression, and asked, "How much? how much? You Jew, you Midas."

"Five thousand pounds."

"Humph! give it me," he said, stretching out his hand.

"On condition," said Paul.

"What is it? I shan't live very long, so conditions don't much matter now."

"Sign this paper, and you shall not only have the five thousand, but my note of hand for five thousand more, to be cashed in six months, if you are alive."

"Make it three months, —— it, make it three?"

"Be it so," said Paul.

"Read the paper, and, —— it, let's drop this parleying—there's all sorts of devils and spiders coming on the walls again."

Paul read a brief paper, somewhat similar to the one which Winford had previously refused to sign. This second one he had drawn up in a more strictly legal phraseology, having made it his study for months.

"No, —— you, I'll not sign it," said Barns, after a pause.

There was a knock at the door, and a servant entered.

"Now, Tom, what is it? what the devil is it?"

"Please, sir, I would rather tell you privately."

"Then come here and whisper, you thief."

The servant obeyed, and the whisper set the master swearing and cursing; in the midst of which a stout shabby-looking man entered, put his hand upon Winford's shoulder, and said, "At suit of Tomkins, you are my prisoner."

Paul's heart beat wildly for a moment, but he soon saw that Winford was arrested at a civil suit, and the momentary fear passed away.

"—— you, am I your prisoner? You infernal thief, who told you so?" exclaimed Barns, nearly choking with rage and disease. "What's the amount, you beast?"

"Three hundred pounds," said the man, calmly.

"Pay the money, Paul; pay the money."

"Will you sign this receipt?" Paul asked, showing Barns the short agreement.

"No, no," and then he fell a cursing again.

"Then, good morning; in five minutes there shall be an arrest of a different kind;" and Paul strode away, looking as resolute as he could, though he was very nervous about the result of this bold venture upon Barns's cowardice.

"—— him, call him back; he's fool enough to do anything; call him back."

Paul was at the bottom of the stairs before he responded to the loud calls for his return.

"Pay the money," said Barns, as Paul re-entered the room.

"Will you sign the receipt, and let us settle the whole business? this gentleman can witness the deed."

"Yes, yes, what does it matter?—a year will see me out—give me a pen."

And the paper was signed. Paul turned back the writing, that it might be witnessed without the contents being read.

The bailiff walked off with the amount at suit of Tomkins, and when he was gone Paul handed the rest of the money to his sometime friend, and casting from him the hand which the arch-deceiver stretched out to be shaken when the

bargain was concluded, he went away
and breathed more freely than he had
breathed for years. But the pangs of
conscience continued to make sad work
with Paul's once stalwart frame, notwithstanding.

CHAPTER IV.

BEARDING THE LION IN HIS DEN.

JOE WITTLE was determined to see
Mat Dunkum, and endeavour to get from
him the secret of the great influence which
Winford Barns possessed over his master.

"It's a werry ticklish job," said Joe,
"but I'll try it on; many a werry ticklish
job has been done by trying it on; so here
goes!"

Joe found it exceedingly difficult to meet
with Mat Dunkum either at the caverns or
at the cottage. Several days had passed
away since he started off to the latter
place, with "here goes" on his lips.

At length the persevering groom
tracked Mat to the cottage, and followed
him boldly. In answer to his modest

knock at the door, a gruff voice said " Come in," and in Joe went accordingly.

" What the blazes do you want ?" said Mat, taking a short pipe from his mouth.

" Well, you see, Mr Dunkum, I couldn't keep away—"

" Couldn't keep away," exclaimed Mat, before Joe had finished what he was about to say, " why I've a good mind to kick you out."

" Don't do that," said Joe meekly, " cos' it wouldn't be fair. for you to hit one so much under your size."

" It would be fair to strangle a whelp like you any day in the week."

" Well, if that's all the reward I'm to have for my good intentions, I'll say good arternoon," said Joe, taking a step back-wards.

" No you don't," said Mat, rising and standing beside the groom with rather startling rapidity ; " what's your game— what are you up to ?"

"Leave go of my collar," exclaimed Joe reddening, "or I'll not answer for the consequences—I'm telling yer."

"Hah, hah, hah!" roared Mat, amused at Joe's threatening attitude. "Here, sit down, and unfurl your yarn at once, or, by Davy's locker, I'll pull you joint from joint."

A mental picture of himself, after such an operation, presenting itself to Joe's imagination, he picked up his scattered limbs, and sat down upon a pair of the principal ones.

"Well, you see, I've brought you this to begin with," said Joe, taking from his capacious pocket a bottle of brandy; "I know it's good."

"Humph!" said Mat, screwing out the cork, "poisoned perhaps; I'll make you swallow every drop if it is."

"I brought it, yer see, Mister Dunkum, as a sort of peace-offering atween you and me; for I've had a dream, and a werry ugly dream."

Mat sat down and resumed his pipe.

"Yes a dream," said Joe, noticing that the circumstance made some impression.

"Well," said Mat, who bethought himself of sundry dreams which had lately troubled his rest, and made him give up sleeping at the caverns.

"I dreamt of you and Mister Barns."

Mat stared at Joe with some surprise, and frowned fiercely.

"And I dreamt as how you was werry ill, and that ere Mister Barns stood by your bed-side and see you die without any compunction."

Mat winced at this, and watched Joe suspiciously.

"Without any compunction. Yes, and more nor that, for when everybody's back was turned he pulled out a knife, and stuck you."

"Humph!" He wouldn't mind doing that, thought Mat.

"And as I'd not seen you for a werry long time, and as a woice in my dreaming

ear said, 'Joseph, bear no malice — go
and see him, he is lonely, he may be dying,' I couldn't refuse, and so I have come:
and if you've no objection, Mister Dunkum, to let bygones be bygones, why I
should sleep all the happier."

"I suppose you liked that young
Grey," said Mat, gruffly.

"Well, I did," said Joe, cautiously.

"And you thought I was a great rascal
—eh? That made you spy about, and
try to get him from me."

"I'm werry sorry I offended you in
that affair, Captain," said Joe, scratching
his head. "But you see his mother was
in such a way."

"His mother! I could strangle her!"
exclaimed Mat. "Don't talk of his
mother."

"Well, I won't if it aint agreeable,"
said Joe, trying to reach the ground with
his toes, and straining his little legs inef-
fectually in the attempt.

"Everybody thinks me a thief and

a brute; and it's through her," said Mat.

"I heard as how she behaved bad," said Joe.

Mat gave a savage grunt, and asked his former question, "Did you like the lad?"

"Well, yes, I did — somehow you couldn't help liking of him."

"No—I hated the cub at first, but, —— me, I began to like him as if he was my own."

"Did you, now?" said Joe, succeeding in putting his feet upon the second stave of the chair, and proudly thrusting his hands into his waistcoat pockets.

"Yes," said Mat laconically, as if dissatisfied at himself for holding anything like a civil conversation with Joe.

"Indeed!" said Joe.

"Here, let's taste your liquor," said Mat.

Joe leaped from his chair, and Mat reached a couple of horn tumblers and filled them.

"Now floor that, first," said Mat, " as a token that it's not poison."

"Certainly," said Joe. "Yer health, Captain, and may you never live to die in such a melancholy way as I see you in my dream at the hands of Mister Barns!"

"Mr Barns, be ——, he's an infernal humbug," Mat replied, tossing off a hornful of brandy.

The truth is Mat had seriously felt the reduction of Mr Barns's purse. The yacht had been sold, and Mat, with difficulty, could but procure the most trifling amounts from his Commodore, as he called Barns.

"Well, I've thought so, do you know, often," said Joe; "but look here, Mister Dunkum, let us shake hands to show that you bears no malice—why should we be ill friends?"

"You thought I was a ruining that boy," said Mat.

"I ain't in a position to say what I thought; but. it seemed as if I was only hackherwated for his good," said Joe,

" and out of no disrespect to you, Mister
Dunkum, who I wish to be friends with."

" Well, on them grounds I'll shake
hands," said Mat, " for I liked that boy,
and may be it wor best as you should get
him away."

The two shook hands accordingly, and
applied themselves to the bottle.

" Since I had that dream, Mister Dunkum, I've been a thinking a good deal
about the hinfluence Mister Barns has
over master, and I've got some ideas about
it."

" Have you ? " said Mat, curiously.

" I'm satisfied as Mister Barns knows
something, as he makes master pay dearly
for, and is nigh a ruining of him."

" And you think you'll make friends
with me to get at it."

" No, no ; now, no questions against a
man's honour. If you think so, don't tell
me anything, and then you'll be on the
right side," said Joe, with an air of frankness.

"I shan't," said Mat, tossing off another horn of liquor.

"It's a werry hard thing, though, to be obliged to reduce your establishment, and give up your residence, 'cos a friend has got a secret, and threatens to split," said Joe.

"Is it come to that?" said Mat earnestly. "Is Mr Massey going to leave the neighbourhood?"

"He is."

"And through Barns?"

"He is," said Joe, looking hard at Mat, and stretching his toes towards the floor —"I'm telling yer."

"I knowed Barns was rather hard on him; but I didn't know it was so stiff as that."

"Why, he's next to ruined—leastwise he's only got a reasonable sort of sum to keep on with—and I shall lose my place."

"Lose your place!" exclaimed Mat.

"Yes, and Harkaway and all the 'osses is to be sold, and Denby Rise guv up."

"The devil!" said Mat, laying down his pipe and putting his elbows on the table, the better to take in all Joe said.

"Yes, and that made me more nor ever wish to be friends along of you, 'cos I've a werry great notion of leaving England. You see I've saved money, a tidy sum, too; and I can do werry fair, no doubt."

"Well, I'm glad you came, mate," said Mat, "and here's my hand on it."

"I'm werry sorry for master; I'd give all I've got to serve him, and to punish that ere Barns," said Joe mournfully.

"It's hard for that pretty young woman as Mr Massey married," said Mat.

"Hard! It's murder. She's one of the best creatures as is."

"For a woman, for a woman, perhaps she may be. What do you think this secret is, then, as gets over the guvnor?" Mat asked.

"Ah, there's the point—I've got it all down except the sum total; but it will

come right in the end, I've got my ideas,"
said Joe.

"*I* could tell you," said Mat, who was
growing more and more confidential now
that he saw Barns's capability of supply-
ing him with money was getting weaker,
and that he had been so selfish in his deal-
ings with Mr Massey. Moreover, the Commodore in his drunken fits had cursed Mat,
and defied him; had twitted him with his
dependence upon him, and called him
" beggar," " smuggler," " thief;" for
which Mat had only recently turned round
upon Barns and threatened to strangle
him, and do other dire deeds of venge-
ance, if Barns did not treat him differ-
ently.

" *I* could tell you," said Mat.

" Could you, now ?" said Joe, eagerly.

" But I shan't."

" Oh!" said Joe, with an air of dis-
appointment.

" It might be worth your while; but
then I aint come here to be a prying

into your affairs," said Joe, "and as the sun's going down, I think it's time I was hoff."

"Stay a bit, mate," said Mat, "what's your hurry?"

"No, I can't, thankee," said Joe; "but I'll look in again, if you've no objection—it's not werry long I shall be in these parts," said the groom, mournfully.

"Well, give us another look in to-morrow about this time; I'll be in," said Mat.

"And you won't kick me out now, Captain, eh?" said Joe, smilingly.

"No more of that," Mat answered; and with this the two parted—Joe Wittle fully satisfied with the progress he had made, and Mat Dunkum in a state of considerable uneasiness and uncertainty about what his course should be, in the changing circumstances to which Joe had referred.

At the same hour of the following evening Joe went to Mat's cottage; and he re-

peated his visits for many days. He pur-
posely avoided the subject, in which he had
felt so much interest, until Mat re-introduced
it, and thereby completely upset Mat's early
suspicions as to the cause of Joe's determined friendship. It was, however, soon
sufficiently manifest to Joe that there was
bad blood between Mr Barns and Mat, and
that through this disaffection a golden key
might unlock the secret that had bound
them together.

Mat had for several years been so accustomed to have plenty of money and to
spare, that the shortening—nay, the almost
cutting off—of supplies made it hard to
bear with Barns's insolence.

"I've only one hobjeck to serve, Mat,"
said Joe, at the end of one of these later
interviews, "and that is the hinterest of
master and mistress."

Mat smoked on in silence.

"My master has no more idea as I
suspecks anything about the hinfluence of
that halligator Barns, no more nor that old

pistol hanging above your head has. I'd give all I have to serve that good dear lady as was so much loved by my old guvner. I would, 'pon my soul—you needn't smile as if you didn't believe it."

" I was only thinking what fools women make of men, whether they be their husbands or their servants," said Mat, " I don't disbelieve you."

" Now look here, Mister Dunkum, I've never asked you to split of anything you knows, and I aint a-goin' to now; but we may both on us be said to be a-goin' down the hill of life; natur's got the drag on my wheels nicely, and I thanks her for it. But we shall both on us get to the bottom soon. There's them as is younger—if we could do 'em a good turn in any way to make 'em not jolt so a-goin' down the rough road, why it's our dooty to do it—and—"

" What the blazes are you driving at ? " exclaimed Mat; " I've nothing to do with dooty; nobody's done their dooty by me."

"Well, now, this is what I was going to say: if there's anything you could tell me, as would floor that ere Barns, I'd gladly share with you half my savings—I don't want money—it aint no good to me."

"No, I'm not going to be bought by you, Joseph," said Mat; "don't come that dodge over me—it won't do. But if all's true as you've said, and considering as that Barns is such a —— infernal selfish thief, and other things settled between us, I'll let you into a secret."

"Yes," said Joe, excitedly.

"Not now, not now; but all in good time. I can't say as it'll do you any good, or anybody else; maybe it will, and maybe it won't."

"Indeed!" said Joe, fidgeting with his fur helmet.

"When Mr Massey leaves Denby Rise, and you goes away, you shall know something, on certain conditions."

After most elaborate arrangements and stipulations, and vows, in which money was not altogether left out of the question, Mat subsequently told Joe a secret that made his hair almost stand on end.

Joe rubbed out the ideal sum in Harkaway's stable, on the night when the mystery was made clear to him, and he thanked God that *he* was not Paul Massey, Esquire.

CHAPTER V.

BESSIE MARTIN.

FOR more than seven months no tidings had come to England from Richard Grey. Since he had announced to his mother, and to Bessie Martin, in a few brief lines, that he had left the employment of Welford and Co., he had not written to any one. Mrs Grey, who had wept many an hour, in secret, over her boy's misconduct, continually finding out fresh excuses for him, watched anxiously for a letter by every post; and every post disappointed her.

But even Mrs Grey's anxiety had not equalled that of poor Bessie Martin, who had grown pale and haggard, with watching and crying. Mrs Beachstone had noticed Bessie's sadness, and had tried to comfort her, but without avail, and at length had determined upon calling in Dr Fell to see the poor little assistant.

Bessie had seriously made up her mind to run away, and go to America, that very week. In fact, she had packed up a little bundle to carry away with her, and had arranged other things, so that her boxes might be sent after her. She had ascertained at what hour the train left Chipswood each morning, and had made up her little agitated mind to walk thither, and take a ticket to Maryport.

Mrs Beachstone's decision with regard to medical advice, had only resulted in Bessie's starting off two days earlier. She must go to Richard. She must see him. There was no help for it. She had written and told him so. Perhaps he was ill; perhaps he had not written to her, because she had said she would run away to him, and he was expecting her. He had not deserted her. Oh, no, he would not do that.

She would go, nevertheless. She could not stay in Helswick; she must get .to America. That very night she would set off. She was just sitting down to write a little note to Mrs Beachstone which she intended to put in the post, asking forgiveness for her ingratitude in leaving so strangely, when the postman came into the shop and gave into her trembling hands a letter with a foreign stamp upon it.

When she was alone she kissed the letter' and put it into her bosom, and seized upon the first favourable opportunity to run to her room and read it. It was a short letter, a cruelly short letter. Bessie pushed her black curls back from her forehead, as she read it, word for word; pushed her hair back and rubbed her eyes, and then gave a deep subdued cry, like one in a death agony.

"If what you say is true, I am very sorry for you, and I enclose you a bill for three pounds, which may be useful; but you must not come here; and you will not do so, when I tell you that, if I once thought I loved you, the dream is over. I was a boy and a fool, and you should not have believed me; besides which, I am an abandoned outcast with neither love nor care for anybody. Make no mistake, Bessie; you are young, and will soon get over the loss of a fellow like me—you had better go to my mother's, she loves you as if you were her own."

Bessie pored over these words until her eyes blazed with indignation and woe. "If what I say is true," "a bill for three pounds," "loves me no longer," she gasped, until she was fain to press her hand upon her heart to keep it from bursting. She could not cry—no tears came to her relief; she could only moan and look about like one bewildered. She could not pray, she could not think; her mind was, for the time, a total wreck. Called to her duties by Mrs Beachstone, she crumpled up the letter and went down-stairs, with her eyes wide open, and her hair dishevelled; but

the sudden remembrance of Mrs Beachstone's purpose recalled her to action,. and
she went back to her room, smoothed her
hair, made a great effort to be calm, and
outwardly succeeded.

She went to bed at the usual hour, but
not to sleep. She threw herself upon
the same bed from which she had risen
on that May morning, in the previous
year, to gather May-flowers — she lay
upon her bed with her blasted hopes, and
with the letter grasped in her hand, but
she did not weep, and she did not moan ;
she lay like a poor stricken thing, too
much hurt for grief.

Hour by hour, the old Helswick clock
struck the time, and at midnight the sil-
very chimes beat out a solemn chant in
the blue star-light of the new year. One
and two o'clock came, and then Bessie
rose.

Lighting the candle, that stood upon
the little oak dressing-table, she put it on
the floor, in the furthest corner of the room,

and shielded it with a towel, hung upon a chair, so that the light might not be observed. She laid a note upon the table, hurriedly drew round her shoulders a thick shawl, and fastened a scarf about her neck. Then taking up a small bundle, ready packed, she blew out the light, and after listening for a few moments, she glided out of the room, and went down-stairs, past the servant's bed-room, down to the second landing, past Mrs Beachstone's bed-room, down into the kitchen, and out into the cold January morning. She stood for a few moments, after she had closed the door, stood upon the very spot where the girls and boys had waited for her on that bright May morning, when she was to be Queen.

And then she set off to walk to Chipswood—ten miles—which was the nearest railway station to the fashionable little town of Helswick. There had been some talk of bringing the railway to the town, but the authorities rose, *en masse*, to oppose it, and so they were left quietly out of the world, and they liked it.

The stars shone down upon the queer little town, and the sea was moaning in the darkness, and everything that could be seen was white with frost. Bessie walked swiftly onwards, on through by-paths until she was out of the town, and then out upon the dreary highway, with tall white hedges on either side.

It was half-past five when she reached Chipswood junction. The signal lamps cast long coloured rays of light upon the dark little box of a station.

There was no light, no fire, in any part of the poor little place at present, except in a tiny house a few yards off, where the pointsman stood, with his back to the fire, waiting for a luggage-train, that could be just heard rumbling along in the distance. Hearing footsteps, the pointsman came out, and being a kind-hearted fellow, he asked Bessie to step inside his box until the train came, which, he said, would be half-an-hour yet. Bessie sat down upon a low seat before the fire, and waited for the train.

" This is a luggage-train as is coming," said the pointsman, " so you needn't mind it; the government is due at six; warm yourself well, miss; never mind me, you look cold and ill."

For the first time since she had received that cruel letter, the tears welled up into Bessie's eyes. The kind words of the old man (who had daughters of his own and could feel for the cold, haggard-looking girl before him) had touched her.

The luggage-train came hissing and groaning and panting by the point-house. The red fire from the engine beamed upon the shining rails, and the air was luminous with flame from the chimney. The men called to each other in the dark morning, and their voices were thick and husky, coming through woollen comforters, which were wrapped about their faces.

At length the luggage-train was shunted

upon a branch line, and the guard went off home, and the engine-driver and the stoker went into the pointsman's box to warm their coffee; whilst the engine stood snorting and fizzing by the hedge-side. Then the pointsman came to Bessie and told her it was time to get her ticket, and she went out and took her turn at the little window, where several men and a woman were taking tickets for various places. After they had all been served they stamped about the platform, in the cold, until the train came up and took them away in its damp and chilly boxes.

It was broad day-light when Bessie reached Maryport. Not in all her life had she seen so much bustle as there was at the railway station, and things did not improve when she was outside the big arched building, where she was hustled by foot passengers, and nearly run over by cabs and 'busses.

A policeman, noticing Bessie's dif-

ficulty, asked her if she had lost her
way.

"I am going to America," said Bessie,
"and I want to find a respectable boarding-
house near the docks."

The policeman said the best thing she
could do would be to take a cab—the fare
was only a shilling; and in a few minutes
Bessie was set down at the door of the
"Maryport Arms," close by the basin from
which the boats for America started.

The landlady, a buxom woman of about
forty, came into the passage whilst Bessie
was making her inquiries. Seeing that
the girl was ill and cold, she took her
into the bar and gave her some hot coffee,
and insisted upon her having a little
brandy in it. Bessie had fainted before
she could put the coffee to her lips; but
she soon recovered again. The landlady,
after eyeing her curiously, yet compassion-
ately, went out to her husband who was
talking to some early customers in the
tap-room.

"Pack her off, pack her off," said the man in a whisper, "unless she has some friends in the place."

"No, no, poor soul, we'll not do that, Jem."

"Ah, there you are again with your sympathy, as you call it; can she pay her bill?"

"For the matter of that I'm sure she can," said the woman; "she's well dressed, and wants to go by the steamer in the morning, and has given me the money to send for her ticket."

"Do what you like," said the landlord impatiently, and the woman went back to Bessie.

"There, my dear, take your things off," she said, proceeding to help her; "now take a little warm coffee, and then we'll see what can be done. What are you going to America for, my love?"

"I don't know," said Bessie vacantly; "I have given you the money, have I not?"

"Yes, dear," said the woman kindly, "have you no friends here in Maryport?"

"No," said Bessie, shaking her head, and looking at the woman with a bewildered gaze—"no, I have not; but Richard has."

"Oh, Richard has," said the woman, untying Bessie's bonnet-strings; "and who is Richard?"

Bessie shook her head again, and leaned back in the chair.

"Where do your parents live?" the woman asked, taking off Bessie's bonnet and putting it, with her shawl, on an old-fashioned sofa, beneath shelves full of glasses, and jugs, and pewter cups.

"I have none," said Bessie faintly; "Richard has, but he does not—" and the poor young creature fainted again, and was carried up-stairs by the landlady and the bar-woman.

They put her to bed, and lighted a fire in the room, and sent for a doctor;

and the next night a man came, with a
small box, like a doll's coffin, and went
away to deposit a still-born infant in the
parish churchyard.

Meanwhile, through the arrival of Mr
Beachstone (who had traced Bessie, by
means of the police, and who had gone
back to Helswick shocked and disgusted
with her dreadful misconduct), the people
at the inn had found out Mrs Grey, who
came and sat beside the bed upon which
Bessie was lying.

Richard's mother was not, however, so
kind to the girl as might have been expected., She read her son's letter, which had
been found crumpled up in Bessie's pocket,
and she blamed her son much less than she
blamed Bessie Martin. But it mattered
little to Bessie who .blamed her; for she
lay there, oblivious to all that was going on
around her. She seldom opened her lips,
but sometimes she smiled and looked so
happy, and so peaceful, that the landlady

of the inn could not help sitting down and
crying; at which times Mrs Grey would
also exhibit sympathetic symptoms, but she
managed to cough her tears away, as she
went about the room preparing some cool-
ing drink, or administering the invalid's
medicine.

Sometimes Bessie's happy smile would
change to one of intense sadness, and then
the tears would start into her eyes. Once
she frowned and evinced signs of great
indignation, and clenched her hand—the
hand in which she had clutched the cruel
letter.

She was insensible for many days, and
then she gradually recovered.

When she was well enough to recognize
Mrs Grey, she evinced great repugnance
towards her, and cried out, " Take her
away, take her away." This brought the
tears into Mrs Grey's eyes; but nothing
could reconcile Bessie to Richard's mother. She clung to the landlady of the
house, who bathed her cheeks and soothed

her; and Mrs Grey used all sorts of
womanly wiles to overcome Bessie's dislike; but the unhappy girl never gave way
for a moment.

"Go, go, go away; I hate you, and all
your house," she said at last, raising her
feeble arm, and making her malediction
sadly solemn and touching—"I hate you
all."

Mrs Grey took the advice of her son
Frank, who suggested various schemes for
Bessie's benefit; but as Bessie grew
stronger, she was more resolute in her determination to have nothing to do with
Mrs Grey. Frank sent a sum of money to
the landlady, with strict injunctions that
she should take care of Bessie, and with a
view to obtaining a situation for her.

When the invalid was well enough to
walk about the room, the kind-hearted
woman made many overtures to her, concerning the Greys; but Bessie scorned
them all, and said the very name was hate-
ful to her.

Then she would not go to America now? the landlady asked.

"No, not now," said Bessie, "not now."

"What will you do then, my poor child?" asked the woman of the inn.

"Do! I don't know, I don't care," said Bessie, gazing out through the window at the shipping.

"Don't care is a bad master," said the landlady.

"Is it?" Bessie asked, with a vague smile.

"A shocking bad master, my love— it has been the ruin of thousands."

"What has 'I do care' then done?— What has 'I love' done,—have they ruined thousands?"

"Oh, you ask such strange questions. I never saw any one put themselves in such a state of mind as you," said the landlady coaxingly. "You mustn't give way so, you must cheer up."

Bessie nodded her head, and swayed

herself to and fro, as she watched the steamers in the great basin.

"I say you must have better heart in your troubles, my dear," said the woman, putting her arm round Bessie's waist.

"Yes," said Bessie, as if answering her own question. "I am very much altered, am I not?"

"No; I don't think so, my love."

"O, yes, I am—very, very much—it seems as if there was no Bessie Martin; no Richard Grey; no Helswick; no Mayflowers; no sunshine," she said sorrowfully, adding in a careless tone—"never mind, I don't care,—it will be all as one some day."

Bessie Martin was indeed changed. The soft expression of her eye was gone, and in its place there was a quick, restless, flashing, dangerous beauty. The roundness of her features was gone; but there was a delicate sharpness left, that showed off, to advantage, her well-shaped nose, her arched brows, and the graceful line of her upper lip.

There was a little shade of pink mingling with the darkly pale hues of her cheek, and her hair hung about her temples, in heavy raven folds. There was a carelessness in all she said concerning her future, an utter abandonment of all plan or purpose, which troubled the woman of the inn, and cost her some sleepless nights. So much indeed did she trouble about Bessie that her husband had sworn the girl should stay no longer under his roof. Sympathy, and all that, was very well in its way; but the house had been upset quite enough, and he would not be humbugged any longer. He couldn't afford to have his wife's health broken down, and he wouldn't.

Luckily, Bessie did not hear the landlord's vows, and the landlady said nothing about them, and thought nothing of them, knowing that as soon as her husband's passion was over, his words were always considered null and void. But by and by Bessie said she was well enough to leave, and should go.

"Go, where? where shall you go?" asked the woman of the inn.

"It doesn't matter where I go. Who cares where I go?"

"I care, my poor child," said the woman.

"Yes, thank you, very much, very much," said Bessie, kissing the landlady's fat round hand; "you have been very kind to me, I shall never forget it; but it is not fit that I should stay here, remembering what I am. No, I must go, and you will not be unhappy soon; you have only known me a few weeks. I knew him (and her face darkened) when I was a child; he told me only last May that he loved me better than all the world, and now you see what I am."

"Do not take it so to heart; you are both young yet,—he may atone," said the woman.

"No, it's all over—I am not the Bessie Martin I used to be—I am a different being altogether; it is no good any one talking to me; I shall go my own way; where I go, or what I do, is a matter of utter indifference to me;" and the bright eyes flashed and the lips were closed, and she swung her arm defiantly.

She was not the Bessie Martin of old, most truly. The change was indeed complete; it was a change of appearance, of feeling, of nature; and often the vacant look, which had indicated the vacant mind for many days, in the sick chamber, would come back to the dark face, and then the woman of the house could get nothing from her, but a vacant, empty laugh, or a few tears.

One afternoon Bessie slipped out unknown to any one; but returned in the evening. A few days afterwards she disappeared at night, and did not return. The landlady of the Maryport Arms set men to search for her. Frank Grey secured the services of a detective officer; but all search proved fruitless. She had left behind her Richard's letter, and the bill for three pounds, torn to shreds and scattered about her bed-room; and on a slip of paper lying beside a plain gold ring (on which was engraven, " Bessie ") was written: " Mrs Robinson, Maryport Arms; wear this for my sake. God bless and reward you ! "

CHAPTER VI.

SUMMERDALE.

SUMMERDALE was a fair inland village, a hundred miles from the sea. It was a moss-grown, slumbering, picturesque place, which had stood aside and let the great world pass by it. Even the swallows, which came there every year, had partaken somewhat of the local indolence, and did not trouble to rebuild the nests, which they occupied family after family.

The houses were built in an irregular square, with stragglers running off, into a couple of dreamy streets, at right angles.

In the centre of the square stood a pair of tall elms, between which reposed the village stocks, that were still used for the one or two drunkards who occasionally

made themselves too obnoxious for toler-
ation.

Outside the square was the village
church and parsonage, both gray with
years and green with ivy.

On the border of the churchyard lay a
long strip of river, just near enough for
the church to image itself in the water,
making the river look deep and mysterious.
A clump of water lilies slumbered on the
limpid blue, and nodded to each other,
whenever the wind moved them.

Besides the church and parsonage, Summerdale had several other public buildings
—a police station (two rooms in the parish
constable's house), a dissenting chapel, and
a school-house. Like the cottages, these
were thatched, and aged, and warm. The
outer beams were shown in the outer
plaster, and there were ledges over the
door-ways, and flowers everywhere.

They were mostly an old race of people
at Summerdale, gray and moss-grown like
their houses. On summer evenings they

stood in their doorways, or sat outside the ale-house on forms placed beneath the bow windows. The children were happy contrasts to the old people—bright, and fresh, and sweet, like the roses and clematis and woodbine that bloomed over door-ways, and beneath windows.

Paul Massey had found out this place through the works of an artist, who had wandered thither, and made sketches, to the infinite wonder of the villagers. The limner had painted the river with the church-shadow in it, and the water-lilies; he had drawn the twin elms, with the worm-eaten stocks beneath them, and a group, such as Goldsmith has described in " Lovely Auburn," dancing on the green; he had indicated the church porch, and the parsonage in the trees, with the sun setting upon them; he had done a vignette in the churchyard, with some lines from Grey's Elegy written beneath, to add greater force of beautiful sadness to the picture; he had painted a peaceful moonlight scene at the

outskirts of the village, showing the quiet
old houses nestling together; and he had
done another view, on a calm summer
night, with the blue smoke ascending from
the old stunted chimneys.

On a little holiday tour, Paul had
brought his wife and daughter to this quiet
happy place, and after certain necessary
negociations, had taken an old house that
had been empty for several years: it had
not been unoccupied sufficiently long to
earn for itself the character of being haunted; but the children had begun to look
suspiciously upon it, and had thrown
sundry stones through the windows.

A good old family had died out in the
good old house, and as it was one of the
most important residences in Summerdale,
the villagers were glad to see it once more
occupied. It was a house of the Eliza-
bethan period, chiefly built of oak, and such
as you will see in many parts of Worcester-
shire and Warwickshire. All the windows
projected, and were filled with small

squares of glass. The front door was pon-
derous and heavy, and opened into a large
square hall, from which the ground-floor
rooms branched off on either hand. The roof
rose in three separate pointed angles, with
a pigeon-cote in the centre one. There
was a pleasant garden in front, and an
orchard behind, with crooked apple-trees
in it that bore big red gnarled-looking
fruit.

Mrs Massey liked the house much, and
when Paul had left Denby Rise, they came
to Summerdale, and settled down, in peace.
The white-haired vicar had visited them;
and the principal residents in the village
square had waited upon them, as a deput-
ation from the rest, welcoming them to
Summerdale, and wishing them long life
and happiness. The four bells in the
church tower had been rung in their
honour, and Mrs Massey was delighted
with the kind attentions that were paid
to her.

The little excitement which their arrival

had occasioned, however, soon subsided, and Summerdale once more assumed its old quiet. The villagers had ceased to stare at Kate Massey in church, and to wonder at the cost of her beautiful dress with its ermine trimming, and its sash with the golden buckle.

When they were ill, the old women soon grew into the habit of looking for Mrs Massey's visits; and the old men accustomed themselves to count on Paul's good advice and practical help, in cases of need. The rector said the Masseys had relieved him of half of his parochial duties, and the village schoolmaster almost daily acknowledged Paul's valuable assistance.

Mrs Massey was happy in this sunny Summerdale, and Paul tried to be so. They read together the books in which Uncle Mountford had delighted. They pursued together the same studies. In twelve months there was scarcely a flower, or fern, or moss, or leaf around Summer-

dale with which they had not made themselves acquainted. Then there was Anna's
harp, and her favourite piano, which made
such music in Summerdale as had never
been heard there before. Paul Massey cultivated and produced flowers that astonished and delighted everybody. Little Kate
Massey scoured the fields on a Welsh
pony, and was the heroine of all the boys
and girls in Summerdale; she was their
princess, their constant wonder. She had
a pair of merry grey eyes, and long auburn
curls. Her laugh was soul-stirring, so
fresh was it and so musical; and her
mother was never tired of her girlish
prattle.

Everybody has his own ideas of happiness; but there are not a few who will ac-
knowledge, that to be comparatively " well
off" in such a place as Summerdale, is a
high type of happiness. To possess a cultivated intellect, and the means of using it
peacefully, in a quiet retired inland village,
where you may ramble amongst flowers in

the day-time, and spend your evenings with
Shakespeare, and Spenser, and Homer, and
Goethe, and Moliere, and Scott, and
Tennyson, and Thackeray, and Charles
Dickens, in company with a wife who can
enter into your thoughts and share your
happiness; to make yourself valuable to
the small community, and be their mentor,
their succour in time of need; to know
that you are mentioned in the prayers of
all those about you; and to be enabled,
two or three times in a year, to go off into
the bustle, and whirl, and hurry, and bad
breath of some big city, in order that you
may come home again to appreciate your
perfect peace there all the more.

Is not this happiness? To one who
has seen the world, most surely. To a
well-regulated mind, most certainly. To
be the wife, ministering to all these joys,
and playing the second part to her husband
faithfully and fondly, was happiness indeed
to Mrs Massey. But the sad shadow,
which Paul could not always conceal from

her, would have its influence upon her, and
set her wondering if Paul were really
happy; and if he were not, whether she
did all that a wife and mother could do.
For Paul was not happy. Paul never
would be happy again. He was resigned,
he was penitent; he had learnt to pray too,
but not for himself—for her, for them, for
that affectionate wife and that dear child.
What a change love and a disturbed conscience had wrought in that Paul Massey of
old—that Paul Massey, the chivalrous, the
merry!

Sometimes Paul felt that he would be
happier in a large town—in London, for instance, where people can lose themselves
amongst great crowds. But he could live
cheaper at Summerdale, and that was a
consideration now; for Winford Barns
had very seriously diminished the noble
fortune of which Paul was master, when
Miss Lee's patrimony had mingled with his
own.

"We have never heard anything of poor Joe Wittle," said Mrs Massey, sitting over some wool work, one evening, whilst Paul was smoking a cigar at the open window.

"No," said Paul, "and I rather miss the fellow too."

"I believe he was thoroughly devoted to us. Kate, would you not like to see Joe?"

"I should, Ma, very much," said Kate, a girl of about twelve years, who was sitting beside her father.

Paul patted her head, and smiled.

"It was rather strange his insisting upon leaving us; we might have kept Joe. Poor fellow, I suppose he thought he might be a burthen to us. 'No, sir,' he said, when I pressed him, 'you may see me again; but at present, I shall rather leave, more particularly as Harkaway is to go with the rest.'"

"Poor Harkaway! But we must not

regret, Paul. Who can regret in this beautiful place?"

Anna could not smother a little sigh for Helswick, notwithstanding.

"Joe Wittle said he would bring me something from foreign parts, Pa, when he bade me good-bye," said Kate.

"Did he, my love? then he will, some day, you may depend," said Paul, leaning a little forward to wave his hand to some one who had entered the garden.

"Who is it, my dear?" asked Mrs Massey.

"Only Anthony Evans," said Paul, and as he said so, a masculine, weather-beaten man came up to the window.

"Good evening, Anthony," said Paul.

"Good evening, sir, a beautiful evening," said Anthony; "how's the good lady, sir?"

"Very well, thank you," said Paul; "but come in, and she shall answer for herself."

Anthony went in accordingly.. He was a man of about five and forty, well-dressed, but evidently one who had sprung from the working order. He had an intelligent, open countenance, that was tanned with toil and travel. He wore a thick cloth coat, and brown waistcoat and trowsers, and looked what he really was—a man, who had emigrated to the colonies as a mechanic, and had made money. He had been away from England more than twenty years, and had returned, he said, more out of curiosity than anything else, having no ties in his own country, and but few pleasant remembrances of it.

"And what really brought you to this out-of-the-way place?" asked Mrs Massey, after Anthony Evans had sat down, and put his hat under the chair.

"Well, you see, I came home with a man who belonged to these parts, and we had to pass through this village, ma'am."

"Yes," said Mrs Massey, noticing some little hesitation in Anthony's manner.

"It was a fortnight after your arrival here," said Anthony, hesitating again.

"Yes," said Mrs Massey.

"Really, my dear, are you not too inquisitive?" said Paul, smiling affectionately upon his wife.

"Mr Evans will tell me if I am; will you not?"

"Oh, it's not at all inquisitive," said Anthony. "To tell you the truth, Mrs Massey, I have often wished to talk to you about this."

"I am so glad to hear you say so," said Mrs Massey, laying down her wool work.

"You see we stopped at the 'Crown'— the ale-house, you know, in the village,— the man and me,—and they were talking of you and Mr Massey there."

Paul suddenly became very much interested in the conversation.

"Yes," said Mrs Massey, nodding pleasantly.

"They were saying how good you

seemed to be, and what a capital thing it was for the village that the old house was let. Somebody asked where you were coming from, and the parish constable said from a place called Helswick."

Paul felt afraid of the conversation; he had no reason to be afraid, but his conscience troubled him at the strangest times.

"And, you see, I once knew Helswick," Anthony went on, stammering a little, and fidgeting with his foot.

"Oh, I am so glad," said Mrs Massey; "but," suddenly changing her tone, "you would know it before I did."

"Yes, ma'am," said Anthony, "a good many years ago;" and there was something very sad in the way in which he said "a good many years ago," as though there were dear memories and associations attached to those years that were gone.

Paul Massey breathed again freely, and relighted his cigar.

"Did you know Denby Rise?" Mrs

Massey asked, "the house in the valley beyond Helswick."

"Know it, ma'am," said Anthony, with ill-disguised emotion, "I put every window sash into it."

Then Anthony, pausing suddenly, as if he had said more than he intended, turned the conversation to Helswick again.

"A nice pleasant town Helswick," he said.

"Yes; but, dear me, how strange that you should have helped to build—I suppose that is what you mean, Mr Anthony? —that you should have helped to build Denby Rise."

Anthony made no reply.

"Why, I thought Denby Rise was much older than that," said Paul Massey, for the mere purpose of saying something.

"No," said Anthony.

"Then you must be much older than you look," said Paul.

"I am, oh yes, no doubt," said Anthony, as though the fact of his being older

than he looked was a great relief, and a
subject for particular congratulation.

"You have worn well, Mr Evans; I
hope I may wear as well," said Paul.

"And you know Helswick well, of
course?" said Mrs Massey, leading the conversation back again.

"Every corner of it," said Anthony.

"The fall, over the rocks?"

"I've played in several cricket matches
there, Mrs Massey."

"The valley above Denby Rise?"

"Oh, yes; I have walked hundreds of
times by the brook there, when— "

Anthony paused, and hesitated. Again
he had been going to say more than, upon
consideration, he thought judicious; which
did not escape Mrs Massey's notice.

"Yes—when?" she said, endeavouring
to lead him on; and with a little show of
inquisitiveness, Paul Massey thought.

"When I was working at Denby Rise,"
Anthony replied; but that was not what
he had originally intended to say.

"You know the caverns, of course?" said Mrs Massey, interrogatively.

"All of them," said Mr Evans, "and I've heard the sea beating into them, and heard the gurgle of that brook thousands of miles away: I shall never forget a sight or a sound belonging to Helswick."

Then there was a short pause, which was again broken by Mrs Massey.

"If I seem inquisitive, Mr Evans, you must really forgive me; but you have awakened my interest, and I thought you were going to tell us why you selected Summerdale for a residence during your stay in England," said Anna.

"Didn't I tell you, ma'am? Oh, no, not exactly. Well, you see I had nowhere to go in particular, and when I heard you were from Helswick, it sounded a little bit home-like, and I thought I'd stop here, and perhaps I might get to know Mr Massey, and we might talk about Helswick."

"And how did we make each other's acquaintance?" Mr Massey asked.

" Well, you see I thought I'd just pass the time of day."

" Oh yes, I remember," said Paul.

" And we got talking, and I told you about my travels, and you were good enough to invite me here," said Mr Evans.

" And right glad I am to see you," said Paul, " or any one else who makes Summerdale his home."

Then the conversation became general as to the beauties of Helswick, and the coast. Anthony Evans was enthusiastic in his references to the caverns, and the fells, and the old ruins. But he sighed now and then, and it was evident that talking of Helswick was as painful to him as it was pleasant.

" Then you have not seen your native place since your return ? " said Mrs Massey inquiringly.

" Yes, it was my native place," said Anthony Evans, as if rather in response to his own thoughts than in reply to Mrs

Massey. "I was born in a little cottage not far from the church, ma'am; but I was apprenticed in Maryport."

"And you have not seen Helswick since you came back to England?" said Paul, repeating his wife's inquiry.

"No—I would rather talk of it than see it," Anthony replied; "I don't think I could bear to see it."

Mrs Massey, noticing that there was a hidden sorrow which was being touched, now endeavoured to divert Mr Evans' thoughts from Helswick, and to her relief tea was brought in, as was customary at eight o'clock. But Anthony Evans would not accept her invitation to partake of it; he said he would much rather be excused that evening; he should take a walk in the fields, and return to his lodgings.

"Look in again, then," said Mr Massey, "whenever you feel inclined."

"Thank you, I am much obliged," said Anthony, taking up his hat, and striding forth into the hall and out into the garden.

Mrs Massey watched his retreating form, and said: "I pity that man, Paul; I am sure he is troubled with the memory of some great grief: he is what the world would call a rough, ordinary mortal, I suppose, Paul, without much feeling too."

"The world, love, is a very bad judge of people," said Paul.

"How happy are we," said Anna, "who care nothing for the world and its judgment."

"You are happy, Anna; are you not?"

"Very, very happy," Anna replied.

"And Katy, what says Katy? Why, she has gone to sleep."

"And it is sufficient to look upon her face to see how happy *she* is," said Anna.

And thus they chatted on, whilst the tea urn hissed upon the table, and the lamp-light glimmered on the oak wainscoting, on

the old-fashioned fire-place (where no fire
was needed on this summer evening), on
the tall bronzes above the mantel-shelf, on
the favourite harp, on the water-colour
drawings and oil paintings, and on the
happy face of the child asleep.

CHAPTER VII.

THE STRANGER.

ANTHONY EVANS became a frequent visitor at Oak House, and was always heartily welcomed there. His intimacy with the Masseys had increased his importance in Summerdale, and his plain unassuming ways, coupled with his pecuniary liberality, soon made him a general favourite.

But Summerdale wondered greatly at Anthony Evans. Summerdale leaned over its half-doorways and watched him to and fro. Summerdale received his nods and kindly-sad salutations with becoming deference. Summerdale smoked its pipe, and shook its head, and said Master Evans had seen the world; had been in foreign lands, where there were savages and kangaroos, and whales, and gold, and all sorts of things.

The old rector would talk to Anthony at street corners, about distant countries; and his Reverence had even been known to sit down in the Crown bar, and listen to the same stories which Anthony had related in the smoke-room. But he was a sorrow-ful man was Anthony; even the villagers could see that.

Mrs Massey often thought that poor Anthony had a secret grief of which it would be happiness for him to unburthen himself; and, as if a fellow-feeling had strengthened the friendship which Paul felt towards this man, Paul would some-times become quite sorrow-stricken over the imaginary griefs which Anna conjured up as Anthony's afflictions.

" I shall go and take a peep at Hels-wick one of these days," said Anthony, in a conversation which had sprung up be-tween Mrs Massey and himself and Paul,

on a casual afternoon meeting in the meadows outside Summerdale.

"It will look beautiful on such a day
as this," said Mrs Massey, watching Katy
gathering flowers which had been cut down
amongst the newly mown grass.

"It was always beautiful when I knew
it," said Anthony, his rough weather-
beaten face lighting up with the memory
of other days.

"The sea is not so clear and green
anywhere as it is off Denby," said Anna;
"you may see the gravel at the bottom in
some of the deepest spots." Then suddenly
turning to Paul, who had been unwell for
many days, Anna said: "You are ill, Paul;
how pale you are!"

"No, no," said Paul, smiling a sickly
fictitious smile, "the scent of the hay and
the flowers we have gathered seems unusually oppressive; all right, love, I am
better now."

"You must really have advice, dear,"
said Anna anxiously; "you have never been

thoroughly yourself, Paul, since you had that dreadful attack at Denby, years ago."

"Never mind me, Mr Evans," said Paul, taking his wife's arm and putting it through his own. "You were talking of Helswick?"

"Yes, I was saying that I should just take a peep, and then go back to Australia."

"Indeed!" exclaimed Paul, "I had hoped we should have you as a permanent resident at Summerdale; we shall miss you when you are gone,—I can hardly say how much."

"That we shall," said Mrs Massey.

"You are very kind to say so," said Anthony, and they went wandering on by the river.

In the evening Mrs Massey, who had thought a great deal about Anthony, and had, in a vague speculative manner, mixed him up with Mrs Grey's story, said: "Paul, I believe I know more about Mr Evans than he imagines."

"Indeed!" said Paul. "In what way?"

"You know how curious I have been about his early life at Helswick?"

"Yes, my love."

"How often I have troubled you with my fancies about it?"

"It is never a trouble to hear of your thoughts, Anna," said Paul.

"But I know I have said so much about the poor man," said Anna, "I pity him so much."

"It is a bitter thing to suffer from a secret grief," said Paul, feeling deeply the truth of his assertion.

Anna set down the earnestness with which Paul said this, to her husband's kind sympathy with Anthony Evans.

"You remember Mrs Grey at Helswick, Paul?"

"Grey?" said Paul doubtfully.

"Uncle's housekeeper, who was your nurse, after that dreadful shipwreck."

"Yes, yes; how ungrateful to forget her for a moment," said Paul.

"You have heard her story—I think I told it to you."

"Something about her husband leaving her shortly after their marriage?"

"Yes," said Anna, "and I believe this Anthony Evans to be her husband."

"Indeed!" said Paul, becoming interested, and forgetting for the moment his own secret sorrow.

"Yes; I am almost sure he is."

"And wherefore? His name is Evans."

"It is assumed. Her husband was a carpenter. Do you not remember how he started when he inadvertently told us that he put the window-sashes into Denby Rise?"

"But he is not the kind of man who would desert a woman," said Paul.

"I should say he is one who would have been an affectionate and good husband," said Anna. "There must have been some foul play; some cruel slander. The poor woman never knew why he left her; but she said he would return, and I

am sure she loved him with all her heart.
He was led to believe some wicked libel
upon her. The fact that he left behind
him, as I remember she told me, all the
money he had, showed that the man was
not naturally unkind. It must be he,
Paul—I am almost sure of it."

"And suppose it is?" said Paul.

"We must be sure before we act,
love."

"And when we are sure?"

"Mrs Grey must be communicated
with."

"Where is Mrs Grey? Still in Maryport?"

"Yes, with her two sons—the eldest I
am told a very fine fellow in every respect.
Poor Harry Thornhill introduced him into
his business house."

Paul winced at the well-known name,
and remained silent.

"I must talk to him about Mrs Grey,
Paul. What do you think?"

"I will not advise you," said Paul;

"whatever your heart dictates will be right."

A week had not elapsed ere Mrs Massey, after repeated attempts, succeeded in bringing Mr Evans to talk more of Helswick, and Helswick people.

Paul, who had been unwell during the day, was walking in the garden, smoking, and answering the curious questions of his daughter, who was growing more and more like her mamma.

Anthony Evans was in the dining-room talking to Mrs Massey.

"And when do you think of going to Helswick?" said Mrs Massey.

"I have not decided," said Anthony mournfully; "I sometimes think I will not go at all."

Anna was almost timidly anxious not to hurt their visitor's feelings; but she was fully bent upon satisfying herself as to his relationship to Mrs Grey, feeling assured, in her own mind, that a mutual explanation would settle the long estrangement.

"Did you know—" began Anna, her heart beating quickly, "did you know a person named Grey, at Helswick?"

Anthony's dark face flushed, and he hesitated.

"Sarah Grey?" said Anna, looking earnestly at him.

"Yes," said Anthony faintly, "I did."

Anna was sure that that "yes" came from George Grey.

"She was such a good woman," Mrs Massey went on—"such a kind soul."

Anthony moved nervously in his chair.

"I knew her for many years. There was a sad story connected with her early life."

Anthony trembled, and said nothing.

"Through some unexplained cause—through some base calumny, no doubt—her husband deserted her. Poor thing! it was a dreadful grief to her; and yet, like a woman, she went on loving him and praying that he would come back."

"She was false to him!—False!" exclaimed Anthony.

"Then you knew her," said Anna, quickly.

"Pardon me, madam—it is a painful subject," said Anthony, calmer for his passionate exclamation.

"I am sure she was a true good woman; I dare be sworn she was," said Anna, not heeding Anthony's agitation. "I saw her every day for years; a more conscientious kind creature did not exist; nor a more affectionate mother."

"Mrs Massey, Mrs Massey, pray say no more—your words are like daggers," said Anthony with quivering lips.

"Then you are not Anthony Evans," said Anna, rising, "but—"

"George Grey," said the wretched man, covering his face with his hands.

"Oh, dear, dear," exclaimed Kate, running into the room, "Pa is so ill."

Mrs Massey was in the garden in a

moment. She found her husband, pale and speechless, leaning against a tree.

"Paul! Paul!" she exclaimed in agony, taking him by the arm.

But there was no response. In another moment, however, Paul's lips moved, and he attempted to walk.

"Paul, my husband!" exclaimed Anna.

"Don't be alarmed," said Paul with difficulty, "I shall be better presently."

"Heaven send he may!" said Anna, fervently.

"Dear papa," murmured Kate, taking his other hand and kissing it.

"Let us go into the house," said Paul faintly, and he walked, with tottering steps, between his wife and daughter.

Anthony Evans, or George Grey, as we had better now call him, only partially recovered from his sudden surprise and emotion, met them at the door, and assist-ed Mr Massey to a chair.

By and by, Paul recovered, and was quite himself again, with the exception of

being a shade paler. He did not know
what had seized him; how he came to be
so suddenly ill: it happened in a moment.

"I am all right again," he said, after
a time, in answer to his visitor. "No,
thank you, I will not trouble the doctor—
there is no need."

"Can I do anything for you, anything
at all?" said the newly discovered Grey.

"No, thank you," said Paul.

"Or for you, Mrs Massey?" he asked,
in a subdued tone.

"No, thank you," said Anna, "you
must hear what I have to say another
day."

"I will," said the man. "Good night,
ma'am; good night, sir;" said Mr Grey;
"and good night, Miss Kate—take care of
papa."

It was a beautiful July evening. The
moon was just rising over the quiet
thatched town. The chestnut trees and
the limes on the outskirts of the moss-

grown old place, were in full flower; and the scent of the new blossoms mingled with the odour of garden flowers. It was only nine o'clock, and yet the people were nearly all a-bed.

George Grey wandered down the quiet streets, and thought of the events of the night, and of days long, long ago. He had loved his wife fervently; but, like many another husband, not sufficiently to believe in her above everybody else, and to defy calumny and scandal.

A doubt of the truth of her shame had never occurred to him until this night. For a moment it had wrung his heart; but only for a moment. He set down the good religious life, which Mrs Massey had described, to penitence and remorse. But he could not help feeling as he passed along the quiet streets, what a terrible loss was his; what a broken, wretched life. Money he had in abundance. What was money to him? One of those poor thatched cottages with a true, kind wife, and with children to love, would, to George, have been greater happiness than anything in the world. Like the best of his order, he yearned for the domestic sweets of the English hearth; but better solitude, better misery, better death, than a home with the blight of dishonour upon it.

CHAPTER VIII.

A PAINFUL DISCOVERY.

THEY had gathered in the hay around
Summerdale; the hops, far away beyond
the church, had been pruned; the bream
and the tench had spawned in the river,
the grayling had made havoc amongst the
flies; and the old town of Summerdale
slumbered on. So slowly and yet so swiftly
did time pass away, that the ripening of the
corn followed, and the gathering in of the
crops, and the browning of the leaves, and
the falling of the apples, ere it was hardly
remembered that the hay was stacked. In
truth the seasons came and went so silently
and so gradually that Summerdale hardly
noticed the transitions.

Paul Massey's health had not improved.

Indeed his condition had caused Mrs Massey so much uneasiness, that she had induced Paul to go to London and obtain advice. She had accompanied him thither, in the early part of the autumn; and all that the great man whom Paul consulted had said to Mrs Massey, after his private interview with Paul, was that her husband must not be over-anxious about anything, must not study too much, or work too hard: it would be good for him to travel.

This was inexplicable to Mrs Massey, but Paul said it was the custom of the profession to exaggerate the ailments of their patients.

"I sometimes think you conceal some great trouble from me," Anna said afterwards.

"No, no, Anna, do not think so."

"Then why should you be cautioned so seriously about being over-anxious, and not taxing yourself too much with study? Why, Paul dear, should the doctor speak as though you were wearing yourself out in some arduous business which afflicts both mind and body ?"

It was very unusual for Anna to question Paul so directly, but this time she would not be put off by mere evasion.

"It is nothing, Anna," Paul said, "nothing."

" Paul, dear Paul, I know you would only deceive me through your great love for me ; but the husband should make the wife a full sharer in his sorrows as well as his joys. The woman is deprived of half her mission, of the best part of her wifely duties, if the husband do not avail himself of her sympathy and assistance in the hour of trouble."

" Do you think the husband who compels his wife to share in all his anxieties and cares, and in all the petty annoyances to which he is subject, a really affectionate husband ?"

" If he lets the wife into a share of his happiness, I do."

" *I* do not," said Paul, decidedly.

"Then there is something which you conceal from me," said Anna, a little reproachfully.

"No, Anna, you are mistaken. I have said so before," Paul replied. "Let us change the subject; I shall soon be better."

This was not the first falsehood that Paul had felt himself compelled to utter, to hedge in that secret which, at times, almost threatened to break its prison, and proclaim itself to all the world.

On their return to Summerdale, almost the first question, after Kate had been kissed, was concerning Mr Evans. Anna's account of her interview with that gentleman had greatly interested her husband.

Kate said Mr Evans had not called during the three days they had been in London; and she had learnt from the gardener that he had left Summerdale.

Both Paul and his wife very much regretted this.

Anna said Mr Evans would be sure to return; and she was right.

In the course of a fortnight he came back again. The trees were stripped of nearly all their leaves; and a bright fire was leaping up the big dining-room chimney of Oak House. Paul was playing chess with his wife, and Kate, with her long brown hair hanging about her white shoulders, was looking on.

A knock at the door startled them; but they were all glad to receive Mr Evans, for he was a pleasant companion, and his history, as you know, was deeply interesting to the Masseys.

"We are very glad to see you again," said Anna.

"Welcome back to Summerdale, mister truant," said Paul, heartily.

"Did you think I should not return?" George asked.

"Oh, no," was Anna's quick reply.

Mr Grey sat down; the chessmen were put aside; wine and spirits were brought forth; and a pleasant chat commenced. The truant soon told them that he had been to Helswick, and that he did not find it much altered.

When Kate had gathered up her wealth of hair, and gone to bed, Mr Grey said to Paul he supposed Mrs Massey had told him about her discovery. Paul confessed that she had, and said how greatly it had surprised him.

To talk about Helswick seemed now a greater relief than ever to George Grey. He told them of every well-known spot, and of the few changes which had taken place. He had heard of his sons, he said, and of his wife, though nobody knew him again. It was a bitter lot his, he said; but it was some comfort to know that those whom he left behind him had prospered—that they had not known want. The thought that they might have done so had cost him many a weary, sleepless night, when he was far away. He was glad she had not suffered, in a worldly sense; a bad conscience was a sufficient punishment to any guilty soul.

How everybody and everything told Paul of his terrible crime! It seemed as if nothing could take place, as if a dozen words could not be spoken, without his guilt being alluded to, in covert bitterness.

Mrs Massey said she was glad Mr Grey had come home in a more settled state of mind.

"Yes," he said, "I shall go back a happier man,"

"Go back, where?" said Anna.

"To Melbourne."

"And when?"

"In the spring."

"But suppose you were to discover that your wife was not guilty," said Anna.

"Ah, it is useless to attempt to buoy me up with false hopes. The proofs were too strong. No, Mrs Massey, I am better contented now. She is living in comfort, and with her sons."

Anna made a memorandum in her mind to make a trip to Maryport; but increased anxieties concerning her husband postponed the intended journey.

Whilst they were talking so cosily round the blazing fire, the wind rose, and blew gustily about the old house, and Paul thought of the sea, as he always did when the wind was high. It blew the elms about in the Summerdale Square, and the old stocks creaked and groaned, as George Grey passed them, on his way home.

The wind blew loudly elsewhere, and at Maryport, amongst other places—screaming amongst the shipping, and shaking the houses.

Indeed, the same wind which troubled Paul Massey, and which rumbled in the chimney of the low, old-fashioned room in which George Grey was fast asleep and dreaming of Helswick, shook the window of the little dining-room, at Purdown, where Frank Grey and his mother were quietly chatting, before retiring to bed.

Mrs Grey had become more affectionate in her manner towards Frank since the night—long ago now—when she had come home, in tears, from that painful interview with poor Bessie Martin, and of late had said much less about her son Richard than formerly, whatever she might have thought.

"I believe I saw that poor girl the other evening, mother," said Frank, with his feet upon the fender.

"Bessie?" asked Mrs Grey, with a sigh.

"Yes; but I may be mistaken—I hope I am. There was rather a noisy upper-box, full of men and women, at the theatre, last night—it was the Mayor's bespeak, as you know—and in the front of the box was a girl that I could not help thinking must be Bessie Martin."

"Poor thing!" said Mrs Grey, looking into the fire, and waiting for Frank to proceed with his story.

"Her hair was very black, her eye bright and large; in fact, every feature corresponded with your description, and there was a vague look of indifference, every now and then, which almost convinced me that I was right in my conjecture. Poor soul, I could hardly follow the play for looking at her, and I was rallied about it by a friend who was with me. He little knew my thoughts, mother. How often people are deceived when they think they are amazingly clever."

Mrs Grey sighed, and looked mournfully up at her son. "Poor Bessie!" she said, "I have wished sometimes that she is dead; but I fear, I fear something worse than death."

"I can hear no tidings of Dick," said Frank, after a short pause, "but I daresay he is all right; he would not have given up his situation, you may depend upon that, mother, unless he had something better to go to; you mustn't trouble about him," Frank continued, cautiously, and like one feeling his way.

"Trouble, Frank! I cannot help it; I have learnt to disguise my feelings of late years, and to check my tongue, but my heart is unchanged, and therefore I cannot help its yearning after your brother. Ah, you don't know what it is to be a mother!"

"No," said Frank, and he could not resist a smile, though he went up to his mother and kissed her forehead, "I do not; but I know what it is to love a mother."

"My dear boy, you have been very kind to me, and I have often behaved ungratefully," said Mrs Grey, the remembrance of some peevish fits occurring to her. "But you must admit, Frank, that you were a little to blame in your treatment of Richard; you did not think enough about his earlier years, and the thoughts and ideas which he had imbibed from Mat Dunkum."

"Don't hesitate, mother—relieve your mind," said Frank, kindly, when his mother paused and looked doubtfully into his eyes.

"If he were never to write to me again, Frank, if I knew that he hated me, I could forgive him; because I know that his mind has been perverted—the same as the mind of another, who left me when you were children."

It was useless for Frank to discuss this question with his mother, and he never did. Had he attempted to do so, Mrs Grey would have worked herself up into a denunciation of everybody, including even poor Bessie Martin, as betrayers of her poor son's innocence.

"Well, now I shall say good-night, mother," said Frank, putting his arm around her.

"That's what you always say when we talk upon this subject; but I do not blame you, my dear boy—good—"

She did not finish the sentence, but exclaimed, "What was that?"

"What, mother?" said Frank, listening.

"That noise."

"Oh, the wind; why, mother, you are getting nervous."

"There have been two burglaries in this parish, Frank," said Mrs Grey, "and this very week."

"It does not follow that there is to be a third here, mother," said Frank.

Two hours afterwards Mrs Grey rose from her bed, and drew up her blind. The wind was still boisterous, and two of the adjacent gas lamps were extinguished.

During a momentary lull she thought she heard footsteps in the garden. Then there was a sound below-stairs, as if a bolt was being removed; then a window was opened.

"How nervous I am, to be sure," she said, "it is but the wind."

But Mrs Grey could not sleep. There was certainly a noise in the kitchen. She went up to Frank's room, but Frank was fast asleep, and she did not like to awaken him.

She was no coward, and she determined to go cautiously, by the back way, into the kitchen. Listening at every step, and creeping on in the dark, Mrs Grey at length reached the bottom of the stairs.

A gleam of light flashed out from the kitchen, and then disappeared. A hurried remark was made in a whisper by some person to another, and then came a second flash of light. Mrs Grey was almost petrified with alarm, notwithstanding her courage.

The light came towards her. She stepped aside, concealed by the door, which was pushed open, and two men passed by her. The light shone upon the foremost one, for a moment, and Mrs Grey had nearly screamed aloud.

They ascended the stairs, cautiously, and entered the dining-room. She could hear them overhead; but she did not move. Had they gone further she would have followed, fearing that injury might befall Frank, whom, for reasons best known to herself, she prayed would continue to sleep.

The minutes were like hours. The quarter of an hour during which the burglars occupied themselves in the rooms above, was like an age to Mrs Grey, as she stood concealed at the foot of the kitchen stairs.

At length footsteps, silent, cautious steps, were heard upon the stairs; the light from the dark lantern flashed again in the kitchen; and in a few minutes more the men were gone.

Mrs Grey came out silently from her hiding-place, and went up-stairs, upon tip-toe, again to Frank's room.

"Thank God!" she said when she found him still asleep; and then she went back to her own room, and crept shivering and trembling into bed.

Cold, cold;—cold at heart, too, the poor woman lay listening to the storm as it increased in anger. She fancied the wind was chasing her wretched son, running him down in some miserable hovel, or dashing him down in the streets. Then it lightened and thundered, as if the heavens had prepared a bolt to blast him, in the height of his iniquity.

When she rose again and tremblingly drew her blind aside, the first grey streaks of morning were in the sky. The wind rumbled in the chimney, the window shook, the rain was roaring down the spouts, and draining from the eaves, in great heavy drops. The wind was banging the garden door (Mrs Grey knew why the lock was broken), which creaked and wheezed on its crazy hinges, as if it had an asthma. Then it rushed by the window, swinging back the shutter below, and sweeping round the corner with increasing rage, taking a tile off a neighbouring house, and depositing it, with a crash, in an adjoining court.

And now another element joined in the fray. The rain ceased, and in its stead great round hailstones, in white clouds, went hissing and clattering in every corner, like a storm of shot-corns into doomed rookeries. Away went the hailstones over chimney and house-top. Away they went, helter-skelter before the driving wind, which increased in strength every minute. It whistled round the tottering chimney-pots, until one close by could hold on to bricks and mortar no longer, and went crashing over the tiles, and frightening a muffled-up watchman as much as if it were a burglar. Scarcely had it reached the street, when the lightning again joined in the fray, and the thunder shook the very earth. All the elements were at war with each other.

Mrs Grey did not notice the picturesque beauty of the storm; but she stood at the window looking out at the opening day, which was in harmony with her own storm-tossed thoughts.

It was a sight for Quasimodo himself,

the birth of this wild, windy day—this day never to be forgotten in the history of the inmates of Tristram Lodge.

Bristling up amongst a host of shining chimney-pots,—some, on the swivel principle, throwing about their great awkward arms as if in very despair,—a hundred gable roofs clustered together under the mysterious morning sky. Loud roared the wind amongst the old timbers. Hail, and snow, and sleet, and rain rushed to and fro in hazy clouds, like affrighted ghosts amongst the gaunt chimney stacks. From roof to roof the gleaming lightning flew, revealing the mysteries of many an old corner, and glaring into a thousand chamber windows on a thousand terrified dreamers. Away clattered a loosened tile, dashing, crashing, clattering, rattling, over the slanting house-tops. The swivel chimney, hard by, turned round its black head with a scream, and the lightning conductor of its taller neighbour trembled like

a reed.   But wind, nor rain, nor hail could
wipe out the occurrence of a few hours
previously.

When the morning had really come,
and the robbery was discovered, Mrs Grey
said nothing.   She was pale, and ill, and
like one beside herself; so Frank made as
little of the affair as he could.   He gave to
the police a list of the articles stolen; it
included about thirty pounds taken from a
bureau in the dining-room, sundry old
coins, a dozen of silver spoons, and as
many forks, an old-fashioned silver watch,
with the initials " G. G." upon the back,
and several other minor things of no importance.

A well-known detective officer examined the house and its fastenings, and
explained how the thieves had got in as
well as if he had seen them.   Near the
kitchen window, through which they had
entered, were several foot-marks, and it
was not unlikely, he said, that these marks
would prove strong evidence against the

thieves, if the robbers were captured, which it was very likely they would be, and that evening.

"Do you think you will take them so soon?" Mrs Grey inquired, with well-assumed calmness.

"Hard to say," said the man, looking at her; "not unlikely, rather think we are on the right scent."

Within an hour afterwards the officer returned with some of the stolen articles; but Frank had gone to business, and Mrs Grey could not identify them. The watch with G. G. engraven upon it was certainly like the one which was missing; but she must decline to swear to it.

"Well, perhaps the master will be able to identify them better," said the man, noticing Mrs Grey's agitation. "There's no need for you to be nervous, marm."

"I suppose it is necessary that we should swear to them before the thieves can be convicted," said Mrs Grey.

"Well, it generally is," said the

officer; " but I'll just fit this boot into the footmarks," he said, taking a boot out of a handkerchief.

Mrs Grey hurried up-stairs, and put on her bonnet and shawl.

" Why some one's been and tampered with them footmarks," said the officer, coming back.

" Tampered with them!" said Mrs Grey, feigning great surprise.

" I must see your servants," said the officer.

Mrs Grey rung the bell, which was answered by a respectable-looking girl.

" Call Mary," said Mrs Grey.

" There, sir, you may question them as you please—I shall be back in a few minutes."

As fast as she could walk, with the wind blowing and hooting at her along the streets, Mrs Grey went to Beckford Square, and saw her son.

Frank was alarmed at her pale face when she entered his room.

"Whatever has happened, mother?—sit down," he said, closing the door.

"They have taken them—they have been to me to identify the things," said Mrs Grey, almost gasping for breath. "I would not say they were our things. They will bring them to you: you must not know them—you must say they are not ours."

"Why, mother? what is the meaning of this?"

"The thieves cannot be convicted unless the goods are identified."

"But we wish them convicted, mother!"

"You would convict your *brother!*" exclaimed the wretched woman, falling sobbing into her son's arms.

Mrs Grey had seen the burglars,—they were Richard Grey and Peter Foster.

CHAPTER IX.

MORE TRIALS THAN ONE.

THE next morning the number of slip-
shod men and women, who lounged about
the city gaol of Maryport, to see the "night
charges" marched to the police court, was
unusually large,—to see the men whom
it was supposed had had a hand in several
serious burglaries, which for a time had completely baffled the detective capabilities of
the police.

It was a bitterly cold day. Snow and
sleet and rain were falling, and the wind
swept wildly along the streets, chilling
everything. But the weather must be bitter indeed that would drive, to their miserable hovels, the class of persons who come

out of back streets and alleys to gaze on criminals.

As the prisoners were brought forth— male and female—some for being drunk, some for brawling, some for thieving, some for stabbing,—they scanned the crowd eagerly, and nearly in every instance found sympathizing faces there.

When Richard Grey and Peter Foster came out, heavily hand-cuffed, there was a great rush towards them; but the two were put into a cab and driven off, and a stout oily-looking rogue, amongst the last batch of prisoners, seemed a little disappointed that he was not to share in this special honour.

Richard Grey had undergone that marked physiognomical change which is inevitably produced by a career of vice. If people would keep their good looks, they must be good. Nature soon sets her seal of infamy upon her infamous children. Richard Grey, the fair-haired, handsome boy of Helswick, with the sanguine blue eyes and florid complexion, was now a gaunt lout of a fellow, with scowling visage and sensual mouth; a fellow with a lowering brow and dull, heavy, villanous eyes. His features were regular and well-shapen still; but there were lines in his face that had changed the once open expression, and he was indeed so much altered, that his own fond mother would hardly have recognized him.

His companion, who was considerably his senior, had changed but little from the time when we first introduced him to our readers. Peter Foster was always an "ill-favoured fellow." He simply looked older now, and dirtier, added to which he was poorly dressed. Richard Grey, on his return from America some months previously, had casually met him in Liverpool, and they had returned to Maryport together. Peter had long been cast off by his parents, whom he had nearly ruined, and Richard had lived a desperate life on the other side of the Atlantic.

No wonder that these two soon found equally abandoned companions at Keem's. It was during the singing and rioting of this place that they became connected with a band of thieves, who had for some time carried on a successful course of robbery, in various parts of the country. They had friends in several of the principal towns of England, and a constant correspondence was kept up with London.

The police of Maryport (whose chief had been reared in Scotland Yard) had a tolerably fair knowledge of the local criminal population. They knew where to look for certain classes of thieves. They knew the set amongst which burglary was favoured; and they could put their hands almost immediately upon ordinary pickers and stealers. But the new importation troubled them so much that the assistance of a Bow Street runner had been secured.

It was not long ere the London detective scented out Keem's Harmonic Bowers,

of which place, attired as a simple countryman, and with all a simple countryman's
manners, he became a regular frequenter.
By-and-by he ingratiated himself with
Peter Foster and Richard Grey, and was
permitted to sit beside the chairman. He
said he had come into some money, and
as he had no other incumbrances, he had
come to spend it, and he should be glad if
they would recommend him to a comfortable sort of inn where he could be jolly for
a week or so.

The chairman undertook to see the
countryman in "a snug crib," and two
friends of Foster's and Grey's (the latter's
alias was Smith, and the former's Banks;
but we who know them will give them
their proper names) went home with the
countryman that night, and had a rare
jollification. The countryman soon grew a
favourite with his new friends; Jack Crib,
the chairman, was particularly fond of him,
and, in his cups, said things which the
countryman treasured up.

The end was that the Bow Street runner became sufficiently acquainted with the company into which he had ingratiated himself to be satisfied that these were the thieves who had bothered the Maryport police. He found it difficult to communicate many particulars to the chief officer, deeming it advisable never to be out of the society of one or more of the men, seeing that several of them were 'cute London thieves, who were almost as wary as himself. On the night of the robbery at Grey's he began to fear that a new comer, whose face he remembered, had penetrated his disguise; so he sat up most of the night drinking, and early the next morning, feigning a besotted state of stupidity, he quarrelled with the landlord of the house and went out brawling, which soon induced a policeman to take him to the station-house. Had he disappeared less suspiciously his birds would have flown.

In less than half-an-hour after the countryman had been taken to the station-house, careful watch was posted throughout the locality, and by dint of good management five of the gang were taken, two being Peter Foster and Richard Grey, and the third the chairman of Keem's Harmonic Bowers, who was discovered to be a receiver on a large scale, and who was—on his own account, we regret to say it—permitted to turn King's Evidence against his patrons.

Thus it was that Richard Grey and Peter Foster were caught, the former with the watch marked G. G. in his possession, and the latter with a newly-made hole in his coat, which a piece of cloth picked up under Grey's window exactly fitted.

By the aid of the oily rogue, Jack Crib, who was transferred from the dock to the witness box, Mrs Grey and her son Frank were spared the necessity of appearing, another case being clearly proved against the prisoners. Two others were remanded, and were, we may state at once, ultimately transported.

The assizes being close at hand, Richard Grey and Peter Foster, after a short examination, were fully committed for trial.

That very week Frank was to have been taken into the firm of Welford and Co., as junior partner; upon the apprehension of his brother, however, he had absented himself from business, and remained at home, giving certain necessary instructions, by letter, with regard to matters requiring attention. Mr Welford had visited him several times, in the kindest way; but Frank persisted that he could not leave home again until the assizes were over at least, and then he had not settled what he might do. Frank kept his word; but at the same time undertook to give any explanation necessary in his department, and attend to all documents that required his attention.

Mr Welford, feeling that it would be best to keep Frank occupied, had all manner of letters, and freight notes, and bills of lading sent up every morning; and the

few days between the committal of the
police magistrates and the assizes soon
passed away.

On the morning of the trial Mrs Grey
insisted upon going to the Court. She
had hitherto said little or nothing about
Richard; having maintained a painful
calmness, which was much worse than a
boisterous grief.

All Frank's appeals, against this wish
of his mother, were vain. Nothing in the
world, she said, should prevent her going
to the Court.

After exhausting every argument to
induce her to change her determination,
after affectionate solicitations and zealous
protests, Frank gave way, and when his
mother was dressed and ready, he insisted
upon going with her.

The December sun was shining upon
the whitened roofs of the houses when
they left Purdown. The city was going on as it went on every day, except
Sunday, when the bells chimed nearly all

day long and the steamers were laid up in the river.

They reached the court as soon as the doors were opened, and took their seats, without a word. By and by eager spectators crowded in, and policemen took up their stations at various points. Lawyers and their clerks seated themselves round the second row of the great table, beneath the bench, and laid down bundles of papers, tied up with red tape, on the shelf which was fastened upon the back of the seat in front of them. Then came barrister's clerks with bags and briefs, and books, which were speedily examined by their masters, in wigs and gowns, who soon filled the seat round the big table. Then the reporters dropped in; and magistrates took their seats on each side of the judge's chair, and ladies were ushered into the galleries above.

Mrs Grey and Frank noticed all this with a dull, blunted gaze, until the trumpets announced the arrival of the judges, and then Mrs Grey took Frank's hand under her shawl, and Frank felt the blood rush into his cheeks. In a few moments everybody rose, and the judge entered; whereupon the usual prosaic preliminaries of opening the Court were gone through, and as this was the second assize-day (and the day which the weekly newspaper of the preceding evening had stated the cases of burglary would be heard), the spectators had not long to wait before Richard Grey and Peter Foster were placed in the dock.

Mrs Grey squeezed Frank's hand, at sight of her younger son—so altered, so degraded; and the sharp agonizing cry which escaped her lips was immediately drowned in a general cry of " order."

It is unnecessary to describe the trial. The charge against the prisoners was fully made out, and the jury deliberated scarcely five minutes ere they returned their verdict.

" What say you, are the prisoners at

the bar, Richard Grey, *alias* Richard Smith, and Peter Foster, *alias* Peter Banks, guilty or not guilty?" asked the usher in a loud voice.

" Guilty," said the foreman.

Mrs Grey, who had been wrought up to a pitch of great excitement and anxiety, fainted as the verdict was given. Close behind her started up a man in half-sailor, half-landman's costume, who raised her in his arms before Frank Grey had scarcely time to notice what had happened.

The prisoner, Richard Grey, turned his head for a moment in the direction where the commotion had arisen, but the man had cleared his way through the crowd, and was out in the open air in a few moments.

"Thank you, I will relieve you now," said Frank Grey.

"I am stronger than you," said the stranger, looking anxiously at Mrs Grey's pale face.

A chair was brought, and water was

brought; but Mrs Grey only partially recovered.

A medical man who was in Court came out, and advised that Mrs Grey should be taken home, and put to bed; she was suffering from more than mere faintness.

A cab was called accordingly, and Mrs Grey was lifted into it, the stranger taking a seat on the box.

When they reached home, Frank Grey led his mother into the house, and the doctor advised quiet. Mrs Grey continued insensible.

CHAPTER X.

THE MAN ON THE BOX.

WHEN the cab stopped, the man who had carried Mrs Grey out of Court slid down from the box and disappeared.

It was some little time before Frank remembered that he had not behaved quite so courteously as he might have done, under the circumstances, to the man on the box. Truth to tell, Frank would much rather have carried his mother out of Court himself. There was a confident officiousness in the rough stranger's manner which did not please Frank Grey. He was not satisfied with himself, nevertheless, for not having thanked him.

An opportunity for his doing so soon arrived. After walking about the neighbourhood for more than an hour, the man who had rode on the box presented himself at the front door of Tristram Lodge, and asked for Mr Grey.

"Mr Grey is engaged—he cannot see any one to-day," said the servant.

"Tell him mine is very important business," said the man, "it concerns his own and his mother's happiness."

"Show him in," at length said Frank, and the man stalked into the trim little room that Frank had furnished, so hopefully, on his mother's arrival at Purdown.

"Oh, it's you, is it?" said Frank. "I am much obliged to you for your kindness this morning."

As he thanked him, Frank pulled out a purse.

"I want neither thanks nor money, sir," said the man, holding down his head. "Mine is business connected with neither the one nor the tother."

"Perhaps you will be good enough to

tell me who you are, then, and explain your business at once."

"May I sit down?" the man asked, dropping, at the same moment, into a chair.

"There is no necessity for ceremony," said Frank, fixing his eyes upon his visitor.

"I don't wonder you have forgotten me," said the man; "I've changed a good deal of late—I was in good feather when you saw me before; but I've gone down since then, and I'm poor now."

"And yet you don't want money?"

"Not from you," said the man.

"Well, let us get on then," said Frank, a little impatiently. Your name is—

"Matthew Dunkum," said the man, swinging his hat between his legs.

"Villain!" exclaimed Frank Grey, rising.

"Yes, worse than that," said Mat, coolly, "but you mustn't lay the blame of all your brother's badness to me; I know your mother does."

"Have you come here, and at this time,

to excuse your infamy?" said Frank, advancing towards him.

"No! to confess it," said the man.

"Go, go—don't stay here; I will not trouble you for a confession. I have often thought that there was some innate wickedness in my brother—I have been inclined to doubt the influence which my poor mother has always said you have had upon him. But now you confess your infamy. I will spare you the miserable revelation, and will thank you to leave this house, without a moment's delay. Yonder is the door."

"Don't send me away," said Mat, looking up with a painful earnestness—"I have a great deal to tell—it concerns *her*, sir— her, your mother."

Frank paced the room impatiently.

"It is a cruel story," said Mat; "do hear it now; maybe I shan't be in the humour to tell it another time."

Frank was touched by the appealing tone of the man's voice, and his quivering lip.

"I knew your father," said Mat, looking down upon the floor again, and swinging his hat.

"No great honour that," said Frank fiercely.

"Don't be too sure of it," said Mat.

"We will not discuss the question, now at any rate. I never knew my father, nor have I any wish to see or hear of him—if he be alive, which I doubt. It has been one of my poor mother's whims that he would return some day."

"He may."

"Let him!" said Frank, defiantly.

"His has been a cruel, hard lot," said Mat; "a cruel, hard lot."

"If this is all you have to—"

"Don't hurry me, don't hurry me," said Mat. "Have patience, and you will thank me for what I am going to tell—you will indeed."

"Go on," said Frank, sitting down and looking contemptuously at his visitor.

"I knew your mother when she was a

girl," said Mat, with a tremor in his voice, " a lovely girl as you could wish to see."

Frank moved impatiently, and stamped his foot.

" I loved her."

Frank rose from his chair; but sat down again irresolutely.

" I was a respectable man then—young, and of her own age, and was the owner of two fishing smacks. I courted her, and we were partly engaged to be married."

This was another bitter pill for Frank's pride to gulp down—to hear such a confession from such a man—but Frank planted his feet firmly on the floor, and swallowed the nauseating dose.

" The young people of Helswick said Sarah was a flirt; but I took it only as their jealousy — of course everybody noticed her. At last George Grey came to Helswick, from Maryport—from this very town—as a carpenter's foreman on the new house then a building in the valley there."

" Don't make more of your story than

necessary; let it be brief, it is bitter enough," said Frank.

"Well then she cast me off," said Mat, raising his voice and swinging his hat fiercely; "she cast me off for him—and I loved her, ay, I'd a give up my life for her. I swore I'd be revenged. I made friends with George Grey; but Sarah feared me, and plotted again me, plotted and plotted, and tried to have me driven from the place. My love turned to hate, —fierce blasting hate."

Frank Grey started at the hissing growl in which Mat exposed the intensity of that bitter hatred.

"I was always thinking of it. I have seen the sea creep into the caverns off Helswick; creep on and on, and at last fill them up, choking every crevice. Revenge filled my heart up, young man, took possession of me entirely."

The man raised his voice, and the veins in his forehead were swollen to distortion.

"Miserable wretch," said Frank.

"Ay, miserable now, but not then. It was happiness to me when my scheme began to work. She defied me—I could see it in her steady assurance, her firm look when she met me. I hated, loathed her; and yet, oh! how I had loved her, worshipped her."

The man's great frame shook with excitement.

"I circulated evil reports about her; I wound myself about George Grey, like a serpent, and at last commanded his ear; one night when I pretended to be in liquor, I spoke lightly of her, and we nearly came to blows; I softened it over though. But my plot had begun to work, and I never left it, I never left it."

"Do be quicker—briefer!" exclaimed Frank, his heart beating as if it would burst.

"At last the plot was worked out," and the harsh voice became nearly a whisper, "I made him believe in her dishonour."

Frank threw himself back in his chair, in silent amazement and horror.

"I need not tell you much more of this part of the plot—I swore to what I said, swore it on the Bible, and you may be sure I had got my scheme so well laid that nobody could doubt her guilt."

Frank clutched the chair, and his breath came quick and hot.

"It was a lie what I had said; but George Grey left her with her two little ones."

"And you were revenged," said Frank so bitterly, that Mat Dunkum cowered beneath Frank's withering scorn; "you were revenged on an innocent woman and her helpless children."

"She had money—George left her money, and she had good friends," said Mat, as if answering his own thoughts. "Mr Mountford was kind to her—she went to be his housekeeper—everybody was kind to her. And I went to the bad. I had my revenge; but I went to the bad. I lost my boats, and was had up for smuggling; but they couldn't prove it against me; if they had, I shouldn't ha' been here. Mountford was on the bench, and I know she had had a hand in it."

"And what profit is this confession now?" Frank asked.

"Let me tell it out—it is a relief to my mind, and things will come right again yet; it's not too late. I saw your father two days ago."

"Good heavens!" exclaimed Frank.

"Let me go on, sir—I shan't be long, don't stop me again. I saw him yesterday, at Helswick. No, I don't mean his ghost, nor anything of that sort; I mean him. I see him wandering about the place; changed, ay, he was changed, but I knowed him though nobody else did, and I've set a watch on him. Don't stop me, sir; let me go on. I am a black villain, I know; but I didn't hate your brother: I was carrying on my revenge, I know, at first; but I got to like the lad, and did something to save him, as you know: I never should ha' thought he'd come to what he has. And when I sat in that Court, and see his handsome face so altered, I could ha' cried, sir, a thing I've not done for more nor twenty year; but I could: it seemed as if he were my own lad, and when his mother dropped afore me, it seemed as if something was a gnawing inside me, and I wished I were dead."

Here the man faltered, and trembled, and hid his face in his hands; and despite his merciless persecution, Frank felt a momentary pang of sorrow for him.

"I picked her up, and when I looked down on that poor face it seemed as if I was blinded; it seemed as if the feelings I once had came back, all of a rush, like the tide in a great wind; and I made up my mind to confess all."

Seeing the importance of this confession—and thrusting back, by his strong will, the mingled feelings which rose up as though they would choke him—Frank wrote down the heads of Mat's story. The man willingly signed the paper. His hand trembled as he did so, and his eyes were filled with tears.

" I shall let you know where your father is, sir, to-day or to-morrow, and then you may take your own course. Let her know as I have confessed it all; I shall never trouble her again, nor you, sir, nor anybody."

Frank said his mother should know of it; and Mat, without another word, sneaked away, with a woe-begone, wretched look, that showed how savagely remorse had gripped him during those few moments when he gazed upon Mrs Grey's death-like features.

It was some minutes before Frank could collect his thoughts. He was altogether at a loss to know what it was best he should do. For the moment, his

brother's fate was forgotten in the discovery which had just been made. Was
this return and recognition of his father,
at such a time, the work of a kind Pro-
vidence? Was the softening of Mat Dunkum's brutal nature the working of the
same Divine Hand? Would it bring comfort to his mother? Would it soothe the
great grief which she was suffering? Or
was it but another misery to make life
still more bitter?

At nightfall—shortly before the rising
of the Court—seven or eight prisoners,
whose sentences had been deferred, were
again placed in the dock. Amongst the
sentences recorded were : Richard Grey
and Peter Foster, each twenty years' trans-
portation beyond the seas. Mat Dunkum
was in Court, with his eyes fixed upon
Richard Grey, when the judge delivered
his brief comments upon the young
man's crime, closing them with that

terrible sentence; and he sat staring at
the vacant dock when the prisoners had
disappeared, and when the hall-keeper
came to lock the doors.

CHAPTER XI.

FRANK GREY FINDS HIS FATHER.

THE snow had fallen upon Summerdale, covering everything with white flakes that hung fantastically upon the branches of the tall elms in the centre of the old square; whitened the black stocks; lay upon the housetops as thickly as the thatch; and muffled the footsteps of the people in the three or four quaint, Dutch-looking streets.

Long after the snow had disappeared in other places, it remained in the village-town of Summerdale: for even the snow fell lazily, and lay lazily down, and was loth to depart, at Summerdale. It came down in big, heavy flakes, and alighted on the first opportunity, until it filled every nook and corner, nestling round chimneys, clinging about door-posts, hanging round window-frames, and covering the highways. So quaint then did the sleepy town appear, with its square-towered church, and its pointed-roofed vicarage, and its timber-fronted school-house, and its thatched cottages with queer gables and little window-panes, that an imaginative writer might have fixed upon it as a scene for strange tales of witcheries and enchantments.

A pale December sun was just disappearing when Frank Grey alighted from the creaking old coach that still ran between a distant town and Summerdale.

He was the only passenger, and was shown into the bar, where a wood fire was lazily climbing up a broad chimney; whilst the reflection of the flame was playing leisurely upon old-fashioned jugs, and cups, and glasses, on a big oak delf-shelf. A shepherd's dog lay asleep on the hearth, and two old men were dozing before their grog on a dark oak settle at one side of the fire-place, whilst the fat and rosy land-lady sat knitting at a round table on the other side.

Frank made inquiries about the Masseys, and resolved on calling upon them on the next day.

After he had done what justice he could to some savoury ham and brown bread, the candles were lighted, and he joined in the lazy talk of the two old men who had wakened up on the arrival of three other persons.

The last comer appeared to be a man of great consideration. The landlord brought forward for him a shiny old chair, and the landlady laid down her knitting to ask how Mr Massey was.

"Better, I think, a little better," said Mr Evans (as we must still call him at the Crown).

"Is Mr Massey seriously ill," inquired Frank.

Mr Evans looked round upon the

speaker curiously, and said: "Not seriously, I hope, sir; might I be so bold as to ask if you know Mr Massey?"

"Slightly," said Frank, "I have come here to see him."

The Summerdale topers nodded at each other, and then looked at Frank, as much as to say: "Indeed! Here is a subject for conversation, friends; a stranger has arrived amongst us, and he knows Mr Massey."

Mr Evans was too well-bred to ask the question which everybody thought he would ask immediately. But the landlady, after looking round the group, and then at the fire, said: "If it's important business, sir, you might go up to-night—we can lend you a lantern, sir."

"Thank you," said Frank, "I will wait until morning."

"It be odd to I," said one of the old men, looking into a mug of hot ale, "it be odd to I if the poor gentleman lives very long."

"Yees, yees!" said another, "as I said to my old ooman, only t'other day, there be that in his faace as 'ud make a man say his prayers."

"I don't like that there dog a howlin' and a howlin' as 'um do; when a dog sets a howlin' a-nights in Summerdale, there be death about surely," said a third.

"Let's hope not, friends, let's hope not—Mr Massey is a young man yet," said Mr Evans; "he'll not die because a dog howls, you may depend."

The old men shook their heads, and the landlady said she had heard that, a week ago, the Town Crier's raven was found sitting on the back of Mr Massey's empty chair, when the servants came down-stairs, and that it was croaking dreadfully. And she had heard that the cook had seen two white beetles in the kitchen.

"We shall alarm you with our Summerdale omens, I fear," said Mr Evans to Frank.

"I don't believe in them," the young man replied.

The old men of Summerdale shook their heads, and looked at each other, and then looked at Frank, not reproachfully, but with a feeling of pity for his ignorance.

"Brought up in a large city, perhaps," said Mr Evans, "where you have so much to do with the realities of life, that you have not time to think of the omens which are noticed by us quiet country people?"

The old men looked at each other again, in admiration of Mr Evans's identifying himself with Summerdale. "He'll tell the poor young man sommat just now," they thought.

"I have been brought up in a large city," said Frank, "and am not superstitious; but I can respect the feelings and opinions of those who are older than myself, and who have more leisure to notice the manifestations of coming events, which nature may make, for aught I know, and particularly in quiet old places like this, which seem almost to belong to a past age."

"You think, then, that intelligence of disaster and death is sometimes communicated to man by means altogether unexplainable by ordinary human rules?" inquired Mr Evans.

"I think of course with Horatio," said Frank, "that there is more in heaven and earth than philosophy dreams of; I think that between two souls bound together by some strong tie of love there may be an intensity of sympathy, almost electrical, which, at the moment of dissolution, may be sufficiently active to communicate to the living one the awful message of death."

Frank spoke so fluently and so well that the old men were astonished. They had not heard any one speak better, except the parson, and a lecturer who, some years ago, had found his way to the platform in the old school-house.

The theme which was thus started, on that cold December night, before the warm

tavern fire, was intensely interesting to
the company, and soon entered the ghost-
story phase. There had been many ghosts
in Summerdale; and even Mr Evans confessed to having thought he had once seen
one in an Australian camp, at the diggings,
but he wished it to be distinctly understood that he proved it to be mere imagination. The landlady was a firm believer
in hobgoblins of all sorts, and the ghost
which had been seen at various times in
Summerdale had been identified beyond
all doubt or contradiction.

It was late when the company buttoned
up their coats, lighted their lanterns, and
went to their adjacent homes. They all
shook hands with Frank, notwithstanding
his disbelief in their particular illustrations
of his vague theory; and Mr Evans, who
looked at him frequently, as if trying to
remember where he had seen the face
before, said, "I am very glad to have met
you, sir; and I hope you will promise not

to leave Summerdale without seeing me again."

"Thank you," said Frank, taking the hand which was so heartily offered to him.

"You have helped us to spend a long night pleasantly—nights *are* long at Summerdale."

So the father and son parted, mutually ignorant of their relationship, yet mutually interested in each other, and both feeling desirous to meet again; and they met, on the morrow.

The next morning Frank presented himself at Oak House. He was shown into the library. Mr Massey and his wife were both there. The husband was lolling in an easy-chair with a book, and the wife rose (as Frank entered) from an ottoman close by his feet.

After some few complimentary inquiries, Frank said: "I received your letter safely, and beg to thank you very much for it."

Paul watched Frank, with a wondering look.

"Yes," said Mrs Massey, "we thought it our duty to write to you, as soon as we were satisfied."

"I had the news two days before," said Frank, "please to read that."

Mrs Massey took the paper, which Mat Dunkum had signed, and gave it to her husband, who, after reading a few lines, returned it to his wife with a sigh, and asked her to read it—he was not equal to the task. Mrs Massey read the paper aloud; and as she did so, Paul thought to himself how a confession might, some day, be made by Winford Barns; and then again, for a moment, came upon him an impulse to relieve himself of some of the burthen which he felt was weighing him down to a premature grave.

"I was sure of it—I knew it," said Mrs Massey. "Your father I believe to be kind-hearted and good; that he has been dreadfully punished, and is a heart-broken man, there is no doubt."

"I begin to believe it," said Frank sadly.

"If we had only come to Summerdale to aid in uniting again these poor bruised hearts," said Mrs Massey to her husband, "we should have no cause to regret Denby."

Paul was about to reply, when Kate came into the room; and then suddenly appearing about to withdraw, Mrs Massey said: "Come in, my dear—come in. This is my daughter, Mr Grey; this is Mr Grey of whom you have heard us speak, Kate."

Frank moved to the fair young girl, who returned his bow, with graceful ease.

Kate looked much older than she was; she might have been taken for seventeen. She was tall for her age, and the constant companionship of her parents had given her confidence, which displayed itself in an unrestrained frankness that was charming: in some girls it would have been forwardness; but in Kate, it was generous amiability. She was more like her mother than like Paul, in appearance; her hair, as we have before said, was a beautiful light brown, and it hung about her shoulders in luxuriant curls.

Frank was struck with her beauty; but he was too much interested in the object of his visit to bestow more than a passing thought upon Kate, who, however, occupied his thoughts for many an hour in the years which followed.

Kate left the room almost immediately after her introduction to Frank, and the business of the morning proceeded. Frank did not tell the Masseys of Richard's shame; he evaded a question about his brother, finding they knew nothing of the tidings which most of the county newspapers had conveyed to their readers. But he told them that his mother was well now, though she had had a severe illness, only recently. He had not exactly prepared her for his father's return; but he had made her fully understand that this journey of his concerned her husband.

"Mother has always believed he would return," said Frank.

"That is his knock," said Mrs Massey, hurriedly, "you had better go into the dining-room—come this way, and leave me to manage the rest."

The dining-room door closed upon Frank as Mrs Massey received Mr Grey in the hall.

Frank sat there for fully an hour, whilst Mrs Massey, with womanly tact, prepared Mr Grey for the meeting. That hour seemed an age to Frank. In that age he had thought all over the events of his life; he had pictured to himself hundreds of men in no way resembling his father; he had almost decided the question, which was still in abeyance, of his continuing in the house of Welford and Co.; he had thought of Bessie Martin; and of his brother, who had been removed from Maryport whilst his mother was still suffering from that shock which the nnsuspecting foreman had given her when he answered the crier's question, "Guilty or not guilty;" and his fancy was just shaping to itself the pretty face of Kate Massey, when the dining-room door was softly opened and the mother of that sweet face entered.

"He is ready to make all atonement; it has been a great pain and a great pleasure to him, the revelation," said Mrs Massey, in an excited whisper.

Frank bowed his head.

"You will pity him—he has suffered, none can tell how much; he has been to Helswick once a week for the past two months; you forgive him for your mother's sake, for his own sake," she went on, hurriedly.

There were tears in Frank's eyes. Mrs Massey needed no other reply. She went gently out of the room, as she had entered it, and returned with the man who had expressed such a strong desire to see Frank again. Their eyes met for a moment—a great sob of joy burst from the long-exiled father—and Mrs Massey left them, as we shall leave them, locked in each other's arms.

CHAPTER XII.

GOING HOME.

HAVING carefully prepared his mother, by letter, for their return, father and son left Summerdale two days after their meeting.

The old coach took them a score of miles, and then they reached a railway station, and booked themselves to Maryport.

The train had to call at many extensive stations, on its way, and it seemed to poor George Grey as if everybody had just returned from long exile, or were going to meet those who had just come home.

Boys leaving school, for the holidays, and were met by fathers and mothers and rosy-cheeked sisters; aunts and uncles, and nieces and nephews, were going to visit each other.

Indeed, George felt that everybody was on their way to see somebody else, from whom they had been estranged for years. He left the carriage at every station, to look at the people hugging each other, and to gaze at the marvellous hampers of geese, and the barrels of oysters, and boxes of oranges, and the bundles of holly and miseltoe.

It was all part of a grand rejoicing in celebration of the returned exile. Frank was delighted at his father's jubilant interpretation of what was passing around him.

How could Frank tell his father of Richard's disgrace? How could he find in his heart to put the smallest barrier between the returned exile and happiness?

"About Dick, what about Dick?" asked the father when they were alone again.

"He is well, sir, no doubt," said Frank, quickly, "but you are full of questions, and tell nothing of yourself."

"What have I to tell?" the father asked.

"A hundred pieces of strange adventure," said Frank.

"We will talk of those over the fire, at home, Frank," the father replied. "Home! It seems all a dream, Frank!"

"Thank Heaven for its reality!" exclaimed the son.

"Ah, Frank, my boy,—I can hardly feel that you are my boy,—you are so much a gentleman, so much higher, so much better in every way than I."

"Now, father, father, talk not so," said Frank, putting his hand over his father's mouth.

"Well, then, I will not; but since you wish me to talk instead of you, I was just going to tell you, if I could, something of the difference between this railway journey and the one which brought me to Maryport on my return, in company with the friend with whom I travelled. I don't think in all my days I suffered so much as I did during that journey from Liverpool to Maryport."

"How, father, how?"

"We commenced our journey on a Saturday. The train stopped at nearly every station—it was a fourth class train. Nearly everybody had somebody to meet them. As night came on, many working men began to get into the carriages, fellows in their fustian jackets, and with their coffee cans. They were going home to their wives and children. Some of them were carpenters and decorators, who had been out for the week, and were going home to spend Saturday night and Sunday with those whom they loved. I knew, Frank, I knew; and I thought of the time when I was a carpenter, Frank, and when I worked at Denby Rise, and how I used to go to Helswick every Saturday night; how I walked by the beach, and how I used to go and court your mother when I was a young man, and how—"

" Nay, father, now you are changing from merry to sad; you were all happiness just now."

" There's happiness in being sad sometimes, Frank, and I can afford to be down a little now; if I am too happy all at once it may drive me mad."

" But think of *this* happy train which is carrying us to Maryport now," said Frank. " We are travelling in company with holiday people, and with friends who are going to join friends they may not have seen for years."

" I do think, Frank, and the contrast to the other train is all the greater. I want you to know how deeply I have been punished. Here was I, just returned to my native country, after years and years of absence; here was I, a stranger and an exile in my own land, a spectator of everybody's happiness; for everybody did seem

happy and content but me. I had no wife
and children to go home to; I had money
in abundance; but there were no arms
held wide open for me; no kettle singing
on the hob; no wife waiting my return;
no children to greet the homeward-bound
father. My companion was a married
man; he did not know that I was married
too; he advised me to find a wife to comfort and console me. By the Lord! Frank,
it was like sending a knife into my heart
to hear him talk. His wife, his children,
his little farm—he could speak of nothing
else, and the train went so slow that he
cursed it twenty times for its tardiness."

"We are going very slowly, too, I
think," said Frank, anxious to attract his
father from the past.

"I wished a hundred times that I had
remained in Melbourne. What did I
want treading English soil again? What
fiend had whispered me to go and have a
kind of last look at the old spot? What
was England to me, when all my prayer

could be, as it ever had been, that those I once had loved so dearly might be sleeping in the church-yard? But still I went on for all that, and re-booked myself when it was necessary, and travelled with my happy companion. It must have been God who led me on, for why I should go to Summerdale I hardly knew. My fellow-traveller was going that way, and he spoke of the country about there; and when I came to think more I didn't feel that I could stand Helswick—I felt as though I must approach it very gradually, from a distance; so I journeyed on with my friend to Summerdale, intending to spend a day or two with him, and then go to Denby and Helswick. But you know the rest; how we found the people talking of the Masseys from Denby Rise, and—"

"Yes, now we are coming to the happier part of it; how you made friends at Oak House; and how I met you there, my dear father."

"And how we have not parted since; and how we will never do so; and how proud I am of you, my boy," said the father, regaining his former buoyancy of spirits.

A young woman, who was put into the carriage, at that moment, by the guard, thought Mr Grey was one of the kindest, nicest, merriest men she had ever seen. For he chucked her baby under the chin, and nursed it all the way to the next station, where he placed it in its father's arms, and told him he was a happy man, at which the young wife dropped a curtsey, and the father laughed to see her blush. George Grey remembered the time when he had dandled Frank upon his knee, and this was the first child he had ever dared to take in his arms since.

It was late when they reached Maryport. The air was cold and frosty. Every lamp burned in the midst of a little halo of its own.

The bustle and excitement was a great

change from Summerdale. Whilst that moss-grown place had put out its lights, and wrapped itself up in its blankets, Maryport was all life and animation. There was a roar of traffic in the streets, and the shop-windows were decorated with holly and evergreens.

"We shall soon be at home now," said Frank, when the cab had dashed through long rows of lighted streets, sometimes plunging into the midst of the busiest, and then darting off through quiet by-ways. "We shall soon be at home."

George felt his heart beating strangely.

"My courage begins to fail me," he said. "Don't let him drive so fast."

Frank astonished the cabman with a request that he would pull in a little—they were in no hurry.

"I shall be all right in a moment, Frank."

"Of course you will, sir," said Frank, taking his father's hand.

After permitting several 'busses and

cabs to pass by him most ignominiously, the driver pulled up, at length, beneath the garden wall of Tristram Lodge, Purdown.

"Follow me at a little distance," said Frank, "and when I call, present yourself."

The father crept on behind his son, and when Frank had satisfied himself that his father was forgiven, he signalled the exile to approach, and left the long-estranged parents to mingle their joys and sorrows.

It was a painful-happy meeting after five-and-twenty years. They would hardly have known each other had they casually met in the streets. But Mrs Grey had dreamed of this meeting so often, had thought of it and prayed for it so frequently, that there was little or no surprise in it to her.

To George Grey it was a great sudden joy of which he had never dared to dream. By the camp-fires of the diggings,

in the counting-house of his Melbourne
business, and on board ship, he had
thought of his wife and children, but
always with a bitter sadness; thought of
them as of the dead and yet of the living;
thought of them as beings worse than
dead; then thought how he had loved
them, and groaned if imagination whispered, " how happy might I have been."

Mrs Grey was almost an old woman
now; old with grief and trouble; but
there was still some of that bloom upon her
cheek, and that brightness in her eye,
which had attracted George Grey when
she was a girl.

To a casual observer George was only
a man of middle age; but his strong will,
his physical exercise, and his iron constitution had kept off some of the marks
which Time sets upon us all.

They might live for a score of years yet,
in which to wipe out the past. But their
happiness must always be clouded; their

sweets must always be mingled with bitters.

Already the consciousness that he was much to blame for not investigating the calumnies which drove him to a mad desertion of all that he held dear, made George Grey bitterly upbraid himself.

"My poor Sarah," he said, after they had sat speechless for many, many long minutes, "My poor dear injured Sarah."

Mrs Grey could not reply.

"I ought to be hanged—I do not deserve this happiness — my poor, ill-used wife."

"I knew you would come back, George," said the woman between her sobs.

"God bless you and forgive me," said the returned wanderer, his heart almost bursting with pity and remorse.

That he should have believed the base falsehoods; that he should have left this poor loving woman to battle with the world alone!

It maddened him now to think of this
—" My poor dear wife."

He was almost like a child, this strong
man who, when two returned convicts tried
to rob his gold-taking, had fought them
both almost to the death; he wept like
an infant, this travel-stained man who had
won a fortune in the rough toil of colonial
life.

" It wasn't your fault, George; I was a
little to blame; and the trick, and ,the
lies looked so fair. Don't cry; it breaks
my heart to see you in tears," said the
woman, kissing his forehead.

When Frank returned, and the three
had sat over the fire talking of the past,
they told the returned exile why Richard
was away; and then he felt that the
sins of the fathers are visited upon the
children.

" It has pleased God," said Mrs Grey,
" to send you to be my comforter at last.
Had not my poor boy stood there before

the judge, Mat Dunkum's heart would never have been softened."

" A husband's and father's curse light upon Mat Dunkum," said George, in his anguish.

" Nay, do not curse him," said Frank, "it was almost pitiable to see him; he called upon me on the day when poor Richard was removed, to say that he should leave the country in the same ship; he said he was the most miserable wretch in the world."

" Curse! Why should I curse?" said George Grey, pausing a moment; "I, who have courted the curse of heaven."

" It *was* hard, George, very hard to see the poor boy."

" Perhaps something may be done for him," said Frank.

" It was not his own fault," said the fond mother; "he was led astray."

" We must make an effort for him," said the father. " If money can do anything, I'll not spare it."

"Poor Richard!" said Mrs Grey, "and poor Frank! I fear Frank has often thought me unkind. He has been the best, the kindest son in the world, George, the most devoted, the most uncomplaining."

"He takes after his mother," said George.

It almost brought the tears into Frank's eyes to hear this eulogium from his mother's lips.

"Well, we must make the best of Richard's position, and do the best for him: it is no use giving way to mere complaining and regret. It is something for me to do, Sarah; an object worth striving for, to restore him to your arms again; perhaps a better son for his punishment," said George, rousing himself.

"Thank God!" said Mrs Grey, "He is merciful as well as just."

"And what of this poor girl—this Bessie Martin?"

"We have heard nothing of her for years," said Frank, "we have concluded that she is dead."

"We have almost dared to hope so," added Mrs Grey.

CHAPTER XIII.

CHRISTMAS.

THE Christmas bells were ringing when the Greys met at breakfast the next morning. The merry Christmas bells were ringing. How happy, how joyful would the sound of the clanging music have been to George Grey had it not been for the thought of that miserable son in irons on the sea!

A fresh pure snow was upon the house-tops, and little icicles hung from the eaves. In the streets, boys pelted each other until they were hot and red; and the bells seemed to urge them on. From every steeple the noisy concerts pealed. The music influenced everybody. Those who were happy became happier still; and even those who were not happy, felt a certain buoyancy of spirit which made them walk quicker, and with a more elastic tread than usual.

George Grey chipped his egg and chatted to his wife; and Frank chipped his egg and thought of that pretty little girl at Summerdale.

"The bells didn't ring when we were married, Sarah," said George; "but it was a snowy morning like this."

"That is just what I was thinking myself," Mrs Grey replied, pouring into Frank's cup a stream of coffee, the aroma of which filled the room, and added to the cozy feeling induced by the crackling wood fire, the soft hearth-rug, and the bubbling urn upon the table.

"I wonder if we have both thought of it, at the same time, before? I dare say we have. What a happy morning it was, Sarah!"

"Not happier than this morning, George, but for one thing."

"No; perhaps not so happy if it were possible that any other morning could be more joyful than that snowy one at Helswick, when we were young. Has Frank done any sweethearting?"

"I think not," said Mrs Grey, smiling. "Do you hear the question your father asks, Frank?"

"No," said Frank, leaving the green meadows of Summerdale, where he had been walking, in imagination, with Kate Massey.

The question was repeated, and Frank gave it a direct negative.

"Have you not an eye upon *any one?*" said Mr Grey, looking good-humouredly towards Frank.

"No," said that deceitful son. For he was deceitful, you know. He had his eye on a pretty fair-haired girl; but then she was so much younger than he; at least she appeared so to Frank, and he dared not confess that he was in love with her.

His feeling for Miss Massey was not

like love, either, Frank tried to persuade himself; but that was a crafty way of satisfying his conscience for telling a fib. Don't you think so?

"I cannot be in love with the girl," he thought. "I only feel as though I should like to protect and watch over her; that I should like to be near her always, and gather flowers for her, and — By Jove! I wish I were a few years younger. I don't know what my feelings might be then. But what would it matter? I could never aspire to the hand of Mr Massey's daughter. As a partner in the firm of Welford and Co., I might perhaps. But *that* dream is over."

Frank was thinking in this wise whilst his father and mother were dressing for Church, and having arrived at the conclusion that even if he were not a little too old to aspire to the love of Kate Massey, it would be absurd to expect that she could ever love him, he dismissed the subject.

The Christmas bells were ringing, we have said—ringing merrily, joyfully, noisily, sweetly, musically. The returned exile, the wife and the son, went to Church, and heard the divine story of the birth of our Saviour. And never went up to the mercy-seat more fervent prayers than those which ascended from the pew in which the Greys worshipped!

It was a new awakening to life for George Grey. The pealing organ thrilled through his soul. Somehow, the Hallelujah Chorus carried his thoughts back, for a moment, to the mighty anthems which he had heard the wind singing in the great forests. And his heart leaped within him when he contrasted the solitary gold miner, away in Australian wilds, with the husband newly restored to his wife, and kneeling by her side, on this Christmas morning, in old England.

The gorgeous reflections of the painted windows fell upon the Church, colouring the holly which was hung about every pillar. The children, in the choir, threw their little souls into the jubilant Hallelu-jahs, until the old place echoed with their music, long after the last glorious strains of the ever-glorious anthem were concluded. But Richard Grey was out upon the sea in iron chains; and Mrs Grey thought of her son, and prayed that the good angels that were about on this good day would have pity on him.

The preacher told the story of Christ in the manger, and of the star that went before the wise men; and then he told of His divine mission, of His crucifixion, of His resurrection, and of His power to save. It was a strange sermon, full of bits of world-wise philosophy and moralisms. Our Saviour's love of children was a point upon which the preacher dwelt at great length; he contrasted their innocence with the sin and wickedness of maturity; he urg-ed his congregation to love them, and to se-cure their love. He said they were a type of the purer life to come; and that there was a moral instinct of what was good in these little ones; he took it as a great good thing to possess the love of a child.

Then he spoke of children in a simply national light, and brought home to his congregation the importance of careful training and education. "It is," he said, "to the safe-keeping of the children of the present day, that Great Britain will have to entrust the highly prized legacy of virtue and liberty, for which the martyrs have bled, and for which our sires have fought in a hundred fields of carnage. Our boys, at college; in our national schools; running wild about our streets; or undergoing punishment in our gaols, will be the statesmen, the philosophers, the authors, the poets, the merchants, the sailors, the soldiers of the next generation. Have you ever contemplated a group of boys and thought so? It is a picture fruitful of many pleasant yet serious ideas, a knot of youngsters in any sphere of life.

"What a happy ignorance youth ex-

hibits of the vastness of its inheritance!
The statesman, in embryo, is intent upon
the quality of a 'tor;' the future poet,
who shall touch the hearts of millions, is
all engrossed in a paper kite; the coming
judge, with a spinning top; the divine,
with a history of 'Blue Beard.' Happy
boyhood! could ye but get a glimpse of
the future, the gigantic machinery of
which must be moved by your hands,
what a fairyland of romance and prodigy
of spectacle would open up to your wondering and bewildered gaze. Happy boyhood! that never thinks of the battles it
will have to fight, the engines to drive, the
telegraphs to work, the ships to man, the
forlorn hopes to make up, the coals to
raise, the perils and dangers that await it
in the future that is dawning!

"No matter what their station in life,
boys inherit the same restless spirit of ambition which is characteristic of our race.
A love of adventure is visible throughout
the whole boy world. At school, the aim

of the young scholar is to rise above his companions. At play, the ambition of the same boy is to be the cleverest at every sport and pastime; and so on, the spirit of emulation may be traced throughout every phase of boyhood. To direct this ambition into the proper channel—to set before the young aspirants for fame, prizes worthy their energies, calculated to develop those faculties which, left to grow of their own accord, often degenerate into vice—is to make clever and useful men instead of scoundrels.

" Children born in the midst of poverty are an integral part of the big world, influenced by the same spirit, prone alike to mischief and adventure; possessing faculties which, cultivated, give stability to our race, adorn our literature, strengthen our commerce, and give additional vigour to our great hives of industry. But unlike the more fortunate of the boy-creation, the children of poverty and profligacy, in most cases, lack the humanizing influences which cast sunny rays over the lives of their happier brethren. Seldom do the ragged little occupants of the dark side of our cities know anything of maternal solicitude. No father directs the course of their ambition, and sets them an example of honour and honesty; no mother weeps over them in sickness, nor soothes their little childish sorrows; no sister shields their trifling faults, awakening sensations of love and gratitude. Theirs is life in the vale of tears—a sombre valley, always in sight of the sunny hill-tops of affluence. Idleness and ignorance prepare mischief, plan ill deeds, and poor children with heaven-born faculties too frequently become criminals, outcasts from society, weeds instead of flowers, on life's highway. For these " waifs and strays " of humanity, national schools, pastoral instruction, Sunday schools, and other agencies have done much, and may do more in the future. Surely the patronage of the State cannot be more legitimately exercised than in as-

sisting in the moral advancement and education of the destitute children of the na-
tion !

"The highest duty of those who live
in the present is the education of the
generation which is rising up around them.
This does not consist in the mere teaching
of the elements of reading and writing.
Education must not be degraded into
mere mechanical instruction. It should
include a serious and determined effort to
implant in the mind of youth noble and
virtuous sentiments, the duty of forbearance, the pleasures of benevolence, the
beauty of patriotism, the manliness of
self-reliance, and above all, the love of
our Saviour.

"It is undoubtedly a grave and serious
responsibility, that of being entrusted with
the development and guidance of the faculties with which children are endowed.
The woman who neglects her duty, as a
mother, has much to answer for to pos-
terity. The father who has not given to

his child some good moral chart, which may be consulted when the sea of life, is beset with darkness and difficulties, has not fulfilled his mission—has neglected his duty to God and man. Parental neglect is not merely a present injury. It is often an hereditary disease that afflicts future generations. We live again in our children, it is said. For the welfare of mankind this is too true. A bad mother has a host of successors. The taint of bad training, and careless teaching, will run through many families.

"If mothers only thought earnestly about their responsibilities, there would be much less of what is called 'young ladyism.' Children are not children now-a-days, they are 'young ladies' and 'young gentlemen.' Children are not called by their Christian names now-a-days, they are misses and masters. The good plain Mary and Jane and Harry and John, which were wont to be understood in the sort of freemasonry that exists be-

tween children, are obsolete amongst the
sons and daughters of *respectable* parents.
Little Mary Smith is Miss Mary Smith
(unless, forsooth, her parents have adopted
the aristocratic substitute of Smythe); and
Harry Brown, riding his father's walking-
stick yonder, is *Master* Harry, even to
his playmate; whose 'ma' would be
shocked indeed were not this same mark
of respect accorded to her snub-nosed
Johnny, who is studying the anatomy of
a fly which has recently undergone the
amputation of its fore legs. Boys may
grow out of this nonsense as they gradually become men, with the exception of those
who grow into things called 'fops;' but,
alas for the girls! in nine cases out of ten
vanity will finish the work which parental
folly has begun, and so the stock of silly
wives and mothers is perpetuated. With
the highest possible respect for the
matrons of England of the present day,
he could not help thinking that there are
excellent lessons to be learnt in economy,

domestic duties, and the bringing up of families, from the lives of some of the ladies whose needlework and home-spun linen are exhibited in our ancient halls and castles. He should like to hear more of the old-fashioned boast, about a young lady being as much at home in the kitchen as in the drawing-room. He would like to hear mothers talk more of the thoroughly domestic triumphs of their daughters, than of their evening parties and ball dresses. He would like it to be an established rule for the daughters of England to have at least as much instruction in cooking, and sewing, and the general management of a household, as in music and the fine arts generally; and as the census always showed a much greater number of women than men, would like to see more female clerks, and less male drapers and waiters."

Then the preacher came back again to the more religious phrase of his sermon, and dwelt upon the Saviour's merciful

consideration for women, showing how he
had forgiven her who had sinned the sin so
seldom forgiven in this world; and he
prayed his congregation to be kind to one
another, and not to let the softening influences of this holy day pass away with it;
it was only a short time that they were
spared to each other, and there was never
a death without a living one left behind to
regret some unkind or hasty word. Let
them continually have in mind the suffering and forbearance, the love, the meekness
of the Saviour; and strive to be worthy of
the grace which the heavenly martyr had
won for all.

"The sin so seldom forgiven in this
world!" Had she, the May Queen of years
and years ago, heard the Christmas bells?
What memories had they brought to her
mind? Had she ventured to pray on this
holy morning? Had the bells brought
back to her the memory of Helswick
rectory, and the Christmas parties at which
she had been present—one of those pure

innocent beings of which the preacher had
preached? Was she listening to the
merry laugh of children, in their holiday
clothes, passing beneath her window in some
London street or alley? Had any good
angel dropped a tear of pity over her sad
lot? Did she languish in illness, on this
holy morning; languish with the bell-
music in her ear, and the thorn in her
heart? Or had she ended her unhappy
life in the great London river? Had an
unknown body been picked up, at ebb-
tide, and laid in a pauper grave, without
a name? and was the forlorn one Bessie
Martin? Was that story of a woman
leaping from Waterloo Bridge, when the
stars were shining on the sullen tide, the
story of Bessie Martin? The newspapers
record many incidents of this kind. Some
good angel had surely kept Bessie from
such an end as this! The woman in Hood's
heart-piercing ballad had been a child
once, happy and innocent. They have all
been dandled on parental knees, those poor

fallen creatures whom you see in the gas-
light; some of them perhaps have been
May Queens; had they died in infancy
they would have been angels now, joining
in heavenly chants, on this holy day, in
the sunny courts above.

Frank thought in this wise as he knelt,
after the sermon; and one prayer, at least,
went up to heaven, on that Christmas
morning, for Bessie Martin.

CHAPTER XIV.

A SUMMERDALE PARTY.

"No, Paul, I cannot think of putting it off; we have kept it up ever since we have been at Summerdale, and I believe it will be good for you," said Mrs Massey, the morning after Christmas day, just as breakfast was over.

"I am not well enough to join in such an affair," said Paul, languidly.

"It will be good for you to do so; I was only asking Dr Fitz a day or two ago, and he said that you ought to be roused, Paul; that a jovial party and a pleasant dance, and a few genial friends, would be better than a dozen of his professional visits."

"I certainly have enjoyed our Twelfth-night parties," said Paul.

"And you shall again, dear Paul, for many years, I hope."

Paul did not reply.

"I have invited the old women to tea for this evening; and the men have had their beef and tobacco, and the children their Christmas toys and fruit, and all the flannel is gone; and the townspeople had their dance in the school-room on Christmas eve, and shall not we have our Twelfth-night?"

"If you will not expect me to dance with all the women, and be merry with all the men," said Paul, turning over the leaves of a favourite edition of Rasselas.

"You must cheer up, Paul; Dr Fitz says so, and *I* say so. And, let me see, we will invite poor Grey and his wife."

"You should say rich Grey," Paul said, "for George told me he had made a great many thousands, and was the owner of half a street in Melbourne."

"Well, then, we'll invite the rich Greys, and be witnesses of their happy restoration to each other; and we'll have Frank."

"Oh! I should like that, mamma," said Kate Massey, who stood beside her mother. "I think Frank a most agreeable young man."

"Do you, miss?" said Anna, smiling at Paul.

"Yes; he is so gentlemanly, and has such fine eyes."

"Indeed," said Mrs Massey, laughing again.

Paul smiled at his wife; but it was a sad, languid, half-and-half sort of smile.

"Come, Paul, Paul, do cheer up; you are becoming quite misanthropic. Now promise me to rouse yourself, and to be merry at least on Twelfth-night. I shall begin to think you are tired of me, and that you find the society of Kate and myself so disagreeable that you are wearying for a change."

Anna playfully patted Paul's cheeks as

she rallied him thus; and he made an effort to enter into her spirit and energy.

"Now, Pa, do be a good darling, merry Pa," said Kate, whipping him with the strings of her hat, which she was just putting on.

"I will try, my pet," said Paul, catching Kate round the waist, and kissing her under the misletoe that hung up in the great dining-room.

"That's right, Paul dear; you will soon be well again if you will only be determined; and you must travel more, love. Our quiet mode of life here—"

"Suits me better than anything," said Paul. "If I am not happy here and with you and Kate, I never can be happy."

"That's a darling Pa; we'll have such a dance, won't we? Let us rehearse a waltz now," said Kate, pulling her father by both hands.

"Not now, dear," said Paul; "but you and I will lead off on Twelfth-night."

"And you'll promise to be very happy and merry?"

"Yes, I will."

"Come then, Kate, and we will send out the invitations at once," said Mrs Massey.

"I am going to see poor old Dame Twerton, Ma, for a minute or two, if you will excuse me; she is very poorly."

"Then come to me on your return," said her mother.

Kate threw her arms round her father's neck, and then tripped away over the hard frozen snow, looking like some bright, happy creature out of a fairy tale.

The invitations were duly despatched, and when the night came the announcements in the great room up the first flight of the broad oak stairs, included the Rev. James Morris (the rector of Summerdale), Mrs Morris, and the Misses Morris; the Rev. Joseph Walsingham (curate of Summerdale); Dr Fitz, Mrs Fitz, and Mr Fitz, junior; Mr Simon Slack (the only lawyer

in Summerdale—happy Summerdale !) Mrs
Slack, Miss Slack, and Miss Mary Jane
Slack; Mr Henry Bennett (of the Elms,
near Summerdale), and Miss Bennett; and
many others of local note, in addition to
Mr and Mrs George Grey and Mr Frank
Grey, of Tristram Lodge, Purdown, Mary-
port.

It was a thoroughly old-fashioned country party. The Summerdale people were
too lazy to be stiff and formal; and they
knew each other so well that it was not
deemed necessary that the meeting should
commence with icy coldness, only to be
brought to a mild state of thaw at parting.

The only strangers were Mrs Grey
and Frank, and they were at home in
five minutes; for being strangers the Summerdale people (however desirous they
might be to know all about them) thought
it becoming to go up to them and shake
hands, and welcome them to Summerdale.

Paul Massey was determined to seem
merry, and he carried out his resolve so

fully, that Mrs Massey was in a whirl
of pleasure all the night; and everybody
laughed and talked and danced so heartily
that every now and then Paul caught the
infection, and was really happy himself.

Frank Grey soon became a great favourite. In the games of forfeit which pre-
ceded the ball, he played his part with
such ingenuity and cleverness, that Mrs
Massey whispered to Paul, "Young Grey
is really the life and soul of the party."

Kate Masey was enchanted with Frank,
and told him so, right out; but then you
see she was only fourteen, though she
looked several years older, and it was
quite proper for her to tell any young
man that she was delighted with him.
Society would be shocked at a young lady
being so candid at sixteen or seventeen,
though we question whether the Summerdale people would have thought there was
anything wrong in it, for they were a
very candid race.

When a girl loved a young man in

Summerdale, and another young man loved
her, it was not the custom for the lady to
deny her love, and torture her lover by
flirting with some one else. They were
truly an old-fashioned lot, these Summerdale folks.

Mrs Grey was very quiet—she would
have been very happy indeed if Richard
had been there.

Mr George Grey tempted the old people
into corners and told them all sorts of
queer stories about Australia; but he did
not inform them how it was he had lived
so long at Summerdale without telling
them that he had a wife and son; he did
not tell them how it was that he had
changed his name: one old matron, who
was more particular than some of her
neighbours, shook her head, and asked
the Reverend Mr Morris if he did not
think there was something very strange in
this. His reply was delivered in a loud
voice, and it was heard by everybody at
his end of the room.

" Mrs Massey told me the whole affair a day or two ago—our friend, Mr Grey (formally Evans), has suffered a great trouble; but he is now happy once more with his family, and we may all rejoice that we have them with us to-night. It had been deemed necessary that he should for a time change his name, but whether as Mr Evans or Mr Grey, we only know him as a kind, honourable, Christian gentleman."

This was quite enough—too much for the old matron in particular; but she vowed she had the greatest respect for Mr Evans, or Mr Grey, and no doubt she had.

It was quite a notable party this, in the memory of more than one or two of those who were present. Mr Henry Bennett, of the Elms, near Summerdale, fell over head and ears in love with Miss Mary Jane Slack. This was her first party in Summerdale. She had only recently returned from a boarding-school at Maryport, and she came down upon the

young fellows at Summerdale with so
many pretty snares and traps, that Mr
Bennett was caught in no time.

But we have nothing to do with the
Bennetts in this story. What are the
Bennetts to us? They are only like the
supernumeraries at a theatre. It is not
even necessary that we should remember
their names. They only "walked on"
at this party; let them walk off as they
please, and make their marriage settle-
ments, and go where they choose. Our
business is with our heroes and heroines—
the people whom we have known and
talked about since our first chapter, which
opened at Denby Rise.

But it is very provoking to the chroni-
cler, who wishes to proceed with his story,
that Frank Grey should have made himself so busy about other people's love
affairs. He started a round game which
the old people said was certainly the most
match-making, and yet the most spiteful,
game they had ever heard of.

Each guest was provided with pieces of paper. One wrote a lady's name; the second wrote a gentleman's; the third wrote down any place where anybody might be; a fourth set down what anybody might be doing; a fifth set forth the result of all this.

" Consequences " the game was called, and Frank Grey was selected to read, first the names, then the places, then all that was going on at the said places, and next the results. It was all quite new to the old people, who shook their sides with laughter, as well they might on hearing that the Rev Joseph Walsingham, and Mrs Grundy, were at Paris, eating frogs and making love, and that the consequences were serious fits of jealousy, indigestion, and remorse. Mr Henry Bennett was obliged to be patted on the back, or he would certainly have choked himself by laughing, with a biscuit in his mouth, when Frank read out, " Mr Henry Bennett, and Miss Slack, under the misletoe, dying for love, and the consequences a hasty marriage at Gretna Green." Frank stammered, and really blushed—there is no mistake about it—when he had to read, " Mr Frank Grey and Miss Massey, in a corner of this room, desperately in love, and they don't know what to do."

It was silly to stammer over this piece of foolery, was it not? But Frank, a really clever, cool-headed fellow, could not help it, and everybody laughed. Kate clapped her hands and threw back her long sunny curls, and looked so beautiful that Frank blundered on to the next paper, and really " did not know what to do."

The eldest Miss Slack believed, in her secret heart, that Frank was confused only because he was disappointed ; for she had hoped that her name would be coupled with his, and—But here we are again with the Slacks. What have. we to do with the Slacks ? Trot along, Pegasus, and let the party be closed.

At twelve o'clock—these old-fashioned Summerdale people never kept late hours— at twelve o'clock the shawls and cloaks and rugs were taken down from their pegs, and the guests went home, some in their carriages, some trudging over the soft white snow, and making long muffled-up odd shadows on the roadway.

When they were all gone, Frank went to his room, and could think of nothing but Kate Massey's beautiful eyes; of Kate Massey's silky hair; of Kate Massey's musical voice.

Frank thought she was the prettiest, merriest, nicest creature he had ever seen.

The stage lady, who played Ophelia in those years long ago, had fine eyes, to be sure, and white teeth, and a lovely arm; but Kate Massey was infinitely more beautiful than Ophelia.

He sat before the fire (they had fires in all the bed-rooms at Oak House during the winter), and thought of Kate for an hour or more; and then he walked to the window, and saw the moon sleeping upon the snow in the garden; the thatched round-looking roofs of Summerdale were just discernible, and the place was so calm and so peaceful in its snow covering; it was like a snow paradise for snow fairies.

In after years that scene often rose up before him, connecting itself, by association, with one of the happiest periods of his life.

CHAPTER XV.

YOUNG LOVE AND OLD LOVE.

WE have drawn the scenes up and down so often in our story, since we first called upon the prompter to blow his whistle for the drop-curtain to fall on certain of our early incidents at Denby Rise, that we have long since ceased to make any special references to the halting-places in this drama.

Our readers will have paused for themselves at the proper times, and have made their comments between the acts.

We stay for a moment here to tell them that the play is drawing on to its close; but that there are still some important acts to come; more sweets and bitters.

By the kind permission and advice of

Samuel Welford, Esquire, Frank Grey had taken leave of absence from the famous business house.

"It will blow over, this affair of your brother's," the old man had said; "you must not leave us; if we consent to your remaining I cannot see why you should persist that you cannot do so, because your name is disgraced. We shall postpone the question of partnership, it is true; but we must have your services, Frank; you may take leave of absence until the nine days' wonder is at an end, and then come back; meanwhile, we can still send to you on any matters of business in your department. Suppose we say you shall have a holiday until the end of the year."

Frank had accepted the kind old gentleman's advice and instructions; but soon after his father had returned he had talked the whole matter over with him; and the father was inclined to advise that they should all move to some other town, and that Frank should start a business of his own.

"I can give you money, Frank," said the father, "thank God, He has enabled me to be of some use to your mother and you after all."

"The best thing, Frank, I think, would be for you to be ruled by Mr Welford—it would be ungrateful to do otherwise—you can tell him what your father can do for you, and whatever Mr Welford says, I think, you should do."

"Perhaps you are right," Frank had replied.

"And perhaps Mr Welford can help your father to get poor Richard's release."

So matters stood, with regard to Frank's position at Welford and Co.'s, when Mrs Grey and his father and himself were prevailed upon to visit Summerdale, as described in the previous chapter.

When they returned, Frank came home with a new crotchet in his head, and a new dream in his heart.

His ambition returned "heavy and thick" upon him. He would live down any disgrace which might seem to have attached to him, through his brother. He would push his way again to the partnership that had been within his grasp. He was not to blame for his brother's sins. Everybody in Maryport knew that he was honourable and upright.

Why should people cast any slur upon him? Why should they associate him with his brother's guilt?

Frank might have spared himself these questions. Nobody had slighted him. Nobody had associated him with his brother's disgrace. All the slurs and slights and distrusts were bred in his own imagination, and existed nowhere else.

Maryport had too much to think of, to lay up lasting memories about a gang of thieves, who had been caught and punished. Maryport had too many ships on the sea, too many banking accounts, too many shops and warehouses; and if it comes to that, too many thieves, to pay any very special attention to special cases of crime.

There were thousands of people in Maryport who did not know Frank Grey himself; and hundreds, who knew him, had never heard that he had a brother; and yet Frank had fancied that every eye was upon him when he went out, and that every tongue said, "That's the burglar's brother—that's the brother of the fellow who robbed his own mother's house, &c., &c."

Frank ought to have known better; but there are many cleverer persons than he, who think they are being talked about when they are not even thought of.

However, Frank returned from Summerdale, determined to live all this down, and he went to Mr Welford and told him so.

The famous old merchant received him, in his gouty chair, and expressed his pleasure at Frank's sensible resolve.

He knew the world, did Samuel Welford;
and he knew that in a big city like Maryport, a clever, enterprising, honest man
would not be cut because he had a low
wicked thief of a brother.

So Frank returned to his desk in the
old room where poor Harry Thornhill
had sat in years gone by; and he laid his
head upon the blotting-pad, and cried
tears of joy and sadness.

The people who had missed him for several weeks shook him cordially by the
hand; and never, by word or look, was he
reminded of his brother's crime.

It was, however, none the less valiant
in Frank to resolve on encountering a
monster, because that monster only existed
in his own imagination. He is a brave
man who can face his own little world,
determined to bear the worst that may
be said of him. Even your own friends
are apt to associate you with the ill conduct of your brothers and sisters. You
may have a brother who is a notorious

scoundrel; you may have a sister who has disgraced herself: " Ah, it runs in the blood," says your little world. If you are successful in life, the little world to which you belong, nods, and winks, and hums and ha's behind your back upon all occasions. Beware if you have had a relation who has done something wrong! Even if your great uncle was turned out of school for insubordination, beware! Your little world will be sure to talk about it; and in all probability they will magnify your great uncle's offence into murdering the schoolmaster. Beware of success!

Whilst Frank Grey was girding up his loins afresh to do battle with the world, his father was devoting himself to the concoction of a variety of schemes for obtaining a remission of Richard's sentence. He wrote to his agents in Australia, and to influential friends there, on Richard's behalf, and spent many an hour in arranging with his wife what they should do for Richard when he would be free.

The devoted mother wrote a long letter to be sent out to her boy, telling him all that had occurred since he left, and begging him to strive and be better.

If he would only pray, and be penitent, and seek forgiveness of God, it was not too late for happiness to come again, she said. If it was any comfort to him to know it, she had forgiven him, with all her heart; his father had forgiven him; and so had Frank.

"We often talk of you, my poor boy," she went on, "and know how you were led away; we know how your good intentions were perverted when you were a boy. Bad company has been the downfall of the best young men, my dear boy; but you must not despond.

"Try to bear your punishment—oh, how my heart bleeds when I think of it—try to bear your punishment, with a contrite spirit. Perhaps I may see you, my poor dear child, again—do try to be good; do try to seek heaven's forgiveness—if you can do this you will find your trials light. Chains and fetters of iron are nothing to the chains and fetters of guilt and a sinful heart. My poor boy, God will forgive you, as I do, if you ask Him."

Thus the poor woman poured out her unchanged affection for her worthless son.

Oh, Richard Grey, Richard Grey, thou hast much to answer for!

But Mrs Grey had some happy hours now, notwithstanding the bitters which Richard had thrown into her cup. It was sweet to lean upon her husband's strong arm, and to feel that there was no shadow upon her fair fame now. It was sweet to walk down the Autumn valley of life with the man she had loved through so many changing years; it was sweet to hear him talk of the old days, and to feel that he was almost her lover again, in this latter time. It was sweet to kneel beside him at night, and to thank God for His answer to her prayers in the days that were gone.

When the Summer came they went
to Helswick, and dreamed they were
young again. They walked on the beach
and through the meadows. They sat on
the rocks near Denby Rise, and heard the
silver bells wandering over the water and
through the meadows, as the people at the
house in the valley had heard them on
the Sundays, years and years ago. And
whilst the tide ebbed and flowed, and toy-
ed with the shells and the seaweed, Mrs
Grey told George of Squire Mountford, of
Anna Lee, of Harry Thornhill, of the
shipwreck, and the strange wedding.

In return for her long stories of the
past, George told her of his early struggles
in the colonies; passing over the cause of
his wanderings, and leading his wife back
to their young days. He pointed out the
spot where he had first seen her, and he
showed her where he had cut her name in
the rock, when he was a carpenter working at Denby Rise.

The Helswick people, and the visitors

who met Mr and Mrs Grey on the beach, never thought what a dramatic story there was in the life of that simple honest pair, who seemed like an old newly-married couple—talking so earnestly and looking so lovingly upon each other, by the sea.

How seldom anybody *does* think of the remarkable histories which many an apparently uneventful life would make! Yet even the common-place episodes of the lives of the simplest amongst us would be sufficient to prove the verity of the Shaksperian maxim that truth is stranger than fiction. Our childish fancies, our school days, our going out into the great world, and our first impressions of its wonders, our fallings in love, our marrying and the coming to have children of our own to repeat perhaps our own individual histories. Every stage of our lives is a romance; every day has its triumphs and defeats, its comedies and its tragedies. And look at the background we have for our life-pictures, the accessories, the shading, the wealth of incident, the materials for reverie and moralizing. Watch, for ten minutes, the ebb and flow of one of the busy arteries that keep up the beating of a big town's pulse. Stand beside Frank Grey on the steps of the Maryport Commercial Exchange, where he has been to look at the messages concerning a little fleet of ships expected every hour, by Welford and Co., to be sighted off the Maryport harbour.

Where do they all go to, where come from—the people you see going up and down the street? Will you ever stand under that gas-lighted portico again, and see the same men and women and children go by? Never! In a few moments the sight will be one of the past. Never again will the same forms flit by in company. There is sadness in the thought. Some of them may die this very night. There is a fearful probability about that.

There they go,—one after another,— like shadows in a dream. Old men who have discovered the truth of the preacher's

summing up of life; young men looking onwards into the future; women with neither
a past nor a future that they care to con-
template; all wrapped up in their own
histories, all with their own individual
feelings, and hopes, and fears, and sorrows;
all with their own particular gifts, predi-
lections, and peculiarities. There is the
vain man, for instance: you know him by
his pompous gait, the head erect, the chest
thrown forward, the arms in full play.
The centre of the pavement is evidently
his particular property, inherited from a
race of conceited progenitors. In singular
contrast, comes the modest man, in whose
cranium the phrenologist would tell you
that self-esteem, combativeness, and de-
structiveness are all much too small, and
that his retiring, nervous, and excessively
milk-and-water character is the result of
these and other deficient developments.
Watch the poor fellow as he wends his
way along the street. He submits to be
pushed and jostled by every one. He

claims not the wall side, neither does he keep to the curbstone. Now he is in the middle of the pavement, now in the road; and whilst the vain man is looking for a comet, or some other celestial phenomenon, the modest man is studying the paving-stones.

Better than either of these two is that man who looks neither too high' nor too low, who is modest and yet bold, un-assuming yet determined, who claims neither side of the footway, but takes that which is most accessible. The fop is a conspicuous character in the street crowd. Affecting a jaunty air and a cigar, he pays no attention to the shop windows, because, by gas-light, he cannot there see his shadow as he passes, and because he has a score of fascinating glances to scat-ter about amongst the shop girls just released from their counters and their customers. Then come the mechanic and his wife, off to some place of amusement; men going home from their work; ambitious juveniles "doing their earliest weeds;" policemen taking an interest in fat girls sent to post letters; boys singing the chorus of a popular song; women shambling along with feet very near the pavement, and women in all the tawdry finery of fashion, with feigned smiles upon their painted faces. How fast they come and go, how fast they are gone for ever— modest man, vain man, policeman, fop, workman, shop-girl!

We know we have gone out of our province in drawing this gas-light sketch, and we are ready to apologize to the patient reader accordingly; but Frank Grey was watching the great stream of life, surging up and down the street, whilst his father and mother were at Helswick, and we have only painted in the scene before which Frank was standing. Perchance it may help to show how foolish the young fellow had been to think that all Maryport had been intent upon the disgrace which had fallen upon his name. Nobody pointed at him as he stood there on the Exchange steps; nobody said " there he is; " nobody sneered at him ; and Frank would not have seen or heard of them if they had ; for though he was waiting there for the messenger about the fleet of ships, he was only thinking of Kate Massey at Summerdale.

CHAPTER XVI.

"FRESH FIELDS AND PASTURES NEW."

MEANWHILE Mrs Massey thought it desirable that Kate should see a little more of the world.

Paul had an uncle at Tyneborough, one William Howard, Esq., with whom he had recently been brought into communication, on account of some family trust deeds in which Mr Howard was interested.

Mr Howard was a banker, the principal in the firm of Howard and Mentz, and he had written to Paul so kindly that Anna suggested a short visit to Tyneborough.

"I can only say," the Tyneborough uncle observed, in his last letter, "that I shall be happy to see you and Mrs Massey, and any member of your family, at any

time. Your father was a man when I was
a boy, being, as I am, the youngest of a
large family—all gone now, alas! But
he was my wife's favourite brother. It
is not my fault I think that his son and
myself have not met or corresponded for
many years; it shall not be my fault now
that business has re-opened our acquaintance if we do not improve it. I am a
widower, and getting old, now; I have
two sons—one in India, one at home. I
need not say that you will be heartily
welcomed by myself and son. We sincerely hope you will visit us."

The letter having been discussed in all
its bearings; and the desirability of
taking Kate out, coupled with the advice
of the doctor that Paul should travel,
having been duly urged by Mrs Massey, it
was decided that they should visit Tyneborough.

And they did visit Tyneborough, accordingly. It was a long journey, but
full of wonders to Kate Massey. When

they once more came in sight of the sea, her young heart leaped with delight, and she talked about Denby Rise.

The effect upon Paul was very different. He knew that rough North-east coast long before he knew Denby; he knew that rough North-east coast when he was a boy, and the contrast between Paul, the merry, reckless youth, in a boat sailing over the bar; and Paul, the man, struck him as the train went roaring along by the water.

The school was close by, where he and Harry Thornhill first met each other; and the tall masts crowded in those docks, and on the river-bank, pointed out the scene of his father's successes as a ship-builder and owner.

He had not the heart to tell Anna this; he was utterly miserable; he wished himself at the bottom of the river.

Mr Howard's carriage was in waiting for them at the railway station, and Mr Luke Howard speedily found out the pas-

sengers, by their luggage. A fine fellow
was this Howard junior, with brown curly
hair, bushy whiskers, and blue eyes. He
was a big, lazy-looking young man of about
thirty-three. He rolled about in his gait,
like a ship in a ground swell.

"So here you are then," he said. "I
saw you claiming your luggage, you know
—I'm Mr Howard's son—how do you do?
Very glad indeed to see you. Here, Jack,
Jack."

At this call a servant came forward,
and removed the luggage; whilst Mr
Luke Howard gave his arm to Kate
Massey, and led the way to the carriage.

Mr Luke Howard laughed and joked
in a lazy fashion all the way; he hoped
they would enjoy their visit; he had made
up a little pic-nic, for the morrow, to Fell-
rocks; and on the following day they
were to go and see the new port which
had sprung up in two or three years, as
if at the call of an enchanter's wand; on
the next day he had arranged that they

should have a sea trip in a friend's yacht; and then, as the next day was Sunday, they could go to church, have a rest, and prepare for the following week.

So this fellow who talked slowly and laughed loudly, and rolled in his gait, and had bushy whiskers, and curly brown hair, and wore his clothes loosely upon his broad limbs, had not been idle in his plans.

Kate was pleased at the prospect, and, as was her custom, she did not disguise her feelings.

Mrs Massey said their nephew was exceedingly kind, and Paul said "Yes" and "No," at intervals, until the carriage stopped before a handsome modern house at the outskirts of the town, where the sound of the harbour bar's moaning could be heard.

It was nearly dark when they reached Pentworth, as Mr Howard's residence was called, and a sharp breeze was blowing the Autumn leaves about.

Mr Howard, a little active man, with

white teeth and a shrivelled face, received his guests with every demonstration of kindness, and introduced to them his great friend, Mr Zebidee Grainger, and Mr Grainger's daughter.

Late in the story, you may think, to introduce four new characters. So it is. It will probably lay us open to critical raps on the knuckles. " The author has not learnt the *art* of story-telling—there is a want of construction in the plot, &c." All this will be quite true, we dare say. There are many things which the author has not learnt, besides these. But he simply begs to say that these gentlemen and this lady presented themselves to his notice, at this particular period of this history, and that he cannot exclude them from this faithful record. He hopes they will turn out to be personages of consideration and importance.

Mr Zebidee Grainger, the friend of Paul Massey's uncle, was a gentleman of

position in Tyneborough. He had risen
by the force of his own ability and exer-
tions. He had, for years, monopolized
the timber trade of the port, and was one
of the leading shipowners. A keen-
looking gentleman, with his hair closely
cropped, and his clothes formally cut, and
his linen scrupulously clean, Mr Grainger
was a person who would have attracted your
attention wherever you might have met
him. A firm, compressed mouth, a quick,
searching eye, there was a hardness in the
general expression and _contour_ of his
features that was not quite in keeping with
his character for piety. But his strictness
in religious matters carried him through
all this contradiction in the matter of
appearance; and he had made the town a
present of one of the largest and hand-
somest chapels in the place.

They were all religious men in the
employ of Mr Grainger, or at least they
attended chapel regularly, and were never
absent from prayer-meetings. Captains

of vessels and timber buyers, too, wiped their mouths, and put them into a careful religious shape before they entered the private office of Mr Grainger; and they came out sadder, if not wiser, men. For Mr Grainger always finished his business with an exhortation that they should fear the Lord.

"This isn't the sort of thing that I like, between ourselves," Mr William Howard said to Paul Massey and his wife, after the pic-nic on the day following their arrival, whilst Kate and Miss Grainger were chatting in Kate's bed-room. "I confess it's not the thing that William Howard admires, but Grainger's a most conscientious man, and it's his way. If he likes it, why, of course, nobody has a right to interfere. Let every man do as he likes, is my motto. I was one of the first to take Mr Grainger by the hand: I allowed him an overdraw, sir, of five thousand pounds when he hadn't a penny. I could see there was mettle in him, and I

knew he would make way, and he has
done. He's a Dissenter, and I'm a Church-
man; but he's got such extraordinary
notions about creeds, that I have only
once discussed the point with him, and I
never shall again. He is a remarkably
clever man, and may do whatever he
pleases in Tyneborough. He might be
sent to Parliament to-morrow, if he
pleased."

Mrs Massey did not like Mr Grainger
notwithstanding, and there was somebody
else who did not—somebody whose affec-
tions Mr Grainger would have given half-a-
dozen ships to win; this somebody was his
eldest daughter—Laura Grainger, who, at
the moment we are supposed to be writing,
is sitting on the edge of Kate Massey's
bed with one arm round Kate's waist and
the other in Kate's hand.

Mr Grainger had been twice married.
Laura was the only child of his first wife.
By his second he had several children,
whom neither he nor anybody else cared

much about, so we shall not introduce them here. Their mother was a strait-laced, red-nosed member of the Primitive Methodist sect; and Mr Z. Grainger had married her because she had money. Laura had never forgiven him for slighting the memory of her mother by such a union; and she had a hatred of what she regarded as her father's cant and hypocrisy.

Perhaps it was wicked for a child to exclude her father from her affection even on this account; but fathers must not lower themselves in the eyes of their children, must not give children cause to withhold their respect, or affection will soon go with it. We do not say whether Laura Grainger had sufficient reason or not for disliking her father; but we know, for our own part, that Laura Grainger was a much more attractive, loveable creature than her father.

A hot, impulsive, warm heart was Laura's. You could see that in her face, at the first glance. She was not beautiful;

we verily believe she had a nose that was anything but classical. Her face was a little too round; but she carried this off with a high plait of hair upon her head, that was very becoming. She was neither fair nor dark; her hair was black, and she bound it close to her head, with the exception of a little cluster of curls, which hung in a bunch behind. Her dress was worn high up in the neck, and fitted her form without showing a wrinkle, and a graceful form it was,—round and supple. Perhaps Laura's most perfect feature was her hand; an eminent northern sculptor had taken a model of it for his study of Venus.

Laura had attained her twenty-eighth year the week prior to the arrival of the Masseys at Tyneborough. Fifteen of these years she had spent away from home. She would not stay at home, and her father had placed her at an educational establishment, some distance from Tyneborough, where she had remained until now.

"I am not a school-girl, please to remember, Miss Massey," she was saying to
Kate, in that handsome bed-room which
had been allotted to our little Summerdale
beauty during her stay at Pentworth; "I
am not a school-girl; but when my education was considered finished, there were
reasons why I should not return home, and
so I have remained at Barnard ever since.
The principal of the establishment was a
friend of my mother's—indeed, they were
girls together, and she is a kind, good
woman, and they let me do as I like; and
I have my own rooms. I come home
sometimes, at my father's command, on a
short stay; we visit here most of the time,
and how glad I am that I should be here
just when you came! For I think you
one of the sweetest, dearest little things I
have ever met. There!"

"And I loved you the first moment I
saw you," said Kate, throwing her arms
round Laura's neck, and giving her quite
twenty kisses.

It was true love, too, this affection, whatever you may think of such a sudden liking. Girls and women mostly do love or hate each other at first sight; and these two, who are kissing each other so fervently, were of all others the most likely to be fond of each other. Of totally different types of beauty, they were not likely to be jealous of each other. Moreover, Kate had never known what it was to have a companion, and had seen so little of the world, that she would have liked Laura, even had Miss Grainger been unworthy of her affection; whilst Laura, having no pretensions to beauty, as she thought, and being a woman of high instinct and noble principles, and generous to a degree, was sure to attach herself to a pretty, unselfish, lively girl like Kate Massey.

And so these two became great friends, and that is one reason why we have not given Miss Grainger a mere passing introduction in this chapter.

"She does everything so gracefully," Anna said to Paul when the connubial candle was put out, after the sea trip; "she sits down and rises and moves with a gracefulness that I have never seen in any other woman. I declare I am as delighted with her as Kate appears to be."

"A pleasant, agreeable girl," said Paul, drawing his night-cap over his reclining head.

"Pleasant, Paul? She is charming; and what a musical voice. That is just the woman I should fall in love with if I were a man."

"Tastes differ, you see, my dear," said Paul; "it's quite evident that it would not be disagreeable to her if Luke were in love with her."

"And don't you think he is?"

"No."

"Then he ought to be, that's all I can say; why she is worth twenty Lukes, good fellow as he is."

"Where are we to go to-morrow?" asked Paul.

"To Greethams, I think they call it—the new port they talk so much of."

"Then we shall have a heavy day, love. I think we had better reserve our ideas about Laura and Luke until to-morrow."

Miserable wretch! he reserved everything, this poor unhappy man; reserved everything, for fear the great secret of his life should rush out. As we have said before, he was growing weak, and morbid, and was continually subject to confessional fits. It seemed as if he must throw off the weight that was upon him. Let him pull his night-cap on, and breathe hard—he is not asleep; miserable sinner!

Mr Massey had hit the right nail on the head when he said that Luke Howard's affection would be agreeable to Laura Grainger. For in truth Laura loved this big, lazy, handsome fellow. She will tell

Kate all about it soon, you may depend, and Kate will hate Mr Luke Howard in consequence, hate him most heartily.

The Masseys met a great many people during these pic-nics and excursions; for Mr Howard was wealthy, and respected, and had a large stake in the prosperity of Tyneborough; and his friends delighted in doing him honour. The gentlemen paid great attention to Kate and Laura, and many young ladies fished for the courteous attention of Mr Luke Howard, who was everybody's friend, and who made himself happy under all circumstances.

Mr Zebidee Grainger did not join these excursions; there was too much that was frivolous mixed up in them to suit his taste; but he was glad for his daughter to be there, glad that she should be thrown in the way of Mr Luke Howard. For it had long been a pet scheme between the two grey-beards—the parents of Luke and Laura—that the houses of Howard and

Grainger should be united by this marriage. Laura was a great favourite with Luke's father. He had known her mother, whom she greatly resembled, and he felt that Laura had natural gifts which would be of value to his son.

"The fellow seems to have no idea of marrying," said Mr William Howard, despondingly, during a confidential chat, as he sipped his grog.

"That is remarkable, indeed," Mr Grainger replied, stirring his weak sherry and water, which was the only "stimulant" Mr Grainger professed to take, though we happen to know that he was in the habit of visiting London once or twice in the year, and giving himself up to about three days of savage drinking at an out-of-the-way inn, somewhere in Pimlico. A wily, keen old man, this father of that noble girl—a sly old wolf to throw off his sheep's clothing, now and then, and be the real animal.

"I think the boy (fancy that big-

whiskered fellow a boy!) likes the girl;
but I can never get him to see what I mean
when I talk to him seriously about her."

"It has not pleased the Lord to give
me her affection, simply because of my
second marriage, but it has pleased Him
to endow her with great qualities; and it
would be the pride of my life to see her
wedded to Luke. There would not be
such a couple in the North."

" I quite agree with you; quite agree
with you, Grainger; but we must wait,
we must have patience, and do the best we
can."

Then the grey-beards talked of trade
and commerce; of the rising port on the
other side of the bay; of some ships which
Mr Grainger thought about selling to Welford and Co., of Maryport. Mr Grainger
thought it would be a good thing to sell
just now; he could easily purchase again;
only four vessels—they were large ones, it
was true; but Tyneborough could soon
build a dozen such.

So there was a letter despatched by Mr Zebidee Grainger (whilst that happy party were sailing round the new port) to Welford and Co., stating that they might have the ships at a certain price. The next morning this communication was opened by Mr Frank Grey, and after a short consultation it was decided that Frank should go to Tyneborough and close the bargain.

What a pity Frank Grey did not know that Kate Massey was at Tyneborough— the pet-companion of Zebidee Grainger's daughter!

CHAPTER XVII.

KATE AND LAURA.

OF course Laura told Kate that she loved that great blue-eyed fellow, Luke Howard.

"You must never tell a soul what I have confessed to you. There now, don't frown, I know you will not. Bless your dear face, I can read truth and goodness written upon your heart as plainly as if you wore it on your sleeve," said Laura.

They were caressing each other in Kate's bed-room, as usual.

"Are *you* in love? Nay, now, don't laugh at me," said Laura.

"I'm not old enough to be in love," Kate replied, archly.

"Not old enough? how old, then, do

you think we should be before we love?"
Laura asked, twirling one of Kate's fair
glossy ringlets round her finger.

"Why, eighteen, at least?" said Kate.

"And are you not eighteen?"

"No, I'm not eighteen," said Kate,
pursing up her pretty lips and nodding
her head merrily at Laura.

"Well, I should have taken you for
twenty at least."

"Should you? Oh, I do wish I were
twenty," said Kate, earnestly.

"You *do* : then you *are* in love," said
Laura, patting Kate's rosy cheek.

"Am I?" Kate asked quite inno-
cently, "perhaps I may be."

Whether she was in love or not, Miss
Massey began talking about a certain
Twelfth-night party, and of a certain gentleman named Grey, who was delightful
company; and then they gossipped about
his position, and about Mr Luke Howard's
position, and Kate quite agreed with
Laura that it was no matter what the pro-

fession or position of a man might be, if a
girl loved him, and he was good and true,
and loved her in return.

But here was Laura's difficulty; she
was afraid that the love between herself and
Luke Howard was all on one side. She
had never breathed her love but to Kate,
in whose bosom she dropped the treasured
secret. Luke was always kind and attentive to her, gave her his arm at dinner,
sat beside her, and handed everything she
wanted, walked with her, and sometimes
sang duets with her, in his big, full, ringing voice. But he was not in the least
afraid of her; that pretty hand never
put his heart into a flutter, and he could
look into those clear eyes without trembling.

If Laura had known how anxious her
father was that she should marry Luke,
perhaps she would have given that father
a little of her affection : and perhaps she
would not; for she might have feared
some foul play, some trick, some strata-

gem, had she known that Mr William Howard was her ally.

"I am often angry with myself," she said to Kate. "I sometimes say I will never come to Tyneborough any more. I find myself doing and saying things which I fear will betray me ; and I would sooner die than let Luke know I loved him, if he did not love me in return."

At that moment Kate uttered a little scream, to the great alarm of Laura.

"What is it, my dear Kate ?" exclaimed Laura, looking through the window at which Kate was pointing. "I see nothing."

"Don't be frightened—how silly I am, to be sure. I thought I saw Mr Grey pass the house. And, hark ! there's a ring at the door."

Sure enough there was a ring, and Laura peeped through a corner of the lowest pane, and could see a gentleman standing beneath the portico. Kate looked over her shoulder, and saw Mr Frank Grey.

"And that is the gentleman you were speaking of. Well, this is charming. Does he know you are here?"

"I cannot think he does."

"How strange! There, now, don't go red and white in that manner," said Laura; "put your hair out of your eyes: why I declare you are trembling like a leaf, you little puss."

"Am I?" said Kate. "Yes, I believe I am. Whatever shall I do?"

"Put your hair out of your eyes this instant, Miss, and let those roses come back to your cheeks. You will be sent for directly: there, that is better, my pet."

And then the caressing went on again with the most fervent intensity.

The intelligent reader will perhaps have guessed how it was that Mr Frank Grey stood at the door of Pentworth.

After settling that little shipping affair with Mr Zebidee Grainger, he had presented himself at the bank of Messrs Howard and Mentz with a letter of intro-

duction to Mr Howard. That gentleman,
Mr Mentz said, would not be at the bank
again that day, as he had company, and
he believed had only just returned from
an excursion.

"Then I will not disturb him," said
Frank. "If you will kindly present my
note to him I will call again to-morrow, I
shall not leave until Wednesday morning;
I am anxious to see your docks and ship-
yards."

"Please thyself," said Mr Mentz, who
was a primitive old man, and spoke very
much like a Quaker, though he did not
belong to the order of Friends; "please
thyself; I can only say that, if thou would
walk as far as Pentworth—it is not more
than a mile—William Howard will be
glad to see thee; and if thou art anxious
to learn something of Tyneborough, he
will tell thee how to go about it."

"Thank you," said Frank; "then I
will act upon your kind recommenda-
tion."

" Thou'll just catch him before dinner if thou goes now—he dines at four."

Frank thanked Mr Mentz again, and directed his steps towards Pentworth, and he was quite unconscious of that little scream of Kate Massey's. An hour afterwards his heart almost stood still at the thought that he might have deferred his visit to Mr Howard until the following day, and then seen him at the bank, and left Tyneborough without dreaming that Miss Massey was near the place. He certainly would not have left Tyneborough without seeing Mr Howard, because Mr Welford had strongly advised him to see that gentleman, as he might be useful to him, in the way of business.

Mrs Massey crossed the hall as Frank entered. You may be sure they were very much astonished; and you may also be sure that as Mr Howard knew that Frank was known to the Masseys, he invited him to stay and dine.

It was some time before Frank summoued up sufficient courage to ask if Miss Massey was there; he was afraid she was not. He was happy, he said, to hear that she was well, and he tried to shield his happiness by excessive courtesy, and to smother it in commonplace remarks about the weather.

What a happy, genial dinner it was! Frank sat between Laura and Kate; on the other side of Laura was Mr Luke Howard; on the other side of Kate was Mr Welton, a Hamburg merchant. They were faced by Mrs Massey, Mr Massey, and several visitors, and Mr Zebidee Grainger was taking his chop at home. Kate looked round at Laura now and then, and smiled, and Mrs Massey watched her daughter, when nobody else did.

Mr Howard was a hospitable host, and he told his stories, and made his jokes at the proper time; though by-the-by they were all about shipping and banking, and making fortunes. He knew every man in

Tyneborough, and how every man had
made his money. Frank Grey, who at any
other time would have been interested in
the old banker's stories, thought little or nothing about them now. When he was not
speaking to Miss Massey, or Miss Grainger,
he was thinking about the former, and in
his heart thanking old Mentz for advising
him not to delay his visit to Pentworth.

There is a custom in the North too
much honoured in its observance—the
custom of permitting the ladies to retire to
the drawing-room very soon after dinner.

The port had scarcely gone round the
table twice, ere the ladies disappeared;
and then Jack, who had attended upon Mr
Luke Howard at the railway station,
handed round cigars, and everybody
smoked, over their port and their claret.
Luke Howard threw himself into an easy-
chair, and sprawled his legs over the fender, and smoked, and laughed, and talked
about the events of the few preceding
days. Old Howard kept his seat at the

head of the table, and gave himself up to walnuts and port, as if he were a young man. Paul Massey was quiet, and moody; and Frank Grey, anxious to propitiate that grave parent, exhibited to the company his thorough knowledge of business, and his acquaintance with books. The other men said what they could,—which was not much,—and smoked furiously.

But this part of the dinner was not agreeable to Frank, who was thinking, most of the time, what the ladies were doing, and wondering when coffee would be announced.

The happy time came at last, and then they all adjourned to the drawing-room. The smoke was hanging about their clothes, and it perfumed the room; but the ladies made no objection, and so far as Frank was concerned all the geniality and happiness of the first part of the meeting went on again.

But we will not dwell upon these mere

details. We need not tell the reader how
Kate played upon that grand piano, which
Mr Howard had bought in London; how
Laura sang, and how Luke Howard was
prevailed upon to try that duet, about the
Fisherman, with Laura. Frank *would* turn
the leaves for Kate whilst she played that
new arrangement of "Home, Sweet Home,"
which Luke Howard insisted was the best
thing out; and Kate was not at all annoyed when Frank turned the leaves at the
wrong time, and she scrambled through
the piece with an amount of success that
would have astonished the author.

And so the evening sped away, until
at last Frank had to take his leave; but it
was arranged that on the morrow a little
party should be got up for a visit to the
docks, and the warehouses, and the ship-
yards, and the anchor works. Mr Grey
was to be of the party, and so was Kate.

Tyneborough was Elysium to Frank,
though it looked more like Pandemonium,
as he went home to his hotel. The fur-

naces were blazing and smoking, and illu-
minating and darkening the sky. The
river was glowing with the lights from the
anchor works and the forges; and the harbour bar was moaning. But the blazing
furnaces were bright, merry, delightful
lights to Frank; and the harbour bar's
moaning was sweet music.

Mr Welton, the Hamburg merchant, who
was staying at Frank's hotel, walked home
with him, and confided to Frank his private opinion that Miss Massey was the
most charming little girl he had ever met;
and that he had serious intentions of telling
her so, if an opportunity offered. Did he
mean to insult the lady? Frank inquired;
because if he did— Oh, no, nothing was
further from his thoughts; he had too much
respect for Mr Howard, and his admiration
of the young lady was too sincere for that.
Well, there was an ambiguity, Frank observed, about Mr Welton's remark, which
was not agreeable, and he must call upon
him to explain. Mr Welton did explain,

all the way to the hotel; and was explaining nearly all the evening afterwards,—in a corner of the coffee-room,—until at last Frank was induced to explain himself; and the end was that the two sat up explaining until long after midnight, to each other's mutual satisfaction.

Frank hardly knew how the time slipped away; the day's surprise had been too much for him, and the prospect of another twelve hours in Kate Massey's society put all other things out of his head.

His Worship, the Mayor, accompanied them through the docks, on the following day; and so, likewise, did Mr Zebidee Grainger, who took occasion, now and then, to remind those around him of the grandeur and beauty of our Lord's works compared with those of man. What were these ships, and those anchors, and that molten iron, and that hot boiling glass, to the sea and the sky above them?

You might have noticed, had you been there, that Mr Zebidee Grainger never committed himself in this way when his daughter was near.

But Mr Zebidee Grainger could not afford to give up all his sermonizing and his pious ejaculations simply because Laura was of the company. That keen, sly old wolf, in the sheep's clothing, had found his purpose answered too well at Tyneborough by a fierce religious zeal; and everybody knew how sincere he was! When the carpenters were on strike in a great builder's yard (of which he was at the time chief proprietor), because Mr Grainger had taken an undue advantage of an engagement, note the congregation held a special meeting at the Zebidee chapel, and prayed that the Lord might turn the hearts of the benighted carpenters, and drive the devil from the yard of His chosen servant. The men knew it was all over with them then; it was almost enough when Mr Grainger met them in a body, and threw twenty texts in their faces; but when the chapel prayed for them — that was too much; and the men returned to work at once, which resulted in a thanksgiving meeting, at which Mr Grainger, going down upon his knees on the bare floor, gave thanks to our Lord for expelling the devil from the works.

Unhappy Laura! Her heart revolted at all this; and between her love for Luke Howard and her fear and dislike of her father, she was ill at ease on this journey through the yards. She saw Frank Grey and Kate Massey lagging behind the rest occasionally, and finding themselves next to each other whenever there were steps to be mounted, or short ladders to climb; and then she felt that she had not fired Luke Howard with that passion which had taken possession of her warm heart.

The day was soon over again; soon, too soon over, and Frank Grey had said good-bye; and had paid Mr Mentz a parting visit, and had paid his hotel bill, and taken his departure for Maryport; whilst Laura and Kate were kissing and confess-

ing upstairs, and lamenting their pro-
bable parting in a few days hence. For
Mr Massey was not well, and had suggested that they should return to Summerdale
at the end of the week. Kate had contemplated a short stay at Pentworth alone;
but Mr Massey thought, as the Autumn
was rapidly drawing to a close, it would
be better that they should all return together.

CHAPTER XVIII.

AN INCIDENT OF LORD MAYOR'S DAY.

IT is extraordinary how much the human constitution will stand. Men who have been dying for years, and who ought to have been killed, time out of mind, by their dissolute and drunken conduct, have lived out the apparently hale men, who have been watching their gradual decay.

Winford Barns was one of those miserable, asthmatical, wheezing, bronchitical mortals, who only enjoy about an hour's life in the twenty-four, and that when they have swallowed as much brandy as would make most men helplessly intoxicated, or raving mad.

This man had not only lived to spend the money which Mr Massey had given him, personally; but he had lived to cash the post-dated cheque.

Moreover, he had lived a whole year in Paris, where he had had such a run of luck, at a celebrated gaming-house, that he had deemed it desirable to quit the Parisian capital " all of a sudden."

Giving up his establishment at High-town, a magnificent festival was got up in his honour at Keem's Harmonic Bowers, prior to his removal to London. The principal tenor had made a song about this chief of the swell scoundrels who frequented the Bowers; and Winford had been attended to his box by a bevy of painted ladies.

Maryport, as he had remarked in a speech upon this occasion, had long been " too slow for him; " so he migrated to Regent Street, where over a magnificent shop, in which was daily exhibited a dazzling array of India shawls, he occupied grand apartments; over a shop which was patronized by Royalty, and which put up

blazing stars above its doorway on the
birthdays of Royal personages, and the
initials of the new civic dignitary every
Lord Mayor's day.

But Winford's course was nearly run.
He had not experienced a lack of money
since his return from Paris, or Paul
Massey would have heard of him, despite
their compact. Night after night, he
frequented the dens and fashionable stews
of the metropolis; and he became nearly
as notorious at the Holborn and the
Argyle, as he was at Keem's Harmonic
Bowers.

Two months after the events recorded
in the previous chapter, he came to an
ignominious and wretched end.

It was Lord Mayor's day. The famous
procession had crushed its way through
the city thoroughfares, and had returned
from Westminster, in a wonderful November sunshine.

The fog of the previous day had disappeared, as if in compliment to the new

Mayor, and out of respect to the metallic armour of his Lordship's knights.

The cabs had been re-admitted to Fleet Street and the Strand, to Cheapside and the Poultry; and her Majesty's ministers had said their ministerial nothings over the Lord Mayor's wine.

Night came quickly, and in an illuminated mist, as it comes in London under the influence of gas lamps and radiant shop-windows.

How like a fairy city London by night! And on this night in particular. For the Londoners not only celebrated Lord Mayor's day with unusual unanimity, because his Lordship was a very popular man; but for some other special reason which we need not explain.

From the top of Ludgate Hill, down through Fleet Street, along the Strand, up the Haymarket, and through Regent Street, to the Circus, and far away, and up and down every street, to right and left, were stars, and crowns, and Prince of

Wales' feathers and initial letters, in jets of gas and variegated lamps.

The streets were all ablaze, until the sky resembled the appearance of the clouds above Merthyr Tidvil, in Wales, or above the Cleveland Valley, or above Tyne-borough, or above the blazing furnaces in Derbyshire.

London bid defiance to November fog that night, though one of those thick rolling battallions of vapour, which come up from the river and the Erith marshes, would have been dense enough to put out nearly all that wonderful luminosity which made the night golden.

As the hours sped on, the city put up its shutters, and the last 'busses began to run along Fleet Street and the Strand. But the more solitary became the Strand and Trafalgar Square, the livelier and the brighter grew an adjacent locality.

The Haymarket lamps from the Hay-market *cafés* sent floods of light across the pavements, and the festal stars and crowns, in gas and oil, showed every detail of the full cabstand that stretched away down the centre of the road.

It was a melancholy sight so brilliantly lighted up,—as if all the gas in London had been set aburning to show the world the ugliest blot upon England's fair reputation.

Etty's picture of the syrens on a sunny sea-coast, with skulls and skeletons lying at their feet, would have been a suitable transparency for that dazzling establishment with the folding doors, which were for ever opening and shutting, and showing a motley throng of men and women in a flashy saloon.

Towards midnight, — when the Haymarket was busiest and brightest, when the big blot on English morality was seen in its covering of lacquer and gilt, —a woman quietly emerged from one of the by-ways, and passed through the crowd, towards Regent Street. She turned a pale face up to the illuminations, and a

few heavy curls of black hair fell upon her
shoulders. She had a sunken, black, brilliant eye and a well-cut mouth; her figure
was slight and graceful. There was something in her manner which would have
set you thinking of the time when those
who passed you in that hideously-brilliant
light were innocent and happy, and
might have made you picture distant
homes from which the pride and hope of
the domestic circle had disappeared. And
then you might have thought that the
"midnight meetings," commenced some
years ago, by a number of religious men
and women, were, after all, perhaps worthy
of support.

Bessie Martin—poor misguided, half-
crazy Bessie—passed on her way, with that
vacant look in her eyes which had alarmed the landlady of the Maryport Arms.

O that some good Samaritan, some
seeker-out of the sinful and unhappy in
London hives, had laid a kind hand on
Bessie Martin's shoulder, years ago!

She passed on, poor fallen soul! She had been a May Queen once, as innocent as the flowers that decked her brow!

Arriving at the shop where the India shawls were hidden by the dark iron shutters, above which a Brunswick star flared and spluttered, Bessie stopped suddenly, and with a startled exclamation.

At her feet lay a man who had fallen, with a heavy thud, before her.

Several other persons were attracted to the spot, including a policeman, who before looking at the form on the pavement, said to Bessie, "You must not go away."

The man was attired in a light dressing-gown, and must have fallen from the open window of the first storey.

The quick eye of the policeman detected this in an instant, and he speedily alarmed the India shawl house.

A doctor was sent for, and two policeman, followed by Bessie, carried the man upstairs.

Need we say that the bleeding wretch

was Winford Barns. He had leaped out
of the window, in a fit of *delirium tremens*.
His appearance, and the evidence of his
valet, soon satisfied the doctor and the
police that such was the case, and they
took Bessie's address, and told her she
might be wanted again.

The man was not dead, and Bessie,
who had been much frightened, lingered
in the room.

Laid upon his bed, Winford opened
his eyes, and looking about the room, fixed
his gaze upon Bessie. Then he made a
vain effort to speak.

Bessie being at this moment about to
leave the room, the dying man raised his
arm, and beckoned her. One of the officers
noticing this, detained Bessie, and Winford
tried to speak again.

Not for an instant did the miserable
sufferer take his eyes from Bessie, except
when he pointed to an ebony box that
stood upon a toilet stand, close by. This
was brought to him, and he tapped it with

his thin hand as if he would have it opened. He tried again to speak, but no sound was heard, except a guttural noise in the throat.

One of the policeman took a small note book from his pocket, and put a pencil into the hand of the dying man, who immediately essayed to write.

After several administrations of brandy, he scrawled, in strange characters, " Ask her name ? "

Bessie was asked her name accordingly; she had never changed her name ; so utterly hopeless and friendless and abandoned had the poor woman become that she was not ashamed to say Bessie Martin.

Winford Barns's face underwent little alteration, at this announcement; but the discovery of Besssie's name seemed to give him some satisfaction, and he wrote, again with great difficulty, " She is my daughter —look in the desk."

And then he expired in a fit of great agony.

The star outside continued to splutter and flare, and the people and the cabs went by as if that tragedy had not just been played out above the store of silks from India.

The policeman looked in the box, as they were requested, and at the bottom, amongst some old letters, they found a packet inscribed, "The Will of Winford Barns."

CHAPTER XIX.

THE BAD MAN'S WILL.

IT was a large piece of paper, and inside it there were notes to the value of £100.

On the paper was written:—"If I don't take £100 out of this before I die it will be because I can do without it. If I possess anything else at my decease it will not be in houses and land—if it is I shall make a codicil, and specify the same. I've lived what is called a fast life, and mean to do so to the last—'it was my father's custom, and so it shall be mine'— and my personality, it is likely, will all be found in the house which has the honour of receiving my last breath.

"Some years ago, no matter how

long since — before the wreck of Paul
Massey's yacht off Helswick, which was
rather a strange coincidence, occurring
where it did, and might be set down as a
punishment by weak fools—there was a
woman I loved. When she died I made
her a promise, which I hereby, to some
extent, fulfil. She had a child which she
sent to be brought up by an old woman
with whom she was acquainted at Helswick. That child was called after her
mother—Bessie Martin, and when I was
at Helswick I learnt that she was alive
and well and comfortable—the old woman
kept a school there, and if she is living now
she will remember that one morning she
received five sovereigns in a packet anon-
ymously—I had expectations then of re-
cruiting my waning fortune, and those
expectations, so far, have not been disappointed.

"To this Bessie Martin I hereby be-
queath the enclosed £100, and all that I
die possessed of, whether in money shares,

notes, jewellery, bills of exchange, furniture, plate, land, messuages, tenements, or anything and everything whatsoever,—to this said Bessie Martin, now or late of Helswick, in the county of Denby, for her sole use and benefit; and I hereby appoint James Mentz and William Howard, Esquires, bankers, of Tyneborough, in the county of Northam, my sole executors to see that this, my last will and testament, is carried out.

"If this is not worded in exact legal phraseology, it sufficiently, and I am advised by a barrister friend of mine, legally explains my intentions, which are that Bessie Martin shall have everything I possess, and that my old friends, the Messrs Mentz and Howard, the bankers aforesaid, shall find her out, and see that she has everything, after they have paid for putting me in the ground, and all proper testamentary charges; and all I hope is, that the little beggar (I mean Bessie Martin aforesaid) will have more to

receive than I expect, and that some thief
of a husband may not marry her for the
sake of her fortune."

The will was duly signed, and witnessed; and the police took charge of the
dead man's possessions—£2000 in notes,
drafts, and gold; a quantity of jewellery,
sundry articles of clothing, numerous tobacco pipes, cigar boxes (full and empty),
and a quantity of other miscellaneous
articles.

An inquest was held on the body; the
northern bankers came to town; and in
due course Bessie Martin entered into
possession of the moneys and goods of her
dissolute father.

The steady old Tyneborough bankers
wiped their hands of the whole affair as
speedily as possible, you may be sure.

They went back to the North, talking
nearly all the way home of the dreadful
wickedness of London.

"And yet they call this London the
centre of British greatness," said Mr

Howard. "If genius doesn't wish to hide her light under a bushel, she must carry it to the metropolis. That's what they say in books and newspapers."

"It's a great mistake, William, a great mistake," said Mr Mentz, "and the sooner thou makes thy son Luke understand that it is a mistake, the better for him and thee."

"I do talk to him, frequently; I do tell him, and I have endeavoured to prevent him doing our business in town, but the boy likes it, and he's a good fellow."

"So he is," said Mr Mentz, "and he's too lazy to go far wrong; but London is not a place for Luke to see much of; humbug and puffery, and debauchery, and extravagance are everywhere in London."

"So they are, Mentz, so they are; I'm glad we are out of it."

"And they talk about their fine arts, their buildings, and their pictures, William: hast thou seen anything in all London to come up to the warehouses at Tyneborough; or the lighthouse off the bar?"

"Certainly not," said Mr Howard; for he liked to humour Mentz; he did not go so far as that in his contrast of Tyneborough with the metropolis; but he heartily hated and despised the big cockney-town.

"Then there is their preachers. Did'st thou ever hear such stuff as yon fellow in St Paul's preached on Sunday?"

"It certainly was not equal to parson Hughes, in our old church."

"Parson Hughes! why, it was far behind Thumper, who preaches in Zebidee Grainger's chapel. There's no power in the London preaching, no oratory, no force. Let them turn to the sermons of some of the old divines, and see how they thundered away at vice and immorality; let them see how the old preachers denounced extravagant dresses."

"True, Mentz, true, the fathers hit
fashion hard."

Strange that these very shrewd, clever
bankers, who were up to so much, had
not seen through Mr Zebidee Grainger!
They would not assist that miserable
Bessie Martin, even in the way of investing her money. Mr Mentz wiped his
hands of her twenty times in almost as
many minutes. But they had lifted up
Mr Grainger—advanced him £5000 when
he was not worth a penny. Perhaps they
were shrewd in this; for the man had
risen rapidly, and had made his mark in
Tyneborough, which was no small achievement, considering the Tyneborough competition.

If the northern bankers had been as
sharp as Mr Z. Grainger, they might have
seen their friend in London. Their friend
saw them—saw them being jostled and
elbowed in the city—saw them, and pulled
his slouching hat further over his long-
haired wig; for he had always a luxuriant

crop of hair when he visited London. He
was the wolf then, you know; he had
room enough in London to be the real
animal; he could throw off his sheep's
clothing, and worry the lambs, and crunch
their bones, and lick his greasy snout to
his own satisfaction. Fancy this fellow
the father of Laura Grainger! He had
been in London two days when the
bankers arrived, and he had scented them
out the second day, and had watched them
under the shelter of an archway—had
watched them and laughed, or rather
growled, we should say, in his sleeve.
" There they go, the two sheep, who think
I am one of them; there they go, the conceited old idiots; there they go." And
then he went to his favourite back-slum
house, and drank whiskey until his eyes
were on fire.

Happy ignorance! The two northern
bankers still chatted as the train went
spinning away along its iron bars. After
finishing off London, and utterly blotting

her out of the map, they talked of Bessie
Martin, and counted up all the families
they had known in which wickedness and
misery seemed hereditary. And here they
had both many pertinent illustrations to
give of Mr Mentz's theory, that once there
was bad in a family, bad there would
always be.

There certainly are families of this kind
amongst the highest and the lowest. It
seems as if the bad seed sown at the beginning must grow, and bear its poisoned
fruit to the last.

There is a weed in every garden, of
which your patient tiller and tender of the
soil is always complaining. At the back
end of the Autumn he made a desperate
attack upon it; he dug and dug until he
had fairly turned up the subsoil, to the
damage of the fruitful loamy earth above.
He had got under it this time, he told
you; there was no mistake about it; look
at the heap in yon corner. Every twig,
every root, every sucker; he had dug at

them, and chopped at them, and picked them out.

On the following day he made a fire of them, and your neighbours complained of the thick suffocating smoke, which climbed, sluggishly, over your wall and crept into their windows.

No matter, there was an end of the switch, or twitch, or bind, or whatever the noxious weed might be. The flowers would have room to strike out their tender roots now that the enemy had gone.

Spring comes, and Summer follows. There are warm rains and sunny days; and with the lilies, and the carnations, and the tulips, and the daisies, up comes the noxious weed again. "There it is," you say to your man, "there it is again;" he knows all about it, and shakes his head, and tells you that the squire's gardener had told him only a week ago that they had been removing a hillock, and had found the tap, or root, of that same detestable weed struck down twenty feet into the soil!

"Once there is bad in a family," repeated old Mentz, "there is no knowing when it's worked out. They were always a bad lot, the Barnses; and Winford's left one behind to perpetuate the family failing under another name."

And yet she might have been good, that poor girl who was so kind to her supposed grandmother at Helswick.

"It will do her no good," said one old Tyneborough banker to the other. "I never knew money do any good to such-like—it mostly makes 'em worse when money comes into bad hands."

Didn't your gardener tell you that the compost and the guano which he had put in, at spring-tide, had brought the weeds up—had made them flourish: "it would bring anything out, good or bad," he said. And so will money; give a man or woman money, and you shall soon see whether they be good or bad. Unhappily, it is too late to try the test upon Bessie Martin.

CHAPTER XX.

"MURDER WILL OUT."

PAUL MASSEY had been seriously ill ever since his return from Tyneborough.

He walked about as usual, it is true; but he was weak, and weary.

London doctors and Maryport doctors had seen him, and prescribed for him; but it was as the Summerdale practitioner had said, "nothing would do. Mr Massey any good;" his system was giving way under a complication of those disorders which years of excessive mental anxiety will engender, in the strongest constitution.

Remorse had done its worst. Paul could no longer bear the weight of conscious guilt.

The loss of physical strength had

brought on a morbid sensitiveness, which betrayed itself so frequently, that Mrs Massey had long since become convinced that Paul's illness was ministered to by some hidden sorrow.

In years past she had often rallied him upon concealing something from her; but since their removal from Denby Rise she had, as will already have been observed, become more serious in the expression of her fears that Paul had a secret.

"Is it some monetary difficulty that troubles you, Paul?" said the patient loving wife, as they sat together on a memorable afternoon in the familiar library of Oak House.

"No, love," said Paul, pressing his hand over his heart, as he had been wont to do for some time, to arrest a sharp pain of which he had often complained during the few previous months.

"You are very poorly this afternoon, my dear," went on Mrs Massey, taking his hand; whilst Kate, who was sitting on an ottoman at his feet, pressed her head affectionately upon his knee.

"I am not so well to-day as I have been for weeks," said Mr Massey, despondingly.

"My dear Paul," murmured his wife, "there is something besides physical pain which is hurting you."

"Kate, my love," said Paul, "take a walk in the garden whilst your mother and I have a little talk."

Kate rose immediately, but not without looking surprised, seeing that it had never been deemed necessary to exclude her from the conversations of Oak House.

"What is it, Paul? Have you been more unfortunate in money affairs than you wish me to think? Don't fear to tell me. I shall begin to doubt your love if you have troublesome secrets to keep from me," said Mrs Massey, when Kate had shaken her curls over her shoulders, and wandered into the garden with a book in her hand.

"I am very ill, Anna," said Paul; and the tone in which he made the confession sounded direfully ominous.

"Let me send for the doctor," said Mrs Massey hurriedly, with her hand on the bell.

"No, no, no," said Paul, "it is no good; we will see by and by."

Mrs Massey looked into his face with alarm: she would have pitied him could she have looked into his secret soul, and seen the deadly struggle that was going on there.

"When was the first time, Anna," said Paul, with a great effort to be particularly calm, "you thought I had a secret from you."

"I cannot tell, my love," said Anna. "I never thought seriously about it until lately."

"And you have thought seriously about it lately?"

"I have; but only for your sake, Paul. You would despise me, and rightly, if you thought I had any weak curiosity which I desire to gratify. But I love you too much not to wish to share your sorrows as well as your happiness.

"Do you remember, Anna, the attack of illness I had at Denby?"

"I do," said Mrs Massey, sorrowfully, "my poor Paul!"

"I said strange things during the fever?"

"You were very ill, Paul; frequently light-headed."

"Do you remember anything I said?"

"I remember one thing."

"What was it?" said Paul, a slight flush tinging his pale cheeks.

"You said you loved me with all your heart and soul."

Paul smiled faintly, and sadly, and pressed the hand that lay in his.

"Do you remember my talking to you strangely, when I was getting better? Do you remember my asking, Suppose I turn out to be a bad, wicked man?"

"It is little that you have said to me, Paul, which I forget."

"Then I will tell you a painful, a dreadful story, Anna; summon all your fortitude to hear it; you will require all your courage to sit it out."

Paul was so pale, and so calm, and his voice was so hollow, that Anna's heart beat fearfully.

"It has been in my mind to tell you years ago, Anna, but I loved you so much, so dearly, that I could not cause you a moment's pain. I do not love you the less now; but something tells me I must respond to your desire to share with me a sorrow which has long afflicted me."

"Dear Paul!" said Anna, now almost as pale as himself.

"I have prayed night after night for guidance; and it seems to have been borne in upon me now at the last, that I should do what I have been on the point of doing many times."

Paul pressed his hand upon his heart,

and looked at his wife so sorrowfully, so sadly, that the tears came into her eyes, and she bowed her head over his hand.

"There was once a youth, Anna, who loved, tenderly and patiently; his name was Harry Thornhill."

Anna started, and looked up, wondering and amazed; but Paul felt as though nothing in the world could stop his story; it seemed to flow from him of its own accord, like that of the Ancient Mariner.

"His name was Harry Thornhill; he was as good and true-hearted a fellow as ever breathed. He had a friend, who on his way to call for Harry at the home of the lady he loved was wrecked, and but for Harry's brave intervention would have been drowned. This friend was Paul Massey, who no sooner saw the lady than he loved her too. He had seen hundreds of beautiful women before, but none so fair as Anna Lee. Nay, hold up thy head, Anna—I am no flatterer. I did not know that she was affianced to Harry Thornhill."

"She was not," said Anna, gently.

"But I loved her with a man's strong-est, purest love."

"Bless you, my dear Paul," said Anna..

Though these tender ejaculations cut Paul to the quick, still he went on with his story.

"And when I learnt that she returned it, the world did not hold a man so happy as Paul Massey. When he found that Harry Thornhill loved her too, a pang of sorrow for his friend was the alloy to Paul Massey's happiness. There is no complete bliss in this world. Time flew on, and Anna and Paul were to be married; whilst Harry Thornhill was to go abroad with his sorrow. A day was fixed for him to take his farewell of Denby Rise, and the visit had Anna's sanction. I had another friend there—one Winford Barns."

Anna instinctively shuddered at this man's name.

"This Barns was a shrewd man of the world,—he saw danger in this visit of Harry to Denby Rise—danger to the ho es of Paul Masse —the soft woman l heart would relent at Harry's misery, would soften at the parting, and pity would beget love. Paul Massey was a hot-hearted fool, who loved so passionately, so madly, that he would have been jealous of the wind kissing the fair cheek that was his."

Paul paused to gather strength for the remainder of his story. He pressed his hand nervously upon his heart, and breathed with difficulty.

" The day of parting came. Winford Barns, like a sneaking wretch, watched Harry Thornhill and Anna Lee; when they were alone he saw the disappointed lover press a ring upon the lady's finger; he heard the lady murmur some tender words; he heard Harry Thornhill say, ' I knew you would, Anna; I knew you would.' "

Anna trembled with excitement.

" What did the lady mean ? What was it that Anna knew she would do ? Whose was that ring ?"

" My own ring," said Anna, interrupt-

ing the story, excitedly, " my own, Paul.
He had taken it from me months before, in
mere playfulness, and in the presence of my
uncle. He returned it when he bade me
good-bye, and asked me to wear it for his
sake, as if he were my brother, my only
brother. I said I would, Paul, I said I
would," and Mrs Massey burst into a flood
of tears.

" Look up, love, look up; I will tell
you the remainder of the story at some
other time."

Paul's resolve was breaking down. In
presence of those tears, he felt that it would
be better that his secret should die with him.
But an inward monitor seemed to say " it
cannot be ;" and he was pressed on to tell
her all, all that terrible story of love and
jealousy, with its ghost which had haunted
him day and night.

It was a selfish thing to do, to make
Anna's life as miserable as his own. He
knew it was selfish ; this tortured him
even whilst his tongue poured the deadly

poison into her ear: but the secret would out—it seemed as if it leaked out of his very weakness.

"Paul Massey has never been jealous since. But on that day the fiend possessed him. He questioned his friend on board the yacht; he asked him to explain the meaning of the ring, — the meaning of those words 'I know you would.' Harry Thornhill was indignant at the meanness of his friend; Harry's proud soul and his pure love for Anna Lee could not brook the vulgar jealousy of the man who had won her heart. Winford Barns, like the arch-tempter himself, stood by to spur Paul's valiant meanness on. High words followed, angry threats were exchanged."

Here Paul rose from his seat, his face was hot, and he clasped his hands together as if in supplication; whilst his wife hung fearfully upon every burning word he uttered.

"Blows followed—great God, forgive me!—No matter that, Harry struck the first. My hand was upon him—it was the hand of Cain—he fell overboard, and was drowned—Paul Massey murdered his friend."

The unsuspecting wife uttered a piercing shriek, and fell stricken, almost to death, at this terrible confession.

Kate heard the cry from the garden, and came hurrying into the room, with the servants.

They found Mr Massey raising his wife from the ground. He trembled so much that his poor stricken burden shook as he endeavoured to raise it. He was pale as a ghost, and his eyes wandered about the room as if he had suddenly gone mad.

Kate hurried to her mother, and the servants brought water. Explanations were neither asked for nor given.

They bathed her temples, and they put brandy between her lips; and by-and-by the closed eyes opened.

Paul looked on, and said nothing; but his death-like gaze alarmed all who saw it.

" I shall be better presently," said Mrs Massey faintly, and they raised her up.

" Take me to my room."

They led her out, and Paul followed them, with his eyes, until all seemed dark and indistinct, and he staggered to a seat just as the doctor, who had been summoned by a thoughtful domestic, entered the room.

Whilst this scene was being enacted, Laura Grainger, in her pretty little room at Barnard, was writing a long letter to her dearest Kate, telling her how happy she had been in her society; how thankful she was they had met; how she should watch over and treasure the friendship they had formed. L. had been very kind to her after Kate left, trying to make up for Laura's sadness at the parting. Oh, if he was always as considerate, as tender as he had been the day after Kate left! They had talked a great deal about Mr Grey, and they all liked him, and she sincerely hoped that he would be successful in his wooing. The day before she

(Laura) had left Pentworth, Mr Welton, the Hamburg merchant, whom Kate would remember, had called. He was in raptures about Mr G., but in greater raptures about Miss Massey. L. had said Kate was a nice little girl, but rather pert: there! what did Kate think of that? Rather pert: that was because her dear Kate did not like him, after she knew how her Laura loved him—her silly Laura. Then Kate's friend, according to promise, enclosed her one of her poems, and told her how she had found things at Barnard on her return: and told her, moreover, that she was afraid that she began to weary of Barnard, and many other things which it is not necessary that anybody but Kate should see.

Was it surprising that when this letter arrived the next evening, that it should lie unopened?

END OF VOL. II.

JOHN CHILDS AND SON, PRINTERS.

Lightning Source UK Ltd.
Milton Keynes UK
UKHW052357211118
332724UK00024B/954/P